The Woodworker's Shop

100 Projects to Enhance Your Workspace

The Woodworker's Shop

100 Projects to Enhance Your Workspace

Percy W. Blandford

TAB BOOKS
Blue Ridge Summit, PA

FIRST EDITION
FOURTH PRINTING

© 1989 by **TAB Books**.
TAB Books is a division of McGraw-Hill, Inc.

Library of Congress Cataloging-in-Publication Data

Blandford, Percy W.
   The woodworker's shop : 100 projects to enhance your workspace /
by Percy W. Blandford.
     p.   cm.
   Includes index.
   ISBN 0-8306-0434-0   ISBN 0-8306-0134-1 (pbk.)
   1. Workshops—Equipment and supplies—Design and construction.
2. Woodwork—Equipment and supplies—Design and construction.
I. Title.
TT152.B57   1989   89-32261
684'.08'028—dc20   CIP

TAB Books offers software for sale. For information and a catalog, please contact
TAB Software Department, Blue Ridge Summit, PA 17294-0850.

Acquisitions Editor: Kimberly Tabor
Manuscript Editor: Kathleen E. Beiswenger
Production: Katherine G. Brown
Cover photograph courtesy of Shopsmith Inc.   HT3

Contents

Introduction

If you enjoy making things in your own shop, you obviously have a keen interest in tools and techniques. This applies whether you have just a few tools and an improvised bench or have built up a comprehensive workshop with a large range of power tools.

Although the products of your shop are the outward evidence of its worth and your ability and you are proud of what you make and others admire, it is the steps that led to completion that provide you with the most interest. A well-made and -designed specimen of craftwork can be very satisfying. To others it might seem the justification for all the time and money expended on a shop full of equipment, but only you know of the personal satisfaction that comes from using your skill to the limit at many stages of construction. You had to solve problems. You had to find ways of doing things for which the available tools and equipment did not seem suitable. You had to improvise or make accessories or special tools so you could do the necessary work more expeditiously and with greater accuracy.

If you use your shop to the fullest, you will find you often need accessories and equipment that cannot be bought, or if they could, their limited use would not justify the expense. Because costs are something to consider, some things you make to use in your shop come about because of the need for economy. Even when ample funds are available, however, the interest and satisfaction involved in making rather than buying are all the justification needed to make what you need for your shop from available materials. Making something in the shop, which will then stay in the shop, is what this book is all about.

We live in an age of stores trying to sell us all kinds of power and hand tools for all kinds of crafts. World communications are such that you can buy tools imported as well as manufactured in your own country. It is possible to buy the best tools in their class, and in many cases, it is best to buy selectively. The power of advertising might tempt you to buy the latest speciality, however. In general, it is better to buy the basic hand and power tools of your craft. They have stood the test of time. With them you can make many other things to use in your shop.

Not so long ago the carpenter doubled as wheelwright and undertaker. He had his shop next to the blacksmith. Between them they made everything their neighbors needed. They also made tools for each other. They did not have a tool store around the corner or a tempting tool catalog to look through. Although you might not want to return to those conditions, they are examples of what could be done with mostly homemade equipment. Look at a piece of furniture or a pair of iron gates of a century or so ago and think of the work you ought to be able to do with your store-bought equipment supplemented by accessories you can make.

Whatever your chosen craft, most shop equipment has to be made from wood and metal. Unfortunately, some woodworkers do not want anything to do with metal, and there are metalworkers rather proud of not being able to work in wood. Both are foolish and missing out on a lot. There is a tremendous satisfaction to be had from looking at something and saying, "I made that," when it has both wood and metal parts fashioned by you. If you have the ability to work in one material, you have proved your manual dexterity and should be able to work in the other material. If you have not done so yet, try it.

Some craftspeople are more at home with wood or metal alone. For them, some of the projects in this book are given in two forms for the alternative materials.

This book contains over 100 projects of varying degrees of complexity, so there is something to suit any degree of skill. There are tools and accessories for a large number of applications and purposes. Whatever you normally produce in your shop, you should be able to find projects that will help you do your work more quickly, more economically, and more accurately. Of equal importance, you will get the satisfaction of using appliances you made yourself.

Although the projects described are functional, rather than decorative, you should spare the time to finish them properly. This will add to your enjoyment in using them. A well-made tool has its own type of beauty in the eyes of a craftsperson.

Note: Unless stated otherwise, all dimensions on drawings and elsewhere are in inches. In materials lists, widths and thicknesses are exact, but lengths are mostly full to allow for cutting to finished sizes.

1

First Considerations

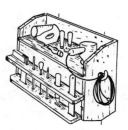

When you are planning to make things for your own use in your shop, you need an overall picture of the general scheme. There is usually a problem of limited space and the way to make the best use of it. Most workshops just develop as you get new ideas and new equipment, which you pack in somehow. It would be better to spend a little time planning ahead as much as possible. If it is a hobby shop, however, some of the happiness and satisfaction of using it comes from a more free-and-easy approach than would be necessary if you depended on the shop for making a living.

For you to get the most satisfaction out of something made for shop use, it has to be justified. You might enjoy making a special accessory or new piece of equipment. You might consider that is sufficient reason for making it, but if it then gathers dust and is rarely used after the first time, was it worthwhile? If it takes up valuable space without being used, that is a further problem. You have to decide whether the item is to be tackled just as an interest project, or if it will have plenty of further uses. If it is your hobby, making it just for the sake of making it might be all the reason you need.

Be careful of overcrowding your shop. You must be able to move about safely. Some addition or accessory might increase the scope of a particular machine, but check that in doing so it will not interfere with your movements about the shop or your operation of another machine. Often, it is better to make more bulky items so they can be taken down or folded. If something you make for use with one power tool can also be used on another, that is a bonus and could be a very good reason for making it.

If your main activity is metalworking, you might not have a great need to swing large pieces, but a woodworker has the 4-foot-×-8-foot problem. That is the size of most plywood and other sheet materials. It is very helpful if you can arrange to handle full-size sheets with a table saw or band saw, and additions elsewhere should not restrict this. Additions to these power tools might make handling sheets safer and more convenient. It is less accurate to cut sheets with portable tools, but if your shop is too restricted to allow safe maneuvering around stationary machines, you might have to settle for the portable tool or move the stationary machine to a larger area.

Dealing with lengths is not such a problem, but when you plan alterations or additions, make sure that you can feed a long piece of wood onto a saw and that there is space for the cut ends to feed off without restriction. Support in both directions increases accuracy and safety. To keep this passage of wood clear in a wood shop is important to you, so be careful to avoid racks or additions to other equipment that could interfere, even if wood has to come onto the saw through a doorway and feed out through a window!

STORING TOOLS AND MATERIALS

In ideal conditions, the shop has plenty of working space, and stocks of material are stored elsewhere, but not too far away. Even then, material for jobs at hand and all the shorter ends that are too good to scrap, which you know will be of some use one day, are more likely to be kept in the shop. In most shops, the stocks of material are kept in and around the working area, and it seems to be the smallest shops where this is most likely.

Tools also have to be stored, and the number of these you accumulate can be surprising, whatever your activity or craft. Nowadays, most hobbyists have stationary and portable power tools. The professional must have them to stay in business. If you call yourself a craftsperson, you will have and use a large number of hand tools. If you want to do more than just copy mass-production methods, you will use quite a lot of hand techniques.

As a result, you have to store power tools and their accessories, as well as your large selection of hand tools. Even if you are naturally untidy, you soon realize that there has to be some order if important things are not to be lost in your shop chaos.

Tools thrown together in a box take up the minimum space. Tools in fitted racks on a wall, in a drawer, or in a cabinet are kept safe and within reach and you know where to find them, but this takes up space. In the average shop you will have to compromise.

There are many tools that do not suffer from being stored together. Others, particularly cutting tools such as chisels and files, should be kept separate so their edges are unharmed. Accessories for some power tools are quite small and could be mislaid. They are better kept in fitted racks near where they are needed.

Work out the compromise to suit your tools, allowing for additions. Remember, you also might need to store materials, and space is limited. Decide which tools must have individual storage. They might require only a nail for hanging or a fitted rack. Not all individual storage has to be vertical. You could make fitted compartments in a drawer. There might even be a lift-out tray to take a second layer.

At the other extreme are the tools that can be loose in a box or drawer. This will leave you wondering about the many tools in between. You might wish to put all your wrenches, punches, screwdrivers, and other hand tools in wall racks. Is there space and would that be justified? There is little point in putting little-used tools on a wall rack if they will only gather dust. It would make more sense to decide which wrenches, screwdrivers, punches, and other tools of a kind you use most frequently. Will they suffer if packed together? Those few could go on racks, while the others are put in boxes or drawers.

ACCESS

Relate storage problems to benches, stationary power tools, and the general layout of the shop. You have to consider the whole workshop area. In general, materials can go where they least interfere with your working activities. Place hand tools in racks or drawers near the bench working area. Consider your movements. Try to arrange things so what you need is where you need it, if possible. (Space problems might dictate otherwise, of course.)

Consider the probable frequency of need with portable power and hand tools as well as accessories and equipment you make. If you make a new piece of equipment or an accessory for a power tool and it has to stay in position, it should be used fairly frequently or you might find it taking up space you would rather have for something else. Then your new piece becomes a nuisance.

Experience will show which tools you use most. Store them within reach. This means installing a wall rack above the bench to hold the tools you always use so that you can reach them with little effort. A drawer directly under the working area will do the same. Other tools that are only used occasionally can go elsewhere, in higher positions on the wall, or in lower drawers under the bench. Tools that are needed for special jobs that only occur rarely can go elsewhere in the shop. They are better kept clean in boxes or drawers as activity in a typical shop develops an inordinate amount of dust.

If rust might be a problem, closed containers are better than open racks. Use drawers or make wall racks with doors. Silica gel, either as crystals or paper, will draw moisture away from steel tools. Include some in storage places for tools and steel stock.

As much as possible, plan the shop and what you make to go in it to suit your physical needs and those of any other regular user. This gives you an advantage over the use of store-bought benches, cabinets, and other equipment.

Fortunately, most people are between 67 inches and 70 inches tall in normal shoes, so it is possible to settle some average shop equipment sizes. For instance, the top surface of a bench should come at about the height of your hip joint. For most people that is between 28 inches and 31 inches (Fig. 1-1A). If you are short, sawing or planing on a bench that is too high for you can be very tiring. A tall person using a bench that is too low does not suffer as much.

A metalworker might have a bench at this height, but the important height is the vise jaw level, which will suit most workers at about 34 inches (Fig. 1-1B). Some workers in more delicate metal forms might favor a few inches higher than that, although the basic height will suit most when sitting on a high stool.

For working downwards, the average craftsperson can use a trestle or other support at chair height or a little higher. A height of 16 inches to 18 inches (Fig. 1-1C) is sufficient.

A wide bench top is valuable if you use it for assembling wood frames and cabinetwork, but if you want to reach across the bench easily, a width of 27 inches is about the comfortable maximum for a bench against a wall (Fig. 1-1D). If the bench is free standing and you might work from both sides, it could go up to 33 inches.

If you visit a store and walk between blocks of shelves, the things the storekeeper wants to attract to your attention are all at eye level or probably little more than 12 inches above or below that. Let this guide you when placing wall racks, tool cabinets, and things you need to reach or see. Put the things you need most frequently between about 54 inches and 76 inches above the floor (Fig. 1-1E), if you are average height. If there is a cabinet projecting from the wall over a bench, leave a clearance of at least 20 inches (Fig. 1-1F). You can reach a little higher than your upper sight line, so position other tool racks there, but if there is more wall space and you are prepared to stand on something to reach it, tool or materials racks can go higher.

A very convenient level to reach from a normal standing position is directly under the bench top. A drawer 6 inches or so deep can store tools, hardware, and a great

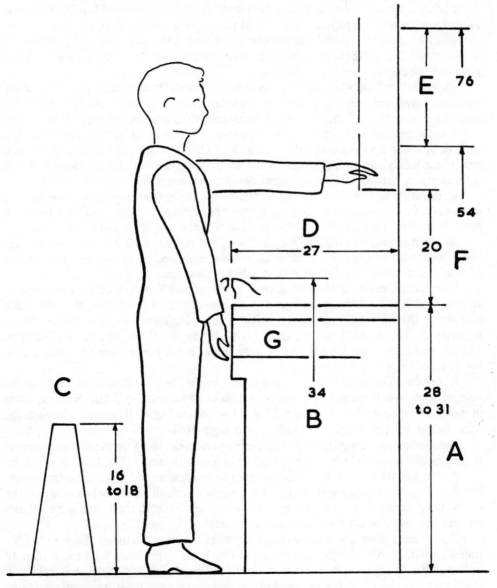

Fig. 1-1. *Arrange shop equipment to suit your height and reach.*

many other items (Fig. 1-1G). If you make much use of your shop, this will probably be the place for all the marking tools, notebooks, spare screws, and the multiplicity of things essential from job to job that you accumulate.

You will want to make use of space at a lower level, but this involves stooping or kneeling. Allow for that. Shelves too close and wide might prevent you from seeing and reaching to the back. Drawers that can be pulled right out might be better. Leaving space for a chest that can be withdrawn could be worthwhile. If you might sometimes want to take a quantity of tools elsewhere, some sort of portable container should form part of the shop equipment.

The foregoing heights are given as they relate to a bench and wall storage. Use them as a guide for other shop equipment. It is probable that your table saw came as a unit on a stand at a set height, probably about the same as your bench, although its table adjusts a few inches. Most workers find it better to have a jointer lower than this, which might be an advantage as large work on the saw table can swing over the jointer.

Opinions vary about the height of a band saw table, but the usual preference is rather higher than a table saw. If it can be high enough to clear the guard on a nearby table saw, it will allow you to swing a large piece of sheet material about the band saw.

As with the band saw, you might have your own preference about the height of a lathe. It is the height of its centers that matters. Experiment with a height around 36 inches.

PLANNING

There are more than 100 ideas for things to make in your shop for your shop in the following pages. If you made them all, there might not be room for you as well.

Many of the things you can make are comparatively small and portable. Hopefully, they will all be of use to you. If you are intrigued by tools and like to gather them into your kit, you will enjoy making them, particularly as most are different from anything you can buy. These are projects to tackle when and how often you wish. You might even make some for your friends or to sell.

Think more about some of the bulky items. Are they for you? Do they suit your needs and shop? If size related to available space is of paramount importance, you might have to discard one project in favor of another—or build a bigger shop!

When some home shop workers make an accessory or piece of equipment for use in the shop, they construct it to the point where it can be used, then never finish it properly. There might be an urgency about the job it is to be used on, and time is never found to get back to finishing it, or the attitude is that it serves its purpose and its appearance does not matter.

Leaving a tool unfinished is unwise. You would not buy an unfinished tool. You will appreciate the tool you make much more if its quality is at least as good as any store-bought tool. Smooth polished wood and clean bright metal will encourage you to do work of comparable quality with the working aid you have made. There is also the impression it makes on other people. If a visitor to your shop sees a crude thing, no matter how effective it is, he will judge your workmanship by it. If he sees a high-quality special tool, and you say you made it, his remarks should help your ego.

2

Working Surfaces

Whatever the activity or craft, you need a surface to work on. For some lighter crafts, you can manage with a normal table. For others, such as basketmaking in the traditional way, you can work on the floor. However, for most crafts you need a substantial working surface, much stouter and more rigid than a common table, if you are to do the work successfully. This is particularly the case with woodwork and metalwork.

The most important piece of equipment in a workshop used for working wood or metal is a bench that can stand up to all the pressures and strains you are likely to put on it. It should be of adequate size and the right height for comfortable working. If you try to work on an unsteady, weak surface that is at the wrong height, you will find it very difficult to get good results.

It is possible to buy benches, some of which are equipped with vises and other holding equipment, for which you might pay a considerable price. You have to accept the bench as it is. It might not be quite the size or height to suit you and might include gadgets that you will never use.

If you make your own bench, it can be individually tailored to suit your needs. It can make the best use of available space. Its height can be arranged to suit you. It can be equipped with just what you require. Most important, the fact that it is one of your own products should inspire you to do better work on it.

A bench might be regarded as just a stronger table, but starting with that definition, you have to do what is necessary to design it to suit your needs. The top has to be stout enough to stand up to the work. Flexing under hammering leads to poor work. If you want it to stand up to the inevitable cuts and scratches, it must have a tough surface, which means choosing a close-grained hardwood. Hardwood also resists flexing better than softwood of the same thickness.

The underframing must also contribute to the rigidity of the top by being stiff enough to take sideways loads as well as downward blows. Within reason, the stouter you make all parts of a bench, the better it will do its job.

Having satisfied these requirements of a bench, you can consider additional uses. Space underneath invites use as storage for tools or materials, but consider the implications. Fitting drawers and compartments might increase rigidity. The more you build in, the stiffer the whole assembly will be. Be careful, however, that storage arrangements do not interfere with the main use of the bench. If something has to go through the bench on occasions, there cannot be drawers below that position. Handles that project forward of the line of the bench top might interfere with a wide piece of work held down in the front. It might be better to make a chest or a block of drawers as a separate unit that fits under the bench but can be taken out.

A bench in a shop is a tool, not a piece of furniture. As such, it can be expected to suffer from wear and hard use while you concentrate on the job being worked on it. There is no need for cabinetmaking standards, but careful jointing is important. You do not want slackness developing in joints, which will reduce the rigidity of the bench. It does not matter, for instance, if joints show through where they will be cut back in furniture or if plywood edges show where they will be hidden in furniture.

TRADITIONAL BENCH

Over the centuries carpenters, cabinetmakers, and other woodworkers have developed remarkably similar benches in many different countries. The requirements are much the same, of course, whatever the place. If these benches evolved over a very long time to provide the best possible service to their users, it is probable that such a bench with very little alteration will suit your needs today.

Until quite recent times, most woodworking processes were carried out by hand. The bench had to stand up to hand work of many types, with some of it imposing heavy and directional loads. It needed to be heavy; even if it was not fixed down, its sheer bulk resisted movement. Its weight and bulk gave a good resistance and reaction to heavy pounding loads, so such things as driving joints together did not lose some of their effect because of the springing of the bench top.

Although machine tools can do many things, there is still hand work to be done. If you want the best results, many things are better done by hand completely or finished by hand after machining. If you have a fairly comprehensively equipped shop, much of the heavy work will be done away from the bench. There are occasions though, such as assembling a frame, when you will be glad of all the rigidity and bulk the bench can offer.

The bench in Fig. 2-1 can be made as long as the type of work justifies or space in the shop dictates but should not be less than 6 feet. The top has two large and thick boards for a working surface and a well between them. The well is a safe place to put tools, but it is removable and can be taken out to allow parts to hang through or clamps to be used. Pieces across the well end allow planes to be put down with the cutting edges clear of anything that might blunt them.

A freestanding bench is made to be used from either side. At each side under the bench-top boards are stout aprons, close up and securely joined to the tops. These are important parts. They give support to the tops and brace the legs. They are square to

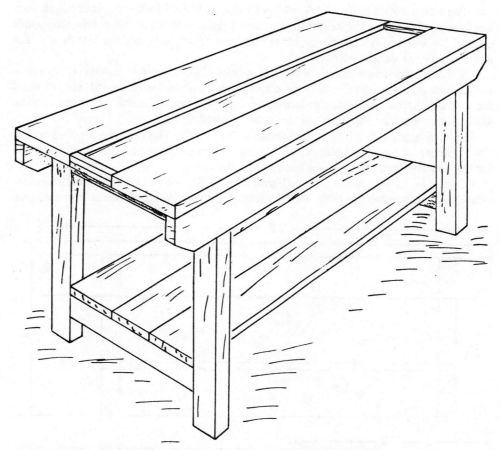

Fig. 2-1. *A bench should be solidly built. This one has a well for tools.*

the top and provide supports for boards on edge, today with one or more vises, but traditionally with pegs and wedging devices.

A bench to be used permanently against a wall might have a narrower and lighter back part on the top but at the same level, and the bench could be stiffened by fixing to the wall. If a bench is to be used against a wall, though it might be used elsewhere at some time in the future, make both sides the same so it can be used as a freestanding bench later.

The traditional bench was usually open between the legs. The craftsman kept his tools in a chest underneath, rather than in built-in storage compartments in the bench. This was because he was a *journeyman*, meaning that he moved between employers and took his kit of tools with him, but the bench belonged to his employer. There could be a shelf between the legs, but if you make a bench and want the facility of clamping through the bench after the well has been opened, do not obstruct the space below with tool drawers or racks.

The bench shown in Fig. 2-2A follows traditional lines. Modify the sizes to suit your needs or space. Relate the height to your own height so that you can comfortably work on top. No vises, dogs, stops, or other additions are shown, but the bench will take any of these, as described later.

Make the working surfaces of top and aprons of close-grained hardwood. Beech is the traditional choice. Ideally, all of the underframing can also be hardwood, but softwood free of large knots and other flaws could be used and would be much cheaper. Strong joints are at least as important as the type of wood.

Start by making the two leg assemblies (Fig. 2-2B). The legs are notched to half the thickness of the apron pieces. Check the widths of the actual pieces you will use for the top and well and arrange the rail lengths to suit.

Corner joints are shown halved (Fig. 2-3A and B), but you could use mortise-and-tenon joints or overlap the parts and bolt them together. Whatever joints you use, glue

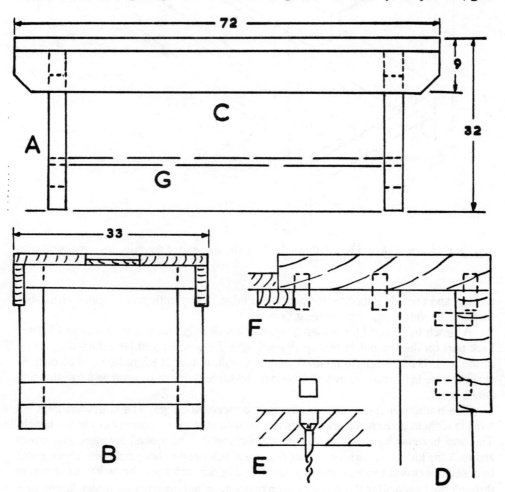

Fig. 2-2. Bench sizes and suggested construction with dowels and screws.

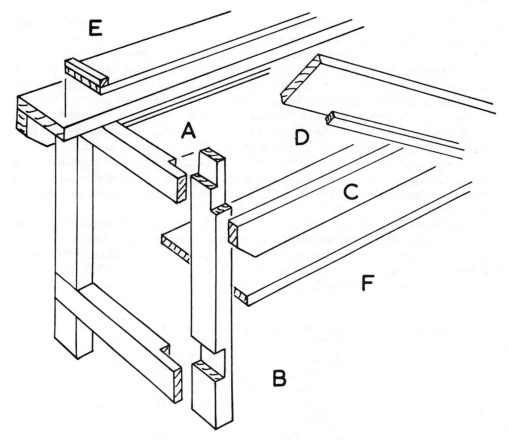

Fig. 2-3. *The parts of a bench with end frames linked with halving joints.*

them as well. Modern glues can contribute a considerable amount of strength. They are something the old-time bench maker did not have. Reinforce halved joints with dowels through them—three ¾-inch dowels at each corner would be appropriate. See that the finished assemblies are square and match each other.

Make the two aprons (Figs. 2-2C and 2-3C). Fit them to the legs with their tops level with the top rails. They can be attached in several ways. Stopped dowels are shown (Fig. 2-2D). It would be simpler to take the dowels right through the aprons, but for the smoothest finish, they are better stopped. You could screw the joints. Counterbore deeply, so there will be no metal near the surface, then plug over the screws (Fig. 2-2E). If possible, make plugs with the grain across, otherwise, use dowel rod. Screws allow you to pull the joints really tight, which is an advantage if you do not have suitable clamps to close up dowel joints.

At this stage, be very careful of squaring in all directions. Assemble on a flat surface. See that the legs are truly square to the aprons and that the assembly is square when viewed from above. Compare diagonal measurements.

Fit the two working surface boards over the rails and the aprons, in any of the ways described for the aprons. Sight along and across the assembly to check for twist. Slight errors can be corrected by trimming the bottom of one or more of the legs.

To support the well piece, put strips underneath (Figs. 2-2F and 2-3D) between the rails. Make the well a push fit between the tops (Fig. 2-3E). Dowel strips across the ends to prevent things from falling off and to act as rests for planes. Put strips underneath to fit loosely between the rails to keep the well in place lengthways.

If you want a shelf underneath, rest two or three boards on the lower rails (Figs. 2-2G and 2-3F). Either screw them down or leave them loose to lift off.

For general purposes, the bench is now ready for use. For precision cabinetmaking or other exact woodworking, however, you might wish to check overall flatness and level the two working surfaces to provide a true datum when you lay out and assemble pieces of furniture.

You could paint the lower parts of the bench, but the top and aprons are working surfaces and are better left untreated. Some commercially produced benches are oiled or even varnished on top, which make them look good in a showroom. If your bench is to get the amount of use you anticipate over many years, there will be times when you need to plane or scrape the top, and this is no place for varnish.

Materials List for Traditional Bench

4 legs	3 × 4 × 32
4 rails	3 × 4 × 33
2 aprons	2 × 7 × 74
2 tops	2 × 12 × 74
1 well	1 × 9 × 74
2 well supports	1 × 2 × 60

METALWORK BENCH

Although a bench of the traditional woodworking type could also be used for metalwork, there is generally no need for the well and, for many purposes, no need for the length unless part of the bench will be used to mount a machine. A basic metalworking bench is intended for setting out, handwork, testing, and assembly. A vise is the only item mounted on it. It is helpful if the top presents a broad smooth expanse. Metal parts spread on the top then will be level, easy to manipulate, all in the same plane, and less likely to snag on anything.

The bench in Fig. 2-4 is drawn 24 inches × 48 inches (Fig. 2-5A), but the same method of construction could be used for other sizes. The top is made of several solid wood boards about 2 inches thick (Fig. 2-5B). Over this goes a piece of ½-inch plywood (Fig. 2-5C). That might be all you require, but you can obtain a good working surface by adding a piece of tempered hardboard (Fig. 2-5D), which can be lightly tacked down and renewed when it becomes worn. Tempered hardboard, however, is surprisingly hard wearing when treated with oil. Ordinary hardboard would require more frequent renewal.

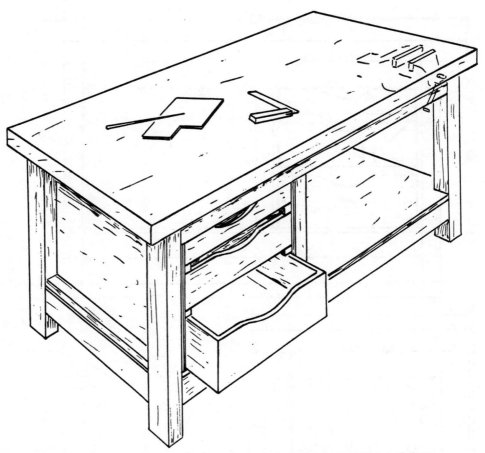

Fig. 2-4. *This bench has a level top. There are drawers and storage space below.*

The bench is shown with three trays fitted as drawers. They are intended to pull out for use on the bench or elsewhere. The top one could be fitted to take gauges, micrometers, and other instruments. The lower ones will take tools and materials. The open part could be enclosed with a door, but the open shelf can take larger items. This model allows a normal engineer's vise to be mounted towards the right-hand end. The whole thing could be made the opposite way around, if that would suit you better.

Make all of the underframing from 2-inch- × -3-inch wood. Joints could be mortise and tenon (Fig. 2-6A) or dowels, but dowels should be at least ¾-inch diameter and taken as deep as possible into the legs (Fig. 2-6B). Make the two end assemblies (Fig. 2-5E). The top overhangs 1 inch at the front and far enough at the back to cover the plywood.

Make the four lengthwise rails. Mark the positions of the 2-inch square uprights (Fig. 2-5F), which are tenoned or doweled. At the lower rails, the uprights can go into the rails directly and the shelf plywood cut around them or taken through the plywood (Fig. 2-6C).

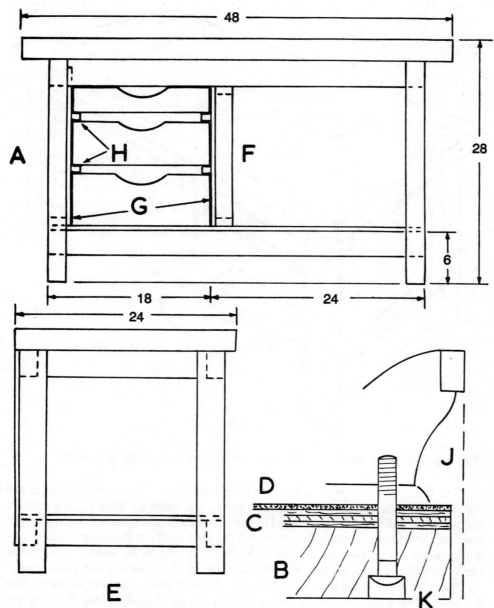

Fig. 2-5. *Sizes of the bench with drawers and how to bolt on a vise.*

Assemble the framing, including the shelf, which will help to keep the assembly square. Cut it around the legs and glue and screw or nail to the rails. Assemble on a level surface and check squareness in all directions. Fit the plywood back securely as this plays a major part in providing stiffness, besides its use in closing the back of the bench.

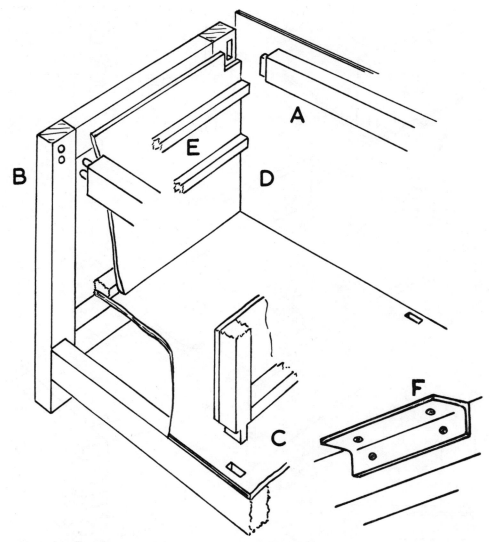

Fig. 2-6. *The parts of the underframing of a bench with drawers.*

Fit plywood panels to the legs and the upright strips (Figs. 2-5G and 2-6D). Stiffen the unsupported edges with 1-inch-×-2-inch strips. Inside the plywood pieces, attach 1-inch square strips to act as runners for the trays (Figs. 2-5H and 2-6E). Arrange the depths of the trays to suit your needs, but they look best if depths are graduated. Be careful to get the strips square to the front and parallel to the bottom shelf, if the trays are to slide easily.

Trays could be made in several ways. Simplest is a box with nailed corners and a plywood bottom nailed on (Fig. 2-7A). It would be better to let the bottom into rabbets (Fig. 2-7B) or even better to let it into plowed grooves (Fig. 2-7C). A stronger nailed

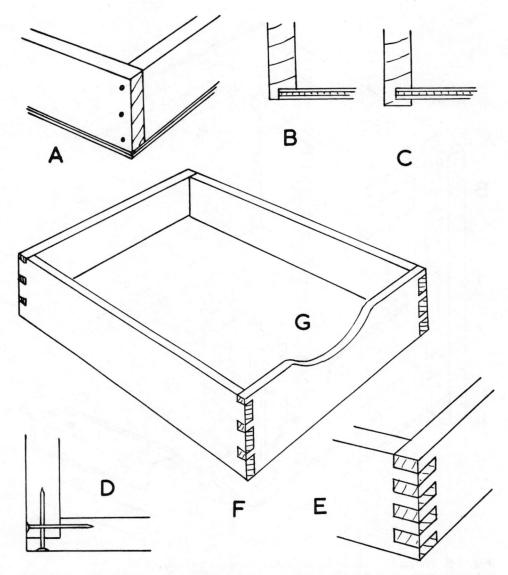

Fig. 2-7. *The drawers or trays can be made in several ways, depending on your choice of joints.*

corner has rabbets that allow nailing both ways (Fig. 2-7D). You could use finger joints (Fig. 2-7E), or you might want to try dovetails (Fig. 2-7F). You could use handles at the fronts of the trays, but you can avoid projections by cutting hollows to put your hand in (Fig. 2-7G). Round the top edges of the fronts.

Make the bench top with three, 8-inch boards or any pieces that will make up the width. Edges could be glued together, but when the bench is assembled, other parts will secure the boards. Glue the plywood to the boards and trim the edges level. Cut the tempered hardboard panels to match and lightly nail them in place.

It is advisable to fit the bolts for the vise before attaching the top to the underframing because they might be inaccessible after assembly. Position the vise so the inner jaw comes a short distance forward of the edge of the bench top (Fig. 2-5J). Drill for bolts as large as the holes in the vise base will allow. Counterbore underneath to allow coach bolts to pull into the wood (Fig. 2-5K). Put the bolts in place permanently before the final assembly of the bench.

Invert the underframing on the underside of the top and join these parts with screws through 4-inch lengths of angle iron. Any available material can be used, but anything between 1 inch and 1½ inches each way and up to ¼ inch thick is suitable (Fig. 2-6F). Two angle brackets at each end and three along each side should be adequate.

You could paint or varnish everything except the hardboard top. This will limit the amount of absorption of dirt and oil. Even if you do not treat the main parts, the trays will be better varnished or painted a light color inside.

Materials List for Metalwork Bench

4 legs	2	×	3	×	28	
4 rails	2	×	3	×	24	
4 rails	2	×	3	×	42	
2 uprights	2	×	2	×	18	
3 strips	1	×	2	×	18	
4 runners	1	×	1	×	24	
1 shelf	24	×	44	×	½	plywood
2 panels	20	×	24	×	½	plywood
1 top	24	×	50	×	½	plywood
1 back	24	×	44	×	½	plywood
1 top	24	×	50	×	⅛	hardboard
3 top boards	2	×	8	×	50	
2 tray ends	⅝	×	3	×	18	
2 tray sides	⅝	×	3	×	24	
2 tray ends	⅝	×	5	×	18	
2 tray sides	⅝	×	5	×	24	
2 tray ends	⅝	×	6	×	18	
2 tray sides	⅝	×	6	×	24	
3 tray bottoms	18	×	24	×	¼	plywood

BUTCHER BLOCK BENCH

If you need a bench with a top that has overall bulk and stiffness, one way of making it is to use wide, thick boards. They might not be easy to obtain, however, and there is a risk of shrinking, splitting, or warping in use.

Until the coming of modern synthetic glues of considerable strength, gluing was the only way of making such a top. It is now possible to laminate narrower strips in what has become known as *butcher block construction*, from the similarity to the way some butchers' chopping blocks have been made.

The advantage of this method is in using readily available wood, with the different grains canceling out any tendency to warp or suffer appreciably from other defects. This top is more stable, and its surface is likely to stand up to wear better than broad, flat boards.

The butcher block method can be used for bench tops of any size. A large one would be suitable for general engineering or heavy metalwork. One of lighter construction would provide a good working surface for leatherwork, jewelry, or any craft where most work needs a broad, truly flat surface that can take occasional hitting or other heavy use.

The bench used as an example in Fig. 2-8 is intended as a stand for a fairly heavy machine, such as a band saw, but the same method of construction is suitable for benches of many other sizes. For a machine, the top area has to be arranged to allow for bolting

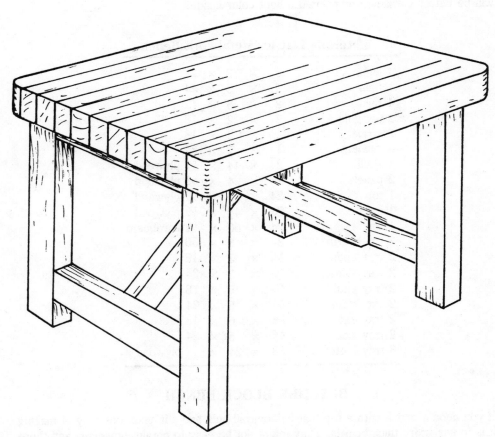

Fig. 2-8. *The top of a butcher block bench is made by gluing many strips together.*

the machine down, usually with some space around the base for putting down work or accessories. The bench height must be arranged to put the working surface of the machine at a convenient height.

The whole of the specimen bench is made of 2-inch-×-3-inch softwood, which is about 1¾ inches × 2¾ inches when planed. Joints could be mortise and tenon, but ¾-inch hardwood dowels are suggested.

For the bench shown in Fig. 2-9A, start by making the two end frames to match each other and with two dowels in each joint (Fig. 2-9B). Make the two lengthwise top rails (Fig. 2-9C) with dowel joints prepared in the same way but do not join them yet.

Set out a side view to obtain the sizes and angles of the diagonal braces (Fig. 2-9D). They cross each other and fit into the angles at the top and to the rails at the bottom (Fig. 2-9E).

Mark the rails in the end frames where the braces will come and drill through for two dowels at each place (Fig. 2-9F). Glue the doweled top rails to the legs and position the diagonal braces so you can drill through the rail holes into them. Glue where the braces cross and hold them together with a clamp while dealing with their end joints. When the assembly is satisfactory, drill through the crossing for a dowel or a bolt. Check that the assembly stands level and that the top surfaces are level. Sight across in both directions to test for twist. Correct any errors by planing.

The top is made of whatever number of strips are needed to make up the width with about 1-inch overhang on the underframing. Although it is possible to glue together all the pieces in one operation, there is a risk of movement when clamping; then parts will not match, and you will have to do some heavy planing to get the surfaces level. It is better to glue strips in pairs first (Fig. 2-10A), followed by gluing pair to pair before joining the whole width. In this way you reduce the risk of unevenness and will only have to do a little planing and scraping to finish the surfaces. Leave some excess length so you can level the ends and round the corners (Figs. 2-9G and 2-10B).

The top could be held down with blocks screwed to the rails and more screws up into the top. You could use metal angle brackets in the same way. However, doweling downwards (Fig. 2-10C) is simplest. Exposed dowel ends on top do not matter for such a functional thing as a workshop bench, but even if you are considering it as furniture, the pattern of dowels complement the strip appearance of butcher block construction.

Materials List for Butcher Block Bench

(all 2-inch-×-3-inch softwood strips)

4 legs	× 19
4 rails	× 16
2 rails	× 20
2 diagonals	× 28
12 tops	× 26

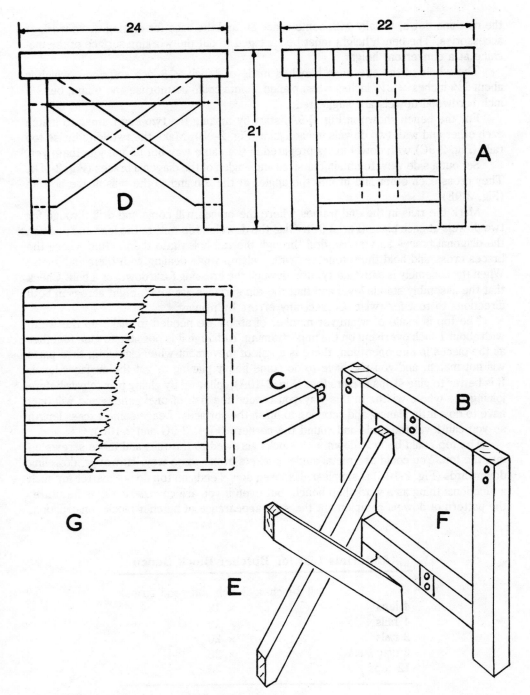

Fig. 2-9. *Sizes and dowel construction of a butcher block bench.*

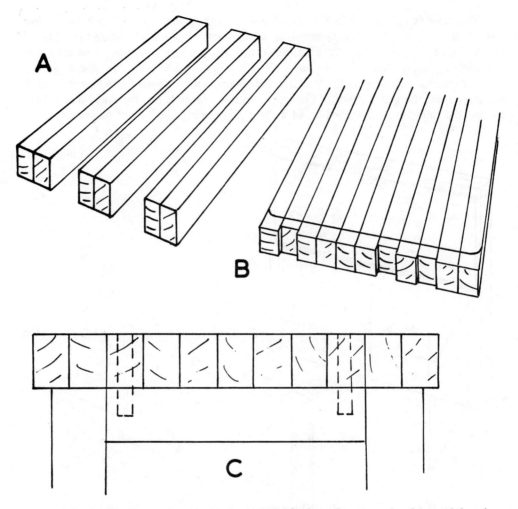

Fig. 2-10. *How to form a butcher block top and join it to the supporting legs and framing.*

FOLDING WALL TABLE

For many lights craft, there is no need for a substantial bench. A worktable can be large enough for spreading tools and materials, although pressures and loads are not expected to be great. In a shop mainly devoted to heavier work, there can also be a use for such a light working surface. It can be used as a drawing board, for laying out assemblies, or as somewhere away from the jumble of tools and equipment for studying plans and books.

There might not be the constant need for such a table or bench, however. Space might be too valuable, and a lighter working surface might only be justified if it can be folded out of the way.

The table or light bench in Fig. 2-11A will fold flat against the wall, only projecting a few inches. How far it projects depends on what you wish to store when the tabletop and its legs are folded. When the assembly is opened, it offers a good working area that is sufficiently supported and access to tools, drawings, or whatever you wish to store.

Arrange the assembly so the length will accommodate two folded legs that will swing out to support the greater part of the top when it is lowered. For the wall table in Fig. 2-12A, the tabletop is 22 inches × 44 inches, and the legs swing out to within 1 inch

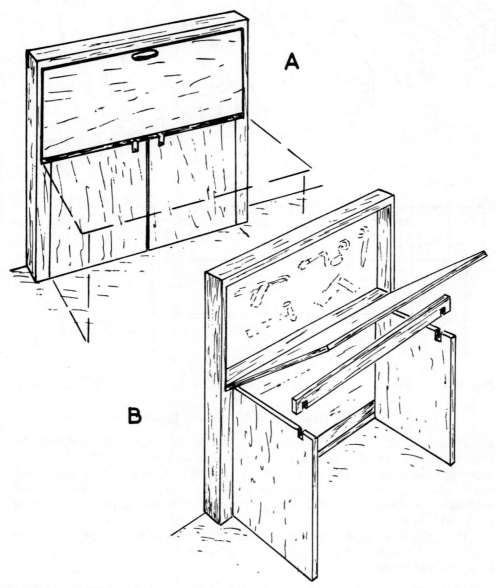

Fig. 2-11. *This worktable's top and supports fold against the wall to occupy minimum space.*

of the front edge. With a 30-inch working height, this gives a wall area coverage of 46 inches × 54 inches. If you need a different size, experiment with leg widths to match the size top you want.

The suggested design is intended to have ¾-inch or 1-inch plywood for the tabletop and legs. Most other parts are softwood. The back can be ½-inch plywood, which can be fitted with tool racks or other storage above the table level. There is a removable rail that notches into the legs below the top to hold the assembly in shape when in use. The rail stows in the lower part behind the folded doors.

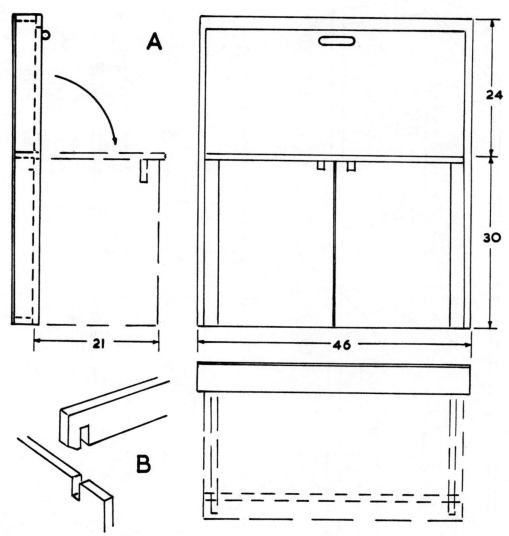

Fig. 2-12. *Sizes and layout of the folding wall table.*

Start by making the pair of ends (Fig. 2-13A) with the positions of the lengthwise parts shown. At the top, position a 1-inch- × -2-inch strip in front of a wider piece (Fig. 2-13B). At table level, set back a shelf by the thickness of the folded tabletop, with a stiffening strip below it (Fig. 2-13C). A 1-inch- × -2-inch strip on edge forms the side support for a leg (Fig. 2-13D). At the bottom, a piece goes across behind the thickness of the folded legs (Fig. 2-13E). There has to be a gap at the edge of the shelf to let the tabletop swing down (Fig. 2-13F). Its under surface will rest on the opened legs (Fig. 2-13G).

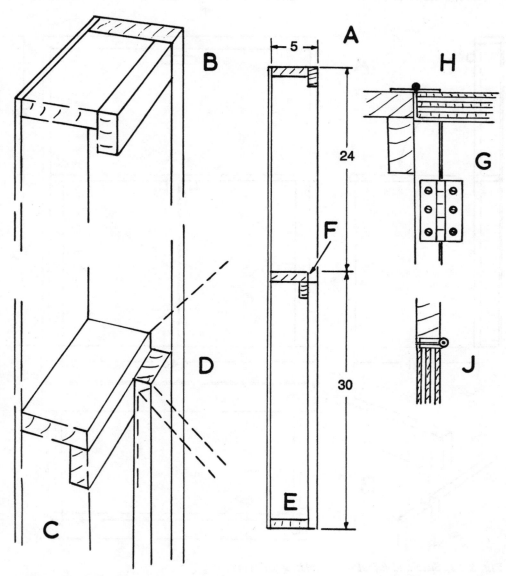

Fig. 2-13. *Details of the back part of the folding wall table and how the parts are hinged.*

Make all the lengthwise pieces and join them to the ends with glue and screws. For a more advanced construction, you could use dovetails at the corners and dado joints at the shelf. Add the strips to which the legs will be hinged. Nail or screw on the back to keep the whole assembly square.

If you want to fit racks for tools and other things, add them now. You could fit narrow shelves for equipment needed for your hobby or craft. You might prefer to provide racks for folded drawings or for your reference books. Details of many sorts of racks are given in later chapters.

Make the tabletop to fit above the top of the shelf and inside the sides and top strip with sufficient clearance for easy working. Hinge it to the shelf so that it will lower to a level position (Fig. 2-13H). Put small stop blocks inside the top corners of the framing to prevent the tabletop from swinging in too far. There can be a handle across the center. For the sizes suggested, use four 2-inch hinges and two spring catches to hold the assembly closed.

Make the legs to fit like doors between the side strips. You could put hinges on the surfaces, but they will look neater within the thickness of the wood (Fig. 2-13J).

Try the doors and tabletop to see that they fit together in the opened position. If this is satisfactory, make a 1-inch- × -4-inch rail as long as the tabletop. Notch this and the legs so that it can be dropped in (Figs. 2-11B and 2-12B) to hold the legs at the correct distance and provide some support for the top. The notches in the doors will then serve as handles for pulling them open. When out of use, the rail will rest diagonally behind the closed legs.

Materials List for Folding Wall Table

2 sides	1 ×	5 ×	56
1 top	1 ×	4 ×	48
1 shelf	1 ×	4 ×	48
1 bottom	1 ×	4 ×	48
2 cross pieces	1 ×	2 ×	48
2 leg sides	1 ×	2 ×	32
1 rail	1 ×	4 ×	48
1 back	47 ×	55 ×	½ plywood
1 table top	22 ×	48 ×	¾ or 1 plywood
2 legs	21 ×	31 ×	¾ or 1 plywood

MOBILE UNIT

If you want to work away from the bench, you have the problem of transporting tools and finding a surface to work on. The mobile unit in Fig. 2-14 can be loaded with the tools and materials you need and wheeled to where it has to be used. Its top is at bench height and can be used with clamps or a portable vise at the edge. There is a secondary use, if you make it exactly the same height as your normal bench—it can be positioned to support long material you are working on. You might prefer to make it the same height as your table saw; then it will support sheet or long material being sawn.

Fig. 2-14. *A mobile unit allows you to take tools about and provides a top to work on.*

As shown, the top is hinged at the back and can be opened to expose a box that will hold all the small things, such as nails and screws. The shelves will take hand or portable power tools. It is possible to add hooks, racks, and toolholders to the outside. What you put there depends on the sort of work you do. One or more large hooks will

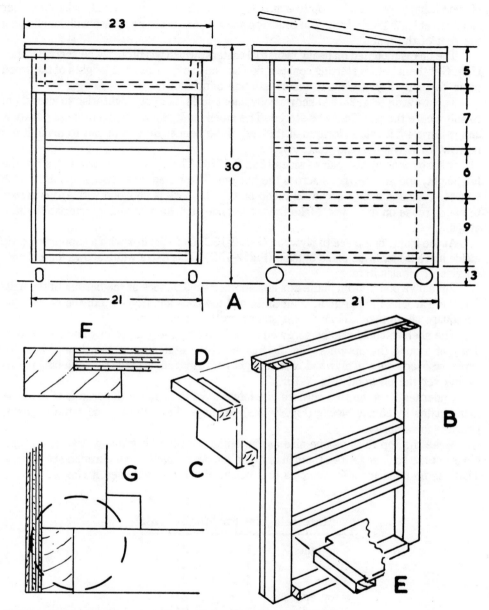

Fig. 2-15. Sizes and constructional details of the mobile unit.

hold coiled cables. You might find it worthwhile wiring the unit with outlets; then one cable from the source can bring power, and you can plug in several portable tools, thus avoiding a multiplicity of wires from the shop points.

Construction is mostly of strip wood on ½-inch plywood, with joints glued and nailed or screwed. Dowels are needed in a few places. The hinged top is drawn as thicker plywood, but if you need a top to stand up to heavier work, you could make a butcher block top at least 1 inch thick. You could replace a worn top after long use without affecting the rest of the unit.

The unit is mounted on heavy industrial casters, which will probably be about 3 inches high. Get them before starting construction so you can measure the heights of the wood parts correctly if you want to match existing benches.

The drawing (Fig. 2-15A) shows convenient sizes, but you might wish to alter them to suit where the unit has to be stored. The mobile unit might make a place to put tools and materials if it can be located at the end of the bench. Be careful not to make it too narrow, or it will become unsteady.

Start by making the pair of sides (Fig. 2-15B). The 1-inch-×-2-inch strips are the full height, and another goes across the bottom. The other crosswise strips are 1-inch square. Glue and nail or screw all these parts. The back is plywood with strips across to match those on the sides. Make the top outside strip long enough to overlap the side strips.

At the front, fit a piece of plywood (Fig. 2-15C) over the box with a supporting strip inside and a 2-inch wide piece outside (Fig. 2-15D). This extra width allows for a clamp-on vise or similar item.

Put a plywood bottom in the box and another similar piece at the bottom of the unit. Cut them around the uprights. With these and the back and front fitted, the unit should be square all around. Check that it stands level without twist.

The shelves could also be screwed in, although you might prefer that they lift out. They fit around the uprights (Fig. 2-15E) and need stiffening across their fronts. To avoid exposed edges of plywood, which might get damaged, arrange the stiffening pieces to lip over the plywood (Fig. 2-15F).

Underneath the bottom corners you might have to increase the area for the caster fixing plates by adding blocks (Fig. 2-15G). Arrange the casters as near the edges as possible for stability.

Make the top to the same size as the outline of the unit framing. Use two 3-inch hinges at the back edge. Let them in until the top bears tightly on the framing all around. There is no need for a fastener as the weight of the top will keep it closed.

Materials List for Mobile Unit

4 uprights	1 × 2 × 28
10 rails	1 × 2 × 21
8 rails	1 × 1 × 21
3 top edges	1 × 1 × 24
1 top edge	1 × 2 × 24
2 sides	21 × 27 × ½ plywood
1 back	21 × 27 × ½ plywood
1 front	6 × 21 × ½ plywood
4 shelves	21 × 21 × ½ plywood
1 top	24 × 24 × ¾ plywood

TRESTLE

The traditional sawing trestle has developed over the years and is difficult to improve. There are many occasions when you need to work on something at about knee height, and a trestle provides the support. If it is a large assembly or long piece of wood, you need two trestles. The standard trestle has a rather narrow top, which does not matter if you are using it with another one, but it might be difficult to steady some pieces of wood on a single trestle.

The trestle in Fig. 2-16 follows traditional construction, but there is an additional broad top to give better support when used alone. The top can be replaced after it has become worn and damaged. You could make just a single trestle or a pair, but the folding steps described next will serve as a second trestle when you have to deal will full sheets of plywood or anything else that is big.

All parts could be softwood, although hardwood for the top will have a longer life. Assembly is with glue and screws. Tightness of joints is important to prevent the legs becoming shaky or loose in use.

Fig. 2-16. *This shop trestle is of traditional form and suitable for any work at knee height.*

The size suggested (Fig. 2-17A) should suit most needs. The height allows for sitting when that is the best posture for work at the bench. Start by setting out the end view (Fig. 2-17B), using the sizes of the wood as a guide. If the legs meet under the top, their outsides should finish about 1 inch each side of the top. Allow for the legs going into notches ½ inch deep in the top (Fig. 2-17C).

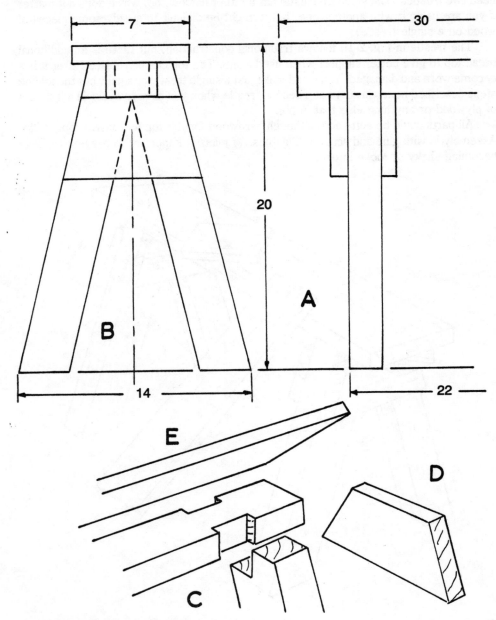

Fig. 2-17. Sizes and construction of the trestle.

Make the top with notches a close fit on the thickness of the legs. With your setting out as a guide, cut the four legs to shape. Use clamps to pull the legs tightly in as you glue them in place. Sight along to see that the leg angles match. Glue and screw on the braces (Fig. 2-17D) close under the top. If they are too long, trim them after the glue has set.

If necessary, trim one or more legs until the trestle stands without wobbling. Bevel around the ends to reduce the risk of splitting. Level the top surfaces. In particular, make sure the tops of the legs are level across because they will support the broad top.

Make the broad top (Fig. 2-17E) large enough to overhang 1 inch all around. If you either counterbore or deeply countersink for fixing screws, the heads cannot come into contact with saws or other cutting tools, but you will be able to withdraw them later if the board has to be turned over or replaced.

If you wish to make a pair of trestles, it is advisable to make all the parts for both at the same time so they match.

Materials List for Trestle

1 top	2 × 3 × 30
1 broad top	1 × 7 × 32
4 legs	2 × 3 × 22
4 braces	1 × 5 × 10

FOLDING STEPS

Because in most shops and at many jobs there are places too high to be reached while standing on the ground, step ladders of moderate height are always worth having. Low folding steps are useful also as alternative trestles, and they make suitable seats when working at a bench. The folding steps in Fig. 2-18 are intended to have the same overall height as the trestle in Fig. 2-16. With the two, you can support a full sheet of plywood or other large piece of wood parallel with the floor and at a convenient height for sawing or doing other work.

The two levels are 10-inch steps. It is always wise to make any ladder or steps with exactly the same spacing all the way to avoid stumbling due to different heights. If you make the steps to other heights, keep to an even spacing.

The steps can be made from softwood, all 1 inch thick. The joints shown are ½-inch hardwood dowels, but mortise-and-tenon joints could be used.

The steps are shown sloping at a 25-degree angle. The rear legs close level with the bottoms of the main sides and are held in the open position with rope (Fig. 2-19A). The side are parallel. Be careful when making the parts not to let the bottoms come closer than the tops. An error the other way does not matter.

Cut a pair of sides (Fig. 2-20A). Cut dadoes about one-third the thickness of the wood (Fig. 2-20B).

Round the forward edge of the step. Prepare its ends with dowels to go through the sides. Round the forward edge of the top in the same way and prepare dowel joints into the sides (Fig. 2-20C). In both cases the dowels go through, so you can drill from outside into both parts of each joint.

Fig. 2-18. *Folding steps at trestle height can be used to climb on or to support work.*

Make the back (Figs. 2-19B and 2-20D) with its top beveled to match the sides. This could be doweled, but it is more satisfactory to screw it to the sides and drive a few screws downwards into it from the top.

Glue together all the parts made so far. Make the lengths of the rear legs (Fig. 2-19C) to fill the space between the back and the bottoms of the sides but with the ends beveled the other way to rest on the floor. Assemble the legs with rails doweled on (Fig. 2-19D). Join the legs to the back with T hinges (Fig. 2-20E).

Drill the legs centrally opposite the lower rails for rope and put holes in the centers of the sides at the same level. Knot rope through these holes with its length adjusted to keep the treads level when the steps are pulled open (Fig. 2-20F).

Materials List for Folding Steps

2 sides	1 × 4 × 25
1 step	1 × 6 × 19
1 top	1 × 7 × 22
1 back	1 × 5 × 22
2 legs	1 × 3 × 18
2 rails	1 × 3 × 15

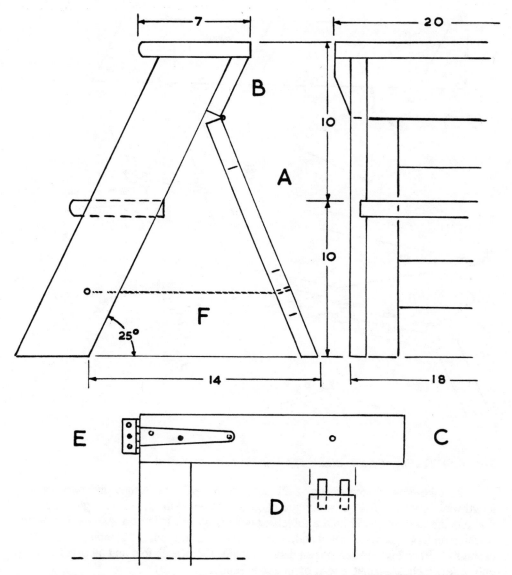

Fig. 2-19. *Suggested sizes for the folding steps and the method of hinging and joining the legs.*

TAKE-DOWN FRAME

Separate trestles will take care of many needs, and a pair will support large work, but they have to be positioned and can move in use. If they can be linked together, you have a much more rigid support under the work. You will know that neither end will move, possibly as just the wrong time during a crucial operation. In most shops, there is insufficient space for such an arrangement to be permanently assembled, especially when it is only needed for occasional use.

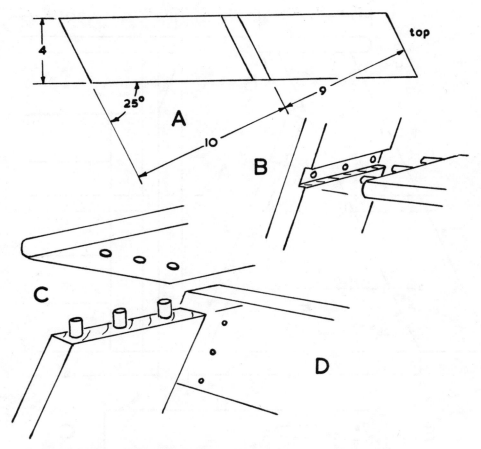

Fig. 2-20. *Folding step side details and how the parts are joined.*

The take-down frame in Fig. 2-21 consists of two end frames and two pairs of lengthwise braces to bolt on when you need the frame. With the sizes suggested (Fig. 2-22A), the assembly will hold a full-size plywood sheet. It is at a suitable height for working on large pieces of wood and, with stout boards on top, for standing on to reach ceilings or other high places. When disassembled, the braces fold and all parts take up only a few inches against a wall or under a bench.

All parts can be softwood, but hardwood tops will be more durable. Construction is shown with mortise-and-tenon joints, but you could use dowels.

Mark out the four legs (Fig. 2-22B). Leave a little extra length at the tops until after the frames have been assembled. Make the rails (Fig. 2-22C) and cut and fit the joints. See that opposite frames match and are without twist. Level the tops of the legs, then add the flat tops, which can have dowels through or be screwed on. The tops overhang about 1 inch all around and can have rounded edges and corners.

Fit the legs with permanently fixed projecting screws to take the braces. There are two possible ways of doing this. You could use ⅜-inch hanger screws (Fig. 2-22D), if these can be obtained with sufficient projection. The alternative is to use ⅜-inch car-

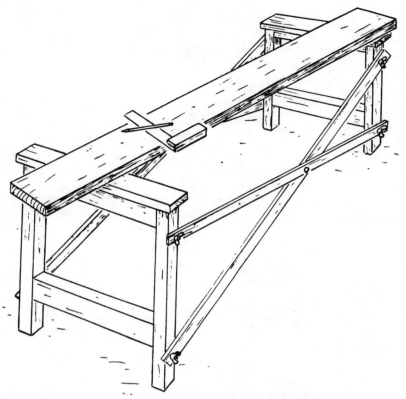

Fig. 2-21. A take-down frame is more rigid than trestles and will support large work.

riage or coach bolts (Fig. 2-22E). The square neck will lock the bolt in the wood and prevent turning.

You can make the braces to lengths to suit your needs, but making them 60 inches between end holes will give an overall length about the same (Fig. 2-22F). Do not cut the ends too close to the holes, or the short end grain might break out. Pivot each pair of braces together at their centers. As it is unlikely that you will want to separate them, use carriage bolts with locknuts.

Use large washers for the end bolts, to reduce wear on the wood, and wing nuts (Fig. 2-22G) or knurled nuts (Fig. 2-22H). You could use plain nuts, but the other types avoid having to find a wrench.

Materials List for Take-down Frame

4 legs	2 × 2 × 24
4 rails	2 × 3 × 21
2 tops	1 × 4 × 25
4 braces	1 × 2 × 66

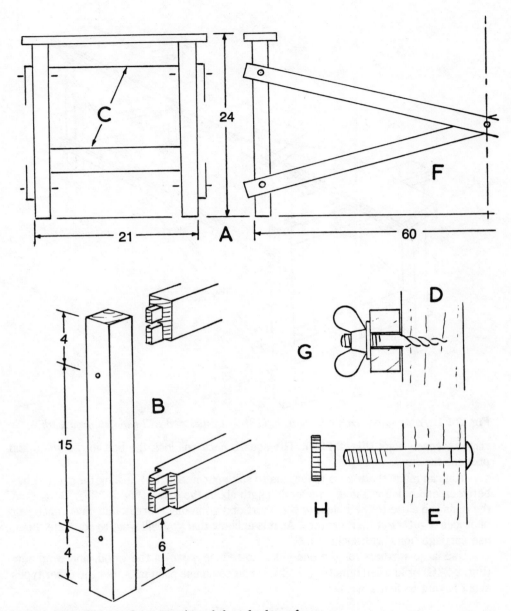

Fig. 2-22. *Sizes and construction of the take-down frame.*

3

Holding Devices

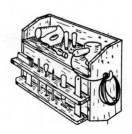

There is always a need to hold material being worked on, particularly when the item is small or unsteady. This applies to most materials but is especially a problem with wood. Nowadays there are a variety of screw-action appliances, but only recently have reliable, standardized screws become generally available. The principle of the screw has been known for a long time, but screws of use to craftspeople were rare. Such screws were usually one-off types with a nut to match that were not made to any standard; therefore they did not match any other screw. Because of the lack of screwed holding devices, earlier woodworkers had to use other ways of holding work.

Many woodworkers relied on wedges or a wedging action. A screw is a wedge wrapped around a cylinder, which uses the same ideas in a different way. Today the vise fulfills most holding needs; but before screws made a vise possible, there had to be some other way to hold wood.

You might think you have all the holding devices you need, but anyone who does much woodworking knows that there are often occasions when you need something different from or in addition to the regular holding tools. That is when some of those almost forgotten devices and techniques can still find a place. Many of them are at least as efficient as the modern alternative, and some allow you to do things more expeditiously. It does not matter how lavishly equipped your shop is, you will certainly find it worthwhile making some of the modern variations of old-time devices, as described in this chapter.

BENCH HOOKS

A bench hook is used over the edge of a bench to support a piece of wood you are working on. You push against it with one hand while working with the other. A bench hook can be used alone or with another matching one for long stock. A bench hook can be regarded as consumable. It can accept damage from a saw, chisel, or other tool that would otherwise harm the bench top. It is obviously easier to replace than a bench top. If made of hardwood, it will have a longer life, but softwood has possibilities.

A bench hook can be cut from a single piece of wood or be built up. A solid bench hook can be made from 2-inch- × -3-inch wood on edge (Fig. 3-1A). A pair will support a long board being worked on (Fig. 3-1B). The size between notches depends on the

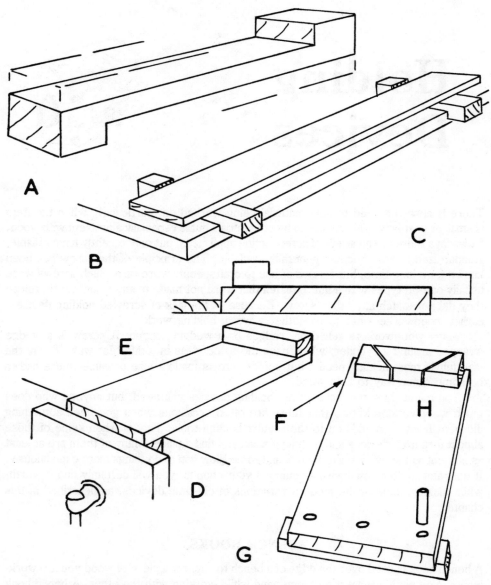

Fig. 3-1. *Bench hooks support work on the bench. They can be cut from solid wood or made by joining pieces.*

widths of boards you use. It should not be more than the width of the front part of the bench if there is a step down to a well (Fig. 3-1C). For many purposes, you use the hooks by pressing the work into them against the edge of the bench, but you get a firmer hold by gripping the work in a vise (Fig. 3-1D).

A built-up wider board is more satisfactory for use alone (Fig. 3-1E), but a pair can still be used for longer work. You can use a wider board alone for such work as handsawing an end or shooting an end with a plane on its side. In a basic wide bench hook, make one piece across the full width, but set the other back about ⅜ inch on each end (Fig. 3-1F). When you use a backsaw, and it drops through, it strikes the hook and not the bench top.

A suitable wider board has a piece about 1 inch × 5 inches with 1½-inch square strips across the ends. Avoid nails or screws, so there will be no metal to damage edge tools. Glue the parts and put dowels through. In any bench hook, whether solid or built up, it is important that the parts across are square to the edges. When making a built-up board, leave the main part too long at first, then mount the cross pieces squarely and trim outside afterwards (Fig. 3-1G).

It is unwise to complicate a bench hook with supplementary uses, but one addition that does not affect its normal use is converting one end into a miter block (Fig. 3-1H). This is suitable for cutting small-section picture molding or similar strips. Mark with a miter square and make the cuts with the same saw you will be using for mitering.

BENCH STOPS

For planing wood resting on the top of the bench, there has to be a stop to press the wood against. If you are right-handed, the stop should be towards the left-hand end of the bench. You can buy a surface-mounting adjustable stop to fit in a shallow recess, but this contains metal, and you only need to hit it once with a newly sharpened plane to wish you had not bought it. It is better to only have wood projecting above the surface. The traditional bench stop was a piece of hardwood through a hole in the bench. It held by friction and was adjusted by hitting up or down with a mallet. Arranging it next to a leg will provide extra resistance to the planing action (Fig. 3-2A).

For the stop to hold at its setting, the frictional grip has to be tight, so fine adjustment might not be easy. It is easier to get the projection exactly where you want and hold it there if you wedge the bottom against a block (Fig. 3-2B). Make the amount of projection nil to about 1 inch. The wedge will give fine adjustment to about half that, then you put a packing under it for further movement. Make the wedge long enough to knock in or out, whatever the adjustment. On a wide top, you could add a second stop square to the first to hold wide boards.

Another way to lock the bench stop at the height you want it, without its frictional grip having to be so tight, is to use a wing nut on a screw (Fig. 3-2C). Make the stop thinner or reduce the lower end. Reduce a 1½-inch square piece to ¾ inch thick for a length sufficient for a slot (Fig. 3-2D). Use a ⅜-inch hanger (or table) screw with a wing nut and large washer (Fig. 3-2E). To drive the screw, lock a plain nut and a wing nut at the top of the thread. Drill for the wood screw part in the leg and start the screw with a tap from a hammer, then turn it in with the wing nut or a wrench. Separate the two nuts and discard the plain nut. If possible, use a washer large enough to cover the

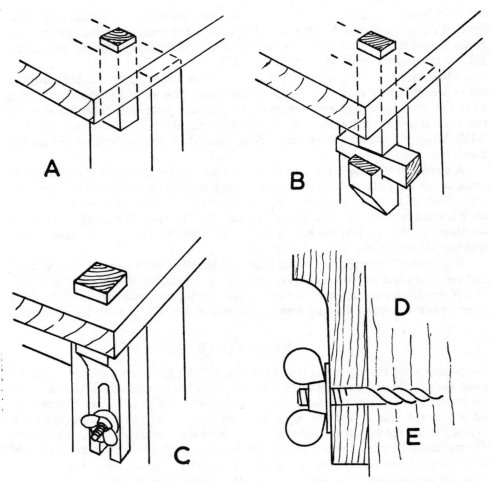

Fig. 3-2. A bench stop can be held by friction (A), by a wedge (B), or a screw (C, D, E).

width of the wood. Alternatively, make one by drilling a hole at the center of a square piece of ⅛-inch metal.

APRON WEDGE

Before the days of screw-action vises, anything which had to be held upright against the side of a bench was secured by wedging. The method used can still be employed today. Even if you have a normal vise at one side of your bench, there can be other places where a wedged support could be used. If the bench is freestanding, the method could be arranged at the other side. You could use the facility at other places in the shop where you need to hold anything upright.

The basic part is a substantial block with a shallow V cut (Fig. 3-3A), bolted horizontally to the bench apron or other upright surface. Thicker wood can go directly into the slot (Fig. 3-3B). Thinner material can be held with a wedge (Fig. 3-3C).

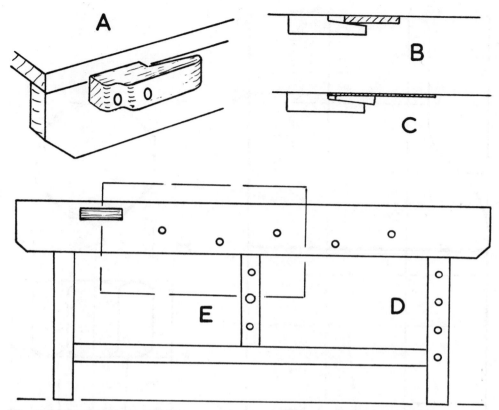

Fig. 3-3. *An apron wedge can take the place of a vise in some situations where wood has to be held upright. Pegs in holes take the weight of large pieces.*

Make the block from hardwood. The size depends on what you want to hold. If it is only plywood, the block can be much lighter than for heavier framing parts. In any case, make it fairly deep to give a good bearing surface—3 inches deep would be reasonable. A suitable size for general use is shown (Fig. 3-4A).

Save the piece you cut out for use as a wedge. Because the levering action on the fastenings is considerable, bolt through rather than rely on wood screws.

The block, as it is, will serve for upright strips of wood, frameworks, or pieces of plywood that reach the floor and for many other assemblies or parts that might not get much pressure. However, if you need to hold a big piece of plywood or a long board against the apron, without it reaching the floor, it will need other support. This was, and still can be, done with pegs. Drill the apron and the bench leg and any other upright to take the pegs (Fig. 3-3D)—¾ inch or 1 inch would be suitable.

If you have a lathe, suitable pegs can be turned (Fig. 3-4B). If you leave square or octagonal heads, the pegs will be easier to grip for withdrawal. In use, you position one or more pegs to provide support (Fig. 3-3E). This is an idea you can also use for long or large work held at one end by a modern vise.

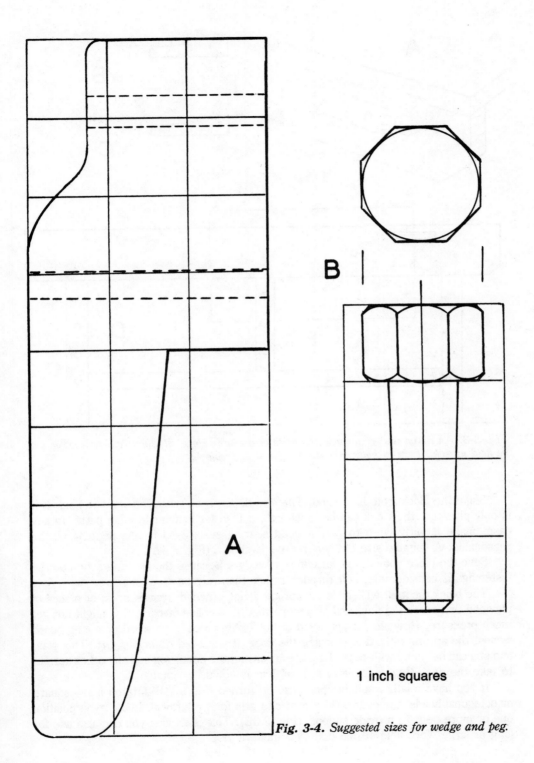

B

1 inch squares

Fig. 3-4. *Suggested sizes for wedge and peg.*

BENCH-TOP SUPPORTS

If you put a thin piece of wood in the vise and its ends overhang, it will sag under pressure. If you are planing or doing other work on the top edge, it will not finish true after pressure is released. To prevent this happening, the wood has to be supported under its lower edge for its full length. The obvious place to provide this support is the top of the bench. The problem then is to hold the thin wood upright. You have a choice of methods of holding the wood, all of which depend on a wedging action in a block on the bench.

The first support works in the same way as the apron wedge just described. A block with a V cut takes the work and a wedge and attaches to the bench with two dowels that can be pulled out of their bench holes when not required (Fig. 3-5A). If you regularly work on wood of quite small section, you might make a support perhaps ½ inch thick, but for the more usual sizes in general woodworking, such as ½-inch-×-3-inch section, the block could be 2 inches thick. A reasonable length is an advantage because it increases the amount of support. A suggested outline is shown (Fig. 3-6A). As with the apron wedge, make the wedge from the piece you cut out.

Dowels should be hardwood as they have to take a heavy shearing load in use. Drill through the block and the bench top at the same time to align the holes. Glue the dowels in the block. Ease the holes in the bench so that you can lift the block away. An alternative to drilling squarely is to angle the drill in the direction of thrust in use (Fig. 3-5B) to let the planing action tighten the block on the bench.

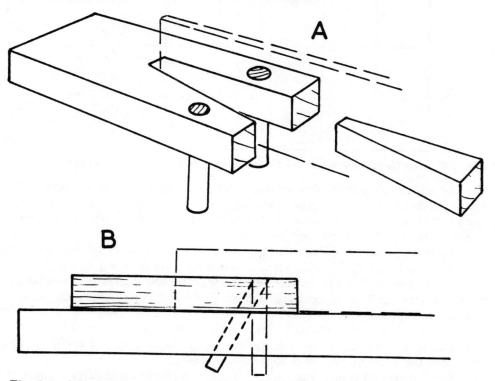

Fig. 3-5. A block with a V cut and dowels into the bench can support wood on edge.

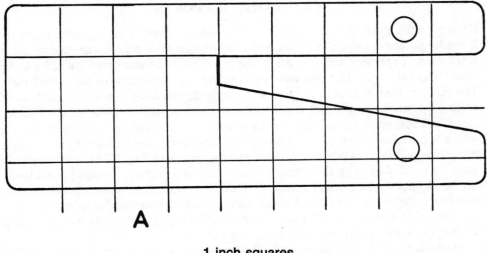

A

1 inch squares

B

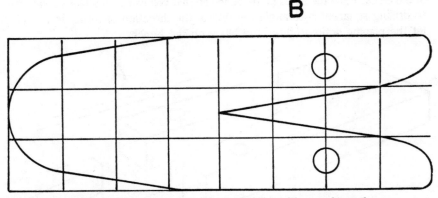

Fig. 3-6. Long blocks with narrow Vs are suitable for holding thin wood on edge.

The wedged block holds thin wood on edge securely, but you have to tap in the wedge and then loosen it on each occasion. Many pieces can be held in a slightly different block without a wedge. If you have to work on a large number of similar pieces, being able to dispense with a wedge will save time.

This block has an acute V opening that is symmetrical to the lengthwise direction of the bench (Fig. 3-6B). Make the block with dowels in the same way as the previous support. The first support is better with very thin wood because it gives sides steadiness, but the second type is good for anything upwards of about ⅜ inch thick, where there is some inherent stiffness.

You will probably find yourself using this block for thicker wood, which might otherwise be worked against the ordinary bench stop. Anything up to the width of the opening of the V can be held so it does not move about.

The third support is ingenious, but not so easy to make successfully. Because of the loads put on comparatively thin parts, it has to be made from a tough hardwood.

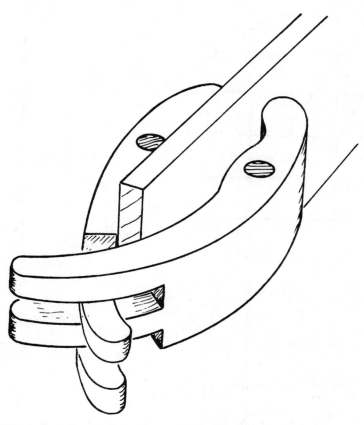

Fig. 3-7. *This support for wood on edge on the bench top grips the wood as it is thrust in.*

The action of forcing wood into the support causes a grip, which increases as the thrust gets greater.

There are two sides pivoting on dowels arranged vertically into the bench top. At the further ends, the sides have fingers that interleave. When a piece of wood is pushed between the sides, the fingers are forced apart and the thickened near ends press against the sides of the wood. As a result of these combined actions, any wood within the capacity of the support will be locked vertically on the bench allowing its upper edge to be planed. The capacity of the support depends on the spacing of the pivots, but in this example (Fig. 3-7), with the pivots at 2½-inch centers, wood from nil up to 1 inch thick can be held.

The pivots are ¾-inch hardwood dowel rods that are glued in the support sides but push fit in holes in the bench top so they can be removed. Because of the risk of splitting during construction if shaping is done first, drill holes for the dowels while the wood is in squared blocks.

The parts are drawn 2 inches thick, with two fingers on each side. This is the minimum to be effective. You could make the pieces thicker with more fingers or have thinner fingers in the same thickness. Much depends on the strength and density of the wood chosen.

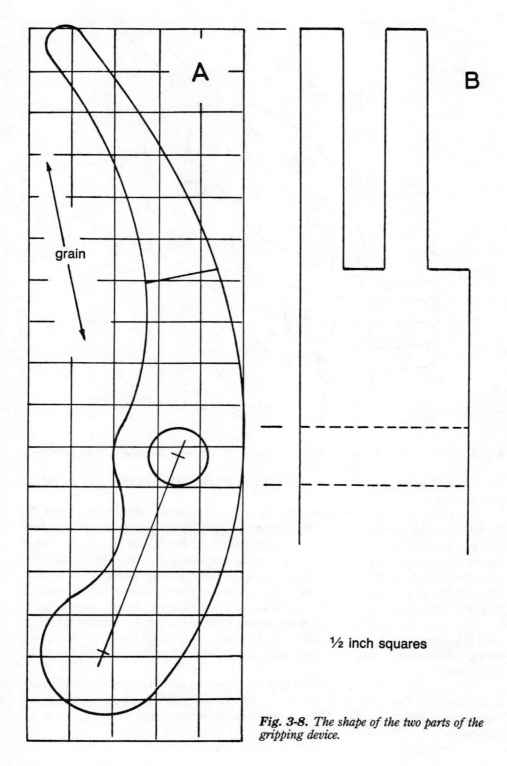

A

grain

B

½ inch squares

Fig. 3-8. *The shape of the two parts of the gripping device.*

Mark the shape of two identical pieces (Fig. 3-8A). Drill for the dowels. This must be done square to the faces, using a drill press, if possible. Cut the outlines and smooth them, keeping square to the top and bottom faces.

Mark and cut the end fingers (Fig. 3-8B). Trim and smooth the meeting surfaces to slide in each other without excessive play. Glue in dowels with enough projecting to go through the bench top and project up to 1 inch.

You might find it advisable to drill holes in scrap wood and test for action before drilling the bench top. If you have worked to the sizes given, and the pivot holes are 2½-inch centers, the jaws should close to grip the thinnest wood while the fingers still have a good overlap. With thicker wood, the finger overlap will increase. Be careful to drill the bench top squarely.

TRADITIONAL VISE

The modern parallel-action woodworking vise is a precision tool and your best aid to good work. Some of the small wooden vises that are fitted to some imported benches have nothing to keep the jaws parallel. They will try your patience and make good work less easy. You need a good vise, but it is always useful to have more than one.

Once good screws and nuts of a size to suit a vise had become available, woodworkers made their own vises. A vise of traditional form is quite effective. Its advantages include a low price, a reliable action, and a grip across a good width at the top. It does not lever out of true, as some simpler wooden vises do. If you have a long screw, its capacity might be greater than any other vise you have.

Vise screws can be wood or metal. Wood screws are necessarily thicker and could be 2 inches in diameter and as much as 24 inches long. Steel screws are about half that diameter but could be almost as long. In both cases there is a nut to put inside the bench apron, which is usually screwed into place.

The vise jaw reaches almost to the floor and is arranged to slope across a bench leg (Fig. 3-9A). At the bottom, an adjustable strut passes through a guide on the leg (Fig. 3-9B). As the vise is opened, the strut is drawn out and a peg is put through one of the holes in it (Fig. 3-9C) to keep the vise opening parallel or slightly closed in at the top. As the top edge of the jaw is being levered against this peg, the pressure at the working end of the vise is considerable.

Drill a clearance hole for the screw you will use. Drill about 6 inches from the top surface of the bench or at about the center of the apron. For normal right-handed use, position the hole to the right of the top of the leg. You can then slope the jaw across to take the strut on the other side of the leg.

Make the bracket to attach to the bench leg (Fig. 3-10A). Hardwood is preferable because it sometimes has to resist a heavy thrust. Make the slot an easy fit over the wood you will use for the strut. That should also be of hardwood and can be a 1-inch- × -2-inch section. Fit the bracket level with the front surface of the leg and with the bottom of the slot about 4 inches from the floor.

Lay the wood for the vise jaw across the apron. A softwood, 2-inch- × -10-inch section is suitable. Position it to overlap the bracket slot and to center the screw in the width. Mark and cut the top and bottom (Fig. 3-10B). Drill for the screw. Fit the nut inside the apron and make a trial assembly to check for satisfactory action.

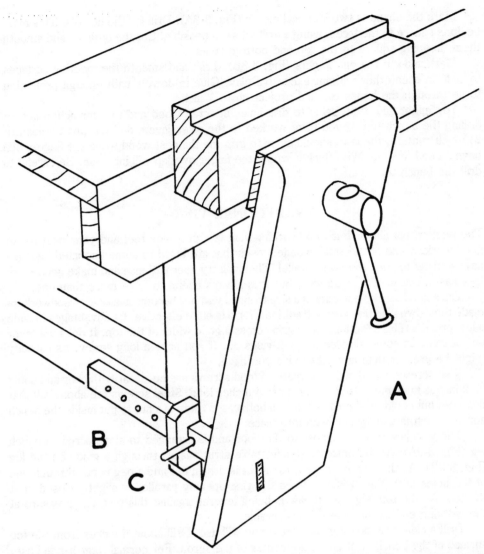

Fig. 3-9. *A traditional vise has a screw at the top and a strip with holes and a peg at the bottom.*

Most vise screws are supplied with a groove a short distance from the head (Fig. 3-10C). This is so you can arrange the jaw to come with the screw as you turn it out. Otherwise you have to pull the jaw back as you unscrew.

To use this groove, you have to provide something in the vise jaw to engage with it. This can be a strip of hardwood shaped to fit in the groove (Fig. 3-10D) and driven into a mortise (Fig. 3-10E). Instead of the flat strip and its mortise, you might find it easier to use a dowel rod in a drilled hole. Shape the end of the dowel rod to fit the groove. When you assemble, use plenty of candle wax in the screw groove to ensure a smooth action. Leave a little of the strip or dowel projecting; you can tap it in further, if it is ever necessary.

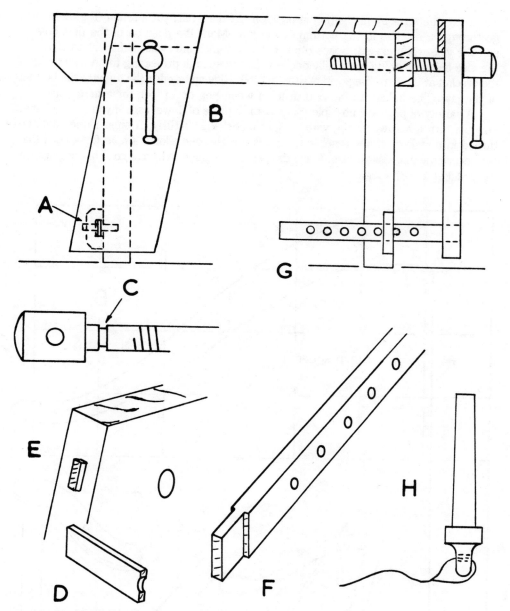

Fig. 3-10. *Size and layout of a traditional vise.*

Put a strip of hardwood across the inside of the top of the jaw, using screws deeply countersunk inside. When the strip has become worn and damaged, you can replace it easily. The vise could close directly against the bench top, but you might prefer to let in a matching piece of hardwood there to act as an inner jaw and protect the bench edge from damage.

Make the strut by measuring in position. At the front, cut a tenon (Fig. 3-10F) to go through a mortise in the bottom of the jaw. Mark the position of the first hole to suit the vise when closed. Space other holes at 2-inch intervals, sufficient to allow for the vise being anything up to fully opened. Leave enough projecting to go well through the bracket at the extreme position (Fig. 3-10G). Glue and wedge the tenon in the bottom of the jaw. The holes can be ⅝ inch for a wood peg or ½ inch for a metal one.

A variety of pegs are possible. Simplest is a piece of dowel rod. If you have a lathe, you can turn a hardwood peg with a slight taper (Fig. 3-10H). A similar one could be turned in metal. In either case, cutting a flat at the end allows a hole for a cord that can secure the peg against loss. Make the peg long enough to have a good bearing against the bracket and the leg.

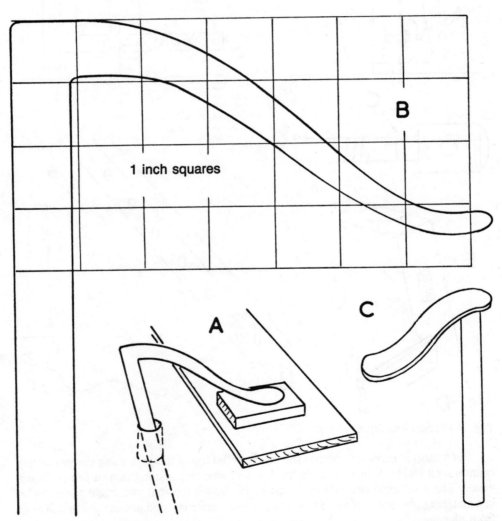

Fig. 3-11. *An iron holdfast fits through a hole in the top of a bench to hold work on the bench.*

HOLDFAST

Besides the occasions when you want to push wood against a stop or prevent it sliding on the bench, you might want to hold the wood down on the bench top. You can use clamps near the edge, but they are no use in the main area of the bench top where you need one or more holdfasts. A holdfast has a rod that goes through a hole in the bench top and an arm that presses down on the wood. It is possible to buy a modern version with a screw for tightening, but a plain type can be made if you have metalworking facilities.

The rod goes through an oversize hole in the bench and a palm on the arm presses down on the wood, usually with a piece of scrap wood to spread the pressure (Fig. 3-11A). You tighten it by hammering the top. You loosen it by hitting it sideways. If you drill plenty of holes in the bench top and have several holdfasts, almost anything flat can be held down. Its maximum thickness will depend on how long you make the rod.

Round iron or mild steel between a ¾-inch and 1-inch diameter is suitable. To forge a solid holdfast, first upset where the bend will come, so you can get a fairly sharp angle there, rather than make a radiused bend, which would not be so good for hitting in use. Taper the arm (Fig. 3-11B) and spread a palm at the end. Round and smooth the palm where it will bear on the wood.

Another way to make a holdfast employs welding. Bend a piece of mild steel at least ¼ inch thick and upwards of 1 inch wide to a similar curve to that of the forged version. Weld it to the top of a round rod (Fig. 3-11C). How long you make the rod in either version depends on your anticipated needs, but it is wise to give it plenty of length—18 inches is reasonable.

4

Clamping Arrangements

"In boatbuilding, you are always finding that you need two more clamps than you actually possess."

That quotation is applicable to many other woodworking activities besides building boats. Not all activities are as demanding of clamping devices, but there are many occasions when you will find you need more clamps or special ones to take care of individual cases where the standard clamps will not do. Fortunately, there are many ways of clamping parts together that can be improvised or simply made. You cannot manage without C clamps or bar clamps, but the other arrangements can supplement them or take their place for special jobs.

You can arrange for the actual method of construction to pull parts together. Screws will ensure a close contact. Tapered pegs through staggered holes will pull tenons into mortises. Dovetail joints will automatically tighten in one direction. These are useful devices that avoid clamps, but they still leave many woodworking constructional situations where some outside arrangement has to be used to draw parts together, particularly when using glue. Even where glues are described as gap filling, that often only means a few thousandths of an inch.

Like the holding devices described in chapter 3, many of the clamping devices you can use depend on wedging. An enormous amount of pressure can be exerted by a wedge, but it does not move an object very far. You can expect a movement of several inches with a screwed clamp, but with a wedge, the movement is probably not as much as 1 inch—packings therefore have to be used.

The amount of pressure is related to the angle of the wedge. A very shallow angle produces the most pressure, but very little movement. A steep angle gets more movement, but each hit produces less pressure. With too steep an angle, the wedge might slip out. It is usual to cut wedges by eye; a slope of 1 in 9 is a typical shallow slope, while you might get away with a 1 in 3 for a steep angle. An acceptable compromise would be 1 in 6.

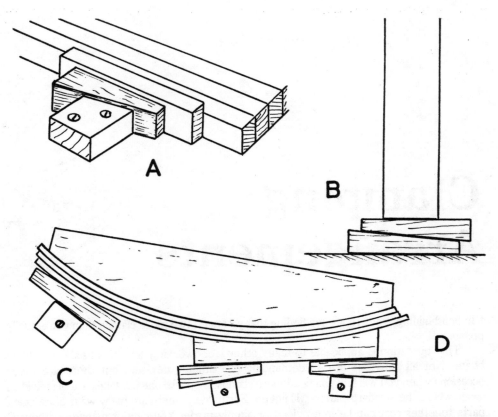

Fig. 4-1. *A single wedge will provide thrust (A). A pair of wedges gives a parallel thrust (B). Wedges can force laminations around a form (C,D).*

A wedge used alone (Fig. 4-1A) might push against a scrap wood pad, but each hit on it tends to move the pad and the job. There are several situations where this is acceptable, but if you want a straight parallel thrust, use a pair of *folding wedges* (Fig. 4-1B). The two wedges should have identical slopes, although they need not be the same thickness. If they are tightened by driving alternately or at the same time, the thrust obtained is parallel. The power exerted should be at least as good as a jack or other screwed device.

You can use scrap wood to make wedges in anticipation of future needs. You can build up a stock of wedges of many sizes and slopes, preferably paired.

A typical application of a wedge is in forcing laminations around a form. If you pivot a block on a single screw into the base board, it will take up an angle to suit the wedge (Fig. 4-1C). Wedging is a simple and very effective way of closing up laminations if you use shaped pressure pads (Fig. 4-1D).

WEDGED BAR CLAMP

Clamps with a long reach are expensive. You probably do not have enough for pulling large framing parts together or for securing several glued boards to make up a width.

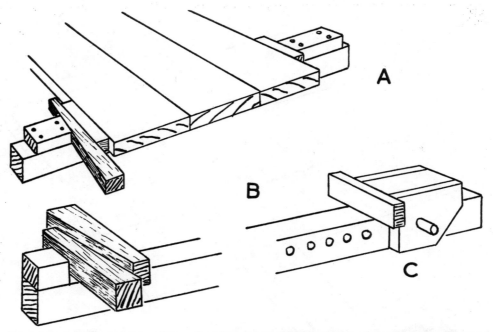

Fig. 4-2. *A wedge can be used in a fixed bar clamp (A). A pair of wedges and a movable head can form an adjustable bar clamp (B, C).*

You could improvise the clamp in Fig. 4-2 for a particular job, or you could make one that is ready for any occasion. For a one-off bar clamp, screw on the stops to suit the job (Fig. 4-2A). Allow for packings against the work to spread pressure and prevent damaged edges. One block is cut at the same angle as the wedge, unless you will be using folding wedges.

For this or any other long clamp, use a bar deep enough to resist bending under pressure. A shallow bending bar will allow the parts being clamped to also bend.

A bar clamp that can be adjusted has one fixed block to take the wedges and another that can be located at many positions along the bar (Fig. 4-2B). Make the blocks as deep as anything you expect to clamp. For general purposes, blocks 1½ inches deep on a bar, preferably hardwood, and 1½ inches × 3 inches and 36 inches long would be adaptable to many applications.

Glue and screw the fixed block at one end. Make the other block long enough to resist tilting. Make cheeks with plywood and put a piece to spread the pressure across these parts (Fig. 4-2C). To allow for the limit of wedge movement of only about 1 inch, drill holes in the bar at 1-inch intervals. To suit the suggested sizes, they could be holes for a ½-inch dowel rod. The peg could be just a piece of rod, or you could turn a wood or metal peg, as suggested for the traditional vise (Fig. 3-10H).

DOUBLE BAR CLAMP

The bar clamp described in Fig. 4-2 will suit many purposes and is the type to use when assembling a frame when there are parts projecting. When you want to join several boards

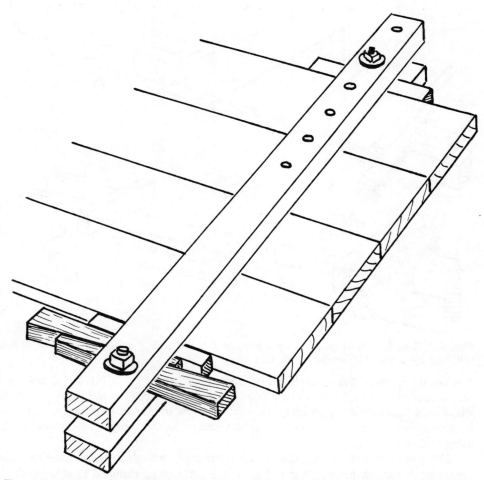

Fig. 4-3. *A double bar clamp with wedges is suitable for a greater width.*

edgewise to make up a width, there is the problem with this or a metal screwed bar clamp. The assembly will bow under pressure, and you have to use weights or other means to keep the assembly flat.

If there are bars above and below the assembled boards, the tendency to bow is minimized and the double bars themselves prevent movement. The double bar clamp in Fig. 4-3 can be closed onto the work or packings put under the top bar, so there is no risk of boards moving in their thickness.

As the bars are not subject to bending loads under pressure, they can be lighter, say 1-inch-×-2-inch strips, 36 inches long. Make the wedges as thin as the thinnest boards you expect to clamp or have a supply of wedges of different thicknesses.

Bolts can be ⅜ inch in diameter. The clamp is shown with one bolt in a single hole and the other in alternative positions, but you could arrange a series of holes at each end. If the rows of holes are staggered in relation to each other, you will get a greater choice of settings. Suppose the holes at each end are 2 inches apart. If you make the distance between the end holes of each group an odd distance, say 11 inches, you get a choice of overall settings in 1-inch steps.

If you use this clamp tight across glued boards, put paper between the bars and the wood to prevent the clamp from becoming glued in place. Varnishing the bars will also reduce the risk of glue adhering to them.

FLOORING CLAMP

When floorboards have to be nailed across joists, or you have a similar constructional assembly, each board has to be pressed tightly against the previous one as it is nailed. There are special flooring clamps made for this purpose, but you can make one to use a wedge action.

For just a few joints, you might nail a block on the joist and wedge against that (Fig. 4-4A). Of course, you have to lift the block and renail at each place.

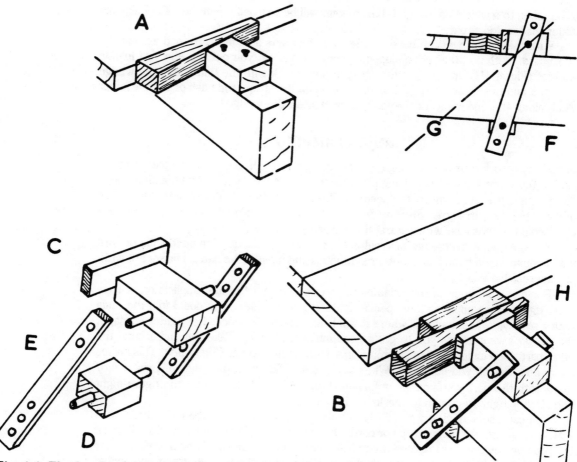

Fig. 4-4. *Floorboards can be forced together with a wedge against a block (A) or with a clamp that can be moved along a joist (B-H).*

A clamp that can be moved along a joist or from one joist to another is more convenient. This flooring clamp is held against the joist by friction (Fig. 4-4B).

Make the block a little wider than the usual 2-inch width of a joist. There could be a piece across its end for the wedge to bear against (Fig. 4-4C). The bottom piece can be 1 inch × 2 inches with a ½-inch dowel through it (Fig. 4-4D). This will probably have enough friction against the sawn undersurface of a joist, but you could glue coarse abrasive paper to it if necessary.

Even if the other parts are softwood, the two straps (Fig. 4-4E) are better made of hardwood—a section ½ inch × 1¼ inches is suitable. If you prefer to use metal, make the pegs from 5/16-inch rod and the straps about ⅛ inch × 1 inch.

Put a peg through the top block. Allow plenty of extension on both sides of both pegs. Taper the ends slightly so that the straps are easy to put on.

Drill a series of matching holes in the straps. For flooring work, you are unlikely to meet joists less than 6 inches deep. The straps do not have to finish vertical to a joist. The clamp holds best with the straps at a slight angle (Fig. 4-4F). If they have to be taken to a wide angle (Fig. 4-4G), a point will be reached when the risk of slipping under load is too great.

With the clamp, you can have a wide piece that acts as a pressure pad against the floorboard. With its other edge sloped to match a wedge, you get the effect of folding wedges (Fig. 4-4H). In use, position the pressure block with the thin end of the wedge against it and the clamp head tight on that. Hook on the straps and push or tap the lower block along the underside of the joist, then tighten the wedge.

ROPE CLAMPING

Simply tying with rope or cord might not prove tight enough to draw wood parts together, but there are ways of increasing the tension of the squeezing action enough to exert considerable pressure where it is needed. This is possible with almost any sort of cord or rope, but the extra strength of modern synthetic fibers makes feasible more pressure than would be possible with natural fiber cordage.

The only modern cordage to avoid is nylon, which is elastic. You need rope or cord with minimal stretch, and all the other synthetics and most of the natural fibers are without appreciable stretch.

For most methods of rope clamping, you need to get the first application of rope fairly tight before applying any special tightening techniques. You could join the ends with a *reef knot*, positioning it where it will bear against the wood. For lighter cordage, the *packer's knot* allows you to get a good initial tightening. Take the end around the other part, then under itself to go around in a figure-eight manner (Fig. 4-5A). This makes a *slip knot*, which you pull tight. When you are satisfied with the tension, twist a *half hitch* with the part you have been pulling (Fig. 4-5B) and slip it over the figure-eight end. Pull it tight to complete the knot (Fig. 4-5C).

You can use a single turn of fairly stout rope, but in general, the best clamping is with several turns of thinner rope or cord. One way of clamping is with a wedge. Tighten the rope on several turns of cord around the parts to be clamped. Drive a wedge under (Fig. 4-5D). Hold the turns square to the work at first until you have driven the wedge

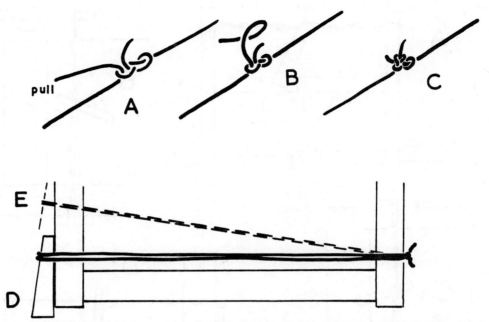

Fig. 4-5. *A simple rope clamp is made by joining the ends (A, B, C) and using a wedge to force the parts tightly together.*

as far as it will go. Get an extra bit of tension by now knocking the wedge and rope further along the edge (Fig. 4-5E).

SPANISH WINDLASS

If turns of tight rope are twisted with a lever, they will pull even tighter. This is seen in the method of tensioning the blade in an old-fashioned bow saw (Fig. 4-6A)—almost obsolete in America, but still seen for saws of many sizes in some European countries. This use of rope or cord to produce a pull is called a *Spanish windlass*, although there is another action that has the same name.

To draw parts of a frame together, turn the cord several times. To prevent the cord marking the wood, put pieces of scrap wood where pressure will come. There is no need for excessive initial tightening. Put a piece of scrap wood through the turns (Fig. 4-6B) and start twisting. Continue twisting until the wood parts have been drawn close, then add maybe one more turn. It is possible to twist so much that you break the cord, but modern fibers are remarkably strong, and you would have to twist far more than normally necessary to break the cord. With a comparatively light assembly, you might break the wood before the cord.

Lock your clamping by jamming the end of the lever against the frame (Fig. 4-6C). If that is impossible, use another cord loop (Fig. 4-6D), which does not have to be very tight.

A similar technique can be used to pull a bundle tight. This could be just a bundle of sticks or a cylindrical shape made up of many staves coopered together. Turn the

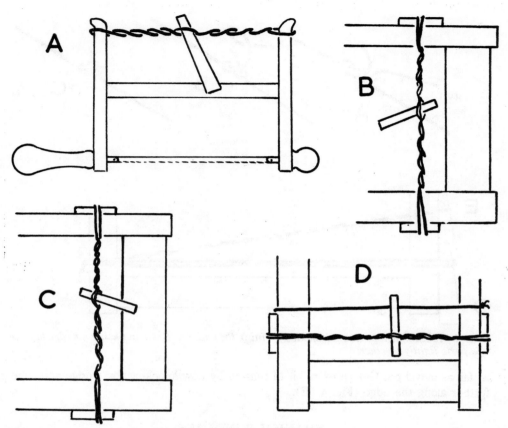

Fig. 4-6. *Cord twisted as a Spanish windlass can exert considerable pressure.*

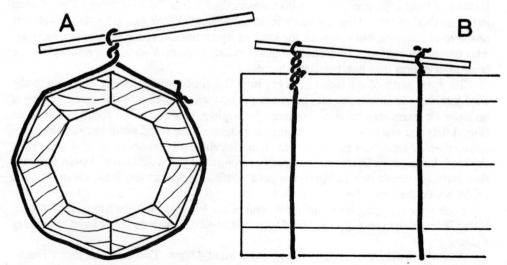

Fig. 4-7. *A twisted rope will pull a bundle tight.*

cord two or three times around the object and join the ends, but leave a little slackness. Put a lever through the turns (Fig. 4-7A) and start twisting. When you have achieved the tightness you need, secure the lever by tying it to another turn of cord (Fig. 4-7B). There is an advantage in having a long lever.

The same method can be used around other shapes. An example is a picture frame. Make four identical blocks to fit over the corners (Fig. 4-8A). Make the inside angles square but make cuts into corner holes to prevent damaging the extreme corners of the frame (Fig. 4-8B). Groove the outside corners (Fig. 4-8C) so the cord cannot slip off.

Put the corner blocks in place and fit a double turn of cord around them with enough slack to admit a lever. Use a lever in the same way as the example in Fig. 4-7 and twist the cord (Fig. 4-8D). After tensioning, turn the end of the lever under the cord and lodge it against the frame (Fig. 4-8E).

All of these applications of the Spanish windlass are providing compression. The other ropework application that is called a Spanish windlass provides a pull. It could be that

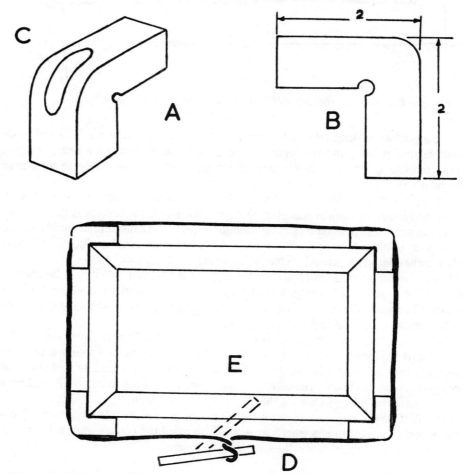

Fig. 4-8. *With suitable blocks, a twisted rope can draw mitered corners together.*

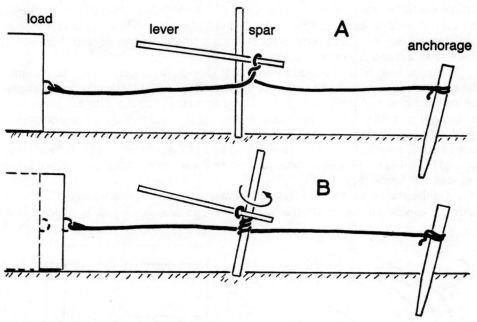

Fig. 4-9. *Another form of Spanish windlass can be used to move a load.*

something you are making requires a strong pull, such as bending a substantial piece of wood around a form, but the technique can also be used to move a heavy weight, such as a machine to a new position. One man can move a car, and no elaborate equipment is involved.

Use a piece of rope strong enough for the load. With it you need a spar about 5 feet long and about 2 inches in diameter, although that size is not crucial. A lighter lever of about the same length must be strong enough to withstand considerable bending load. Hold the spar upright, but not rigidly so. Prevent its foot from possibly slipping by letting it a few inches into the ground. Have an assistant hold the top.

Attach the rope to the load and to a strong point in the direction it is to be moved. That could be a part of a building, a post driven into the ground, or anything that will not move when you start pulling. Give some slack to the rope and position the spar about midway between the load and the anchorage.

Twist a few turns on the end of your lever (Fig. 4-9A). Put the lever against the spar and start twisting it around (Fig. 4-9B). As the load moves, the spar will begin to tilt towards the anchorage. Do not let it slope too much and see that its foot does not move. Your assistant should press down on the spar. If you want to move the load very far, release the twists and shorten the rope, then start again.

For a first time it might be advisable to try a light temporary load. Run through the drill with your assistant to see what happens before using the considerable tension that comes from using a Spanish windlass on a really heavy load.

5

Setting-Out Equipment

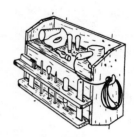

The key to good workmanship is in the preliminary planning and setting out or marking out. It is no use working with great accuracy on something that has been incorrectly measured and marked out in the first place. You might finish with parts that do not fit, with something that is the wrong shape, or worse, with something that is out of square when assembled. Everyone who sees it cannot help noticing the fault.

In the past, most things were built up from boards of available widths. Today, you can still make framed assemblies in this way, but if something has to be fairly wide, you use man-made boards such as plywood, particleboard, and hardboard. Marking large areas is a problem that did not bother craftspeople of only a few generations ago. Most setting-out equipment in use today is intended for comparatively narrow widths. It is helpful, then, to make your own tools to suit the larger expanses of sheet material now in use.

Time taken in preliminary work is well spent. Drawing a detail helps to clarify your thinking. If it is something that is not square but has to be symmetrical, you need to set out the main lines, at least to get sizes and angles. Planning ahead step by step will ensure accuracy and avoid duplicating work unnecessarily. You might also find you can prepare for some later stage conveniently while engaged in earlier work. It is always easier to do all you can to a strip of wood on the bench than wait until it is built into something else that makes it awkward to cut a joint or do other work. There is always a great urge to get on with the job, but time spent in early planning and setting out should result in speedier as well as more accurate work.

SHOP DRAWING BOARD

For modern drafting, it is usual to have a drafting machine with adjustable arms that ensure accuracy in parallel and square lines as well as other functions. In the shop, you have no room or need for such a device, but you might want to make working drawings to see how an assembly will look or how some detail can be worked out. For that purpose you can use a T square and a plywood drawing board.

The drawing board in Fig. 5-1 has the T square fitted into the back. One way of storing the combination is across the end of a bench (Fig. 5-1). If you wish to store your board in that way, measure where it will go and allow sizes to suit, otherwise suitable proportions are shown (Fig. 5-2A). If you can, arrange the storage grooved pieces on the bench to come over the rails. If the bench end is open, that simplifies fitting.

Make the T square first. The blade should be straight-grained hardwood to reduce the risk of later warping. If you have doubts, make the blade slightly thicker. Taper it

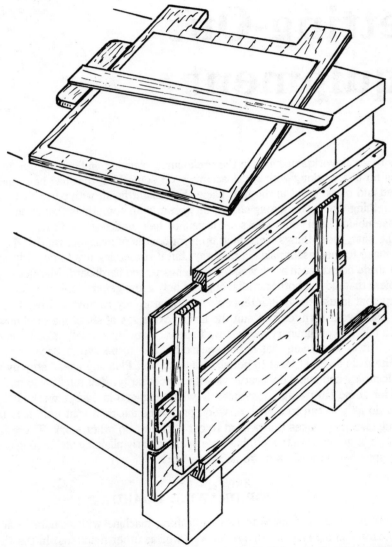

Fig. 5-1. *A shop drawing board can hold its* T *square and fit in a rack at the end of a bench.*

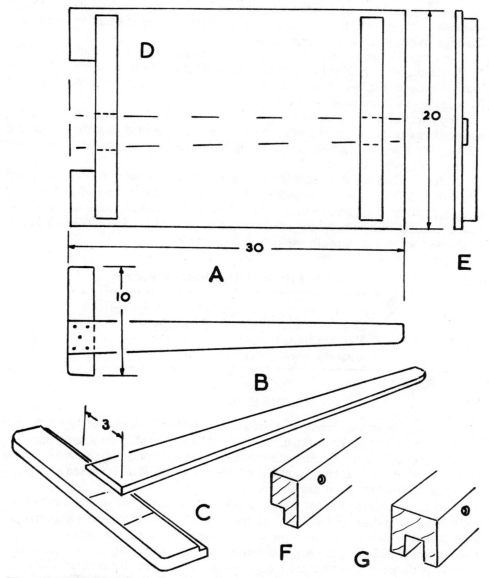

Fig. 5-2. *Details of the drawing board and* T *square.*

and bevel the working edge (Fig. 5-2B). The stock could be the same wood. Cut a small rabbet on the working edge (Fig. 5-2C). Round the other edges and corners.

Mark where the blade edge comes on the stock and glue and screw it on. Use a try square to get the parts square to each other. Obviously, it is valuable to know that these parts are absolutely square, but for ordinary drawing with triangles, everything is related to the blade edge, so perfect squareness at the stock is not so important.

Choose plywood with a good surface for the drawing board. For the occasional service in a shop, it should be sufficient to plane the edges straight and square. If an edge becomes worn, you can plane it again. The alternative is to put a hardwood lip along the edge where you will use the T square.

Cut away the end of the board to give easy clearance on the T square stock (Fig. 5-2D). On the back, glue and screw cleats across, but cut them to allow the T square blade to slide in (Fig. 5-2E). If the board is to be stored in a grooved rack, cut back the ends of the cleats to allow clearance.

You might be satisfied to merely push the T square in when you put your drawing equipment away, but if you put soft rubber or even a piece of cloth under one slot, it will keep the blade from accidentally slipping. Varnishing or polishing the T square will improve its appearance.

A rack on a bench end consists of two pieces with rabbets that fit easily on the board edges (Fig. 5-2F). If there is something about the bench that will not allow the board to go against the legs, groove the pieces instead (Fig. 5-2G). If yours is a two-sided bench, leave the rack open; for one-sided use, put stops at the far side. Wax in the rabbets or grooves will ensure smooth working.

Materials List for Shop Drawing Board

1 board	20	× 30	× ½	plywood
2 cleats	¾	× 2	× 20	
1 T square blade	⁵⁄₁₆	× 3	× 30	
1 T square stock	½	× 2	× 10	

LARGE SQUARE

The largest try square you might have has a 12-inch blade. You might also have a 24-inch roofing square. With sheet material, however, you often need to draw lines square to an edge up to 48 inches long. Any attempt to extend a line drawn with a shorter square will lead to errors at the extremity, unless you are very lucky. What is needed is a square, known to be true and extending the full distance.

The manufactured corner of a sheet of plywood can usually be assumed to be true, and that can form the base for making a large square. You could just cut a large triangle from a sheet of plywood, but it is worthwhile going to the trouble of making something more advanced than that. The suggested square in Fig. 5-3A has a guide to press against the edge of the sheet being marked, a curved edge, and a cutout that is an aid in handling.

You could make a 45-degree square, but that is rather unwieldy. If you make a 60-degree square, the fine point will be rather weak and will soon break. The square is much stronger if the cuts at the corners are near square, as they will be with this curved edge.

Draw the outline and the cutout (Fig. 5-3B). Avoid sharp corners in the cutout. Cut the outlines and sand the edges.

Make the guide by plowing a groove in a 1-inch-×-2-inch strip (Fig. 5-3C). Round the outer edges. Pencil a guideline parallel with the plywood edge to check that the

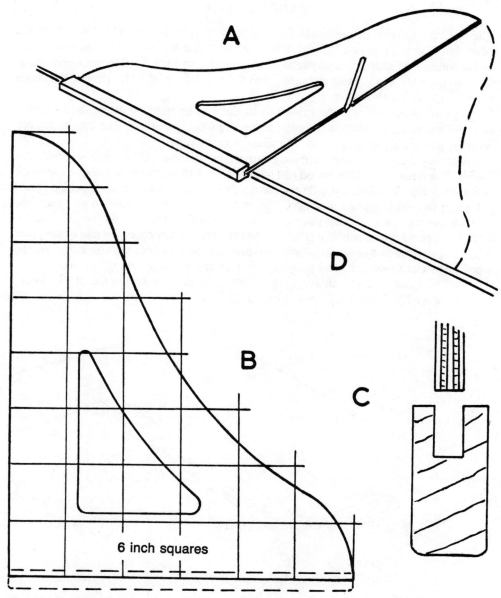

Fig. 5-3. *A large square is useful for marking out panels.*

strip is kept straight and the plywood enters the same amount when it is glued in.

Check the accuracy of the square by putting it against a straight edge and drawing a line along it. Turn the square over and see if it matches the line (Fig. 5-3D). If it does not, plane the edge until it is both straight and square.

PANEL GAUGE

The ordinary marking gauge works fine for scratching lines a short distance from the edge, but if you try to use it for distances approaching 6 inches, it begins to wobble and becomes inaccurate. It is no use making a longer arm if you need to mark lines parallel to an edge but at a greater distance. With the regular use of wider panels, the larger panel gauge is worth having.

A panel gauge works in the same way as the smaller marking gauge, but is bigger and with a steadier bearing on the edge of the wood being marked. The arm length can be what you wish, but a reach of 30 inches is reasonable.

A panel gauge is an interesting project to make, and you will be more satisfied with the tool if you use a good hardwood and finish it by polishing. Some shaping of the stock is shown in Fig. 5-4, but if you do not have a jig or scroll saw, a plainer outline would not affect the efficiency of the gauge. The end of the arm has a point to scratch a line in the same way as a marking gauge, but if you turn the arm over so the plain side is against the panel, you can hold a pencil against the end. In any case, the use of the panel gauge is a two-handed operation. One hand presses the rabbet of the stock tight on the wood edge and the other hand presses down on the marking end of the arm.

This panel gauge has a choice of two ways of locking the arm in the stock. There could be a wedge (Fig. 5-5A) or a screw (Fig. 5-5B).

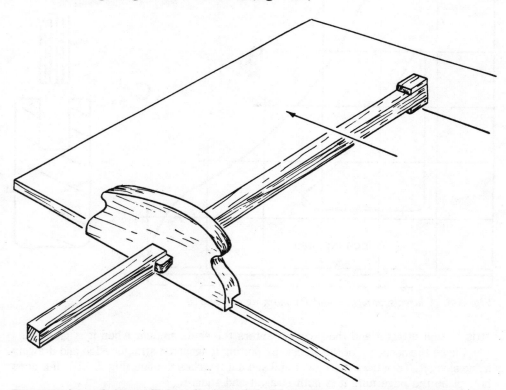

Fig. 5-4. *A panel gauge will draw lines parallel with an edge at a much greater distance than an ordinary marking gauge.*

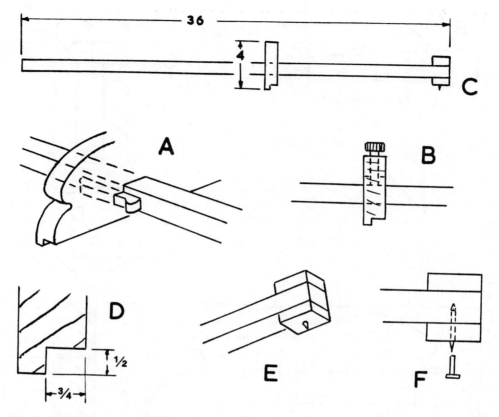

Fig. 5-5. *Size and arrangement of the panel gauge.*

Make the arm straight and square. Leave thickening the end (Fig. 5-5C) until the stock has been made, as the thickness has to be the same as the height of the hole above the rabbet.

Cut the rabbet on the stock (Fig. 5-5D). If necessary, sand inside the rabbet so it will slide smoothly. It is advisable to mark the hole for the arm on both sides and cut it from both sides to make edges clean and the hole square. Try the arm through and check its squareness.

If you wish to fit a wedge, make it first (Fig. 5-6A). Use it as a guide when cutting the slot for it in the stock. When drawn back to the thinner part, the wedge should be clear of the arm; but if you press it in, it should tighten when there is some of the thicker end still projecting (Fig. 5-6B).

For screw locking, choose a screw about ⅜ inch in diameter, preferably with a wing or knurled head. If you have to use one with a square or hexagonal head and wish to avoid the use of a wrench, you can solder a piece of sheet metal into a sawn slot (Fig. 5-6C). A brass screw will look better than a steel one. Drill a clearance hole through the stock for the screw.

At the hole, cut back for a sheet metal pressure plate. Make this high enough to hide the nut (Fig. 5-6D). Cut away for a nut, preferably a square one, close enough for

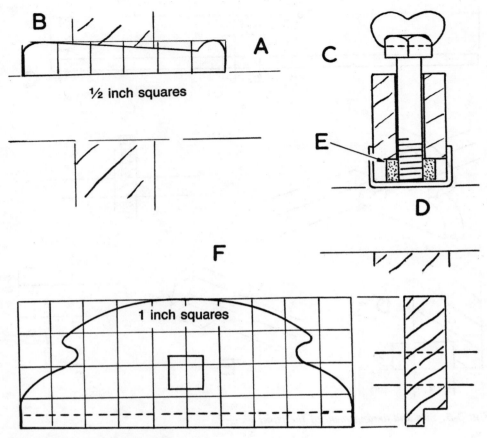

Fig. 5-6. *Sizes of panel gauge parts.*

the wood to prevent it turning (Fig.5-6E). For extra security, use epoxy adhesive. If you have the facilities, you could make a metal block to fit the recess, with a suitable hole tapped for the end of the screw.

Shape the outline of the stock (Fig. 5-6F). Well round all the upper edges to provide a comfortable grip.

At the end of the arm, glue blocks on the top and bottom of the end (Fig. 5-5E). A simple way of making the scratch point is to drive in a nail, then cut it off and file a point (Fig. 5-5F). If you prefer to use a hard steel point, drill undersize and press it in.

Materials List for Panel Gauge

1 arm	1 × 1 × 38
1 stock	1¼ × 4 × 11
1 wedge	½ × ½ × 4

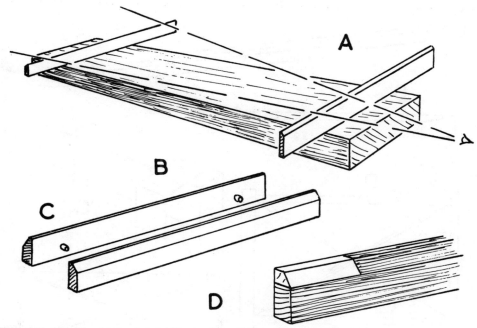

Fig. 5-7. *Winding strips help you see if a piece of wood is twisted.*

WINDING STRIPS

It is possible to machine or hand plane a surface and check with a straightedge that it is true across and in the length, yet it has a twist that might not be apparent until you start assembling parts to it. If you sight along the board, you might be able to see the twist, but it might not be very obvious. A better test is to put two parallel strips across opposite ends and sight over their edges. These are called *winding strips* (Fig. 5-7A). A twisted board is said to be *in winding*. If the winding strips are longer than the width of the surface they are resting on, the effect is to exaggerate the amount of error to make it easier to see when sighting.

Any two parallel strips that you pick up off the bench can be used, but it is better to have a pair hanging on the wall ready to use. Make two matching pieces (Fig. 5-7B). A length of 18 inches should suit most needs. Bevel the top edges. Two dowels glued into one strip can press into holes in the other piece to hold them together for storage (Fig. 5-7C). Put a hole at the end of one piece if you want to hang the pair on a nail.

A refinement is to let in pieces of contrasting color at the ends of one or both pieces (Fig. 5-7D). The easiest way of doing this is to glue in slightly oversized pieces, then plane them level with the adjoining wood. Choose woods that will show a good contrast against the wood of the main parts. A light polish or varnish will finish the winding strips.

ADJUSTABLE SPLINES

The way to check squareness or symmetry is to compare diagonal measurements. If you want to repeat an angle, you can check the diagonal distance between two measured

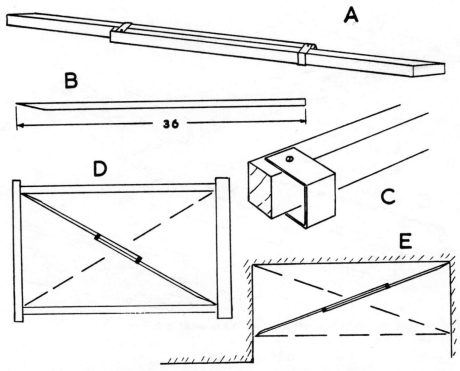

Fig. 5-8. *These adjustable splines can be used for comparing diagonals.*

points. There are other situations where accuracy depends on finding the distance between two points and maybe repeating the measurement on the work. Using an expanding tape measure can lead to errors, as you might read a different graduation one way from another. When you are dealing with internal measurements, there is the additional problem of folding or otherwise getting the tape into a corner.

In some cases it is more accurate to lay a piece of wood across and put pencil marks on the edge, but this is not always possible. A pair of linked and adjustable splines will deal with many of the situations more accurately and easily. Their lengths depend on your needs, but the range of measurements possible is slightly more than the length of one spline to slightly less than double that length (Fig. 5-8A).

Use straight-grained wood. For 36-inch splines, use ¾-inch- × -1-inch section (Fig. 5-8B). Prepare two matching planed strips and taper feather ends.

To link the splines, use thin strip metal (Fig. 5-8C). Brass or aluminum, ¾-inch wide and about 18 gauge, is suitable. Bend it around the strips and screw one to each so you can interleave the splines.

When comparing diagonal measurements (Fig. 5-8D) you can just hold the overlaps. If you need to lock the splines at a particular setting, put a small clamp across the overlap. If there are inaccuracies, pencil marks on one spline opposite the end of the other will allow you to see what the difference is. Room corners are often not as square as they appear. Suppose you want to fit a shelf in an alcove—diagonals with the splines and measurements along the walls will show you the true angles (Fig. 5-8E).

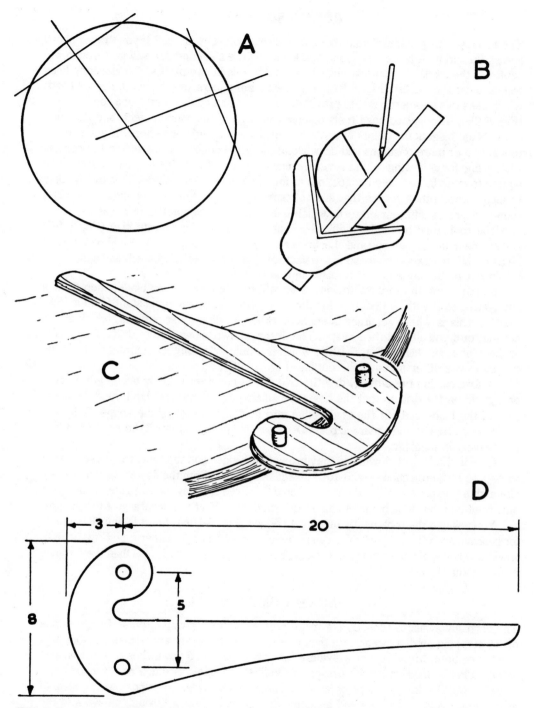

Fig. 5-9. *A round square draws lines square to a curved edge.*

ROUND SQUARE

The name seems a contradiction, but can you think of a better one? If you draw a chord across the circumference of a circle and bisect it, the bisecting line will go through the center of the circle, or point towards it. If you do this in two places, the bisecting lines will cross at the center (Fig. 5-9A). A combination square might have a center head, which uses this geometric fact to provide a means of finding the center of a round object (Fig. 5-9B). The square head rests against the edge of the round object, and the edge of the blade bisects the points of contact, which are the ends of a chord. If you use the tool in two or more positions and draw along the blade edge, you will locate the center. That is fine for centering, but in several branches of woodwork the need is to draw lines square to quite large curved edges, not to find the center of the circle. This might apply to ellipses and other curves that are not parts of circles. For that purpose there is a round square of different pattern, which uses the same geometric principle.

The tool could be made in any size, but this one is of moderate size (Fig. 5-9C) and can be made of plywood and short pieces of dowel rod (Fig. 5-9D). Solid wood could be used, but hardwood plywood is satisfactory. Softwood plywood, such as Douglas fir, would not be strong enough to maintain a good blade edge for long.

Start making the tool by drawing what will be the edge of the blade, then draw a line square to it with the centers for the dowel holes marked equidistant from it (Fig. 5-10A). This is where accuracy is needed—other parts are just outlines, which would not matter if you altered their shape. The design shown allows you to drill a 1-inch hole at the root of the blade (Fig. 5-10B), which is a help in cutting it accurately. Draw the curves of the other parts of the outline (Fig. 5-10C).

Before cutting the outline, drill the two dowel holes, preferably using a drill press or a guide on the drill so that the holes are square to the surface. Drill the hole at the root of the blade and cut the blade edge into it. Cut the rest of the shape. Trim the blade edge straight and square across. Do not round it, but round all the external edges for comfort in handling.

Glue in the ⅝-inch dowels so they project both sides and the tool can be used either way—a ½-inch projection (Fig. 5-10D) should be enough. Trim the dowels square across, although if you have a lathe, their ends could be curved. If any excess glue is squeezed out, remove it because blobs of glue in the angle will affect the accuracy of the square.

You will use the tool mostly on convex edges (Fig. 5-10E), but it is equally suitable for concave ones (Fig. 5-10F). You can reverse it against a rim of either type (Fig. 5-10G). It will also find the center of a round object, but not if the diameter is less than the distance between the dowels.

BEAM COMPASS

The normally available tools do not make provisions for drawing curves of large radius or for stepping off distances more than a few inches, yet there are occasions when you need to do both. Metalworker's dividers can only cope with a few inches, and the largest woodworker's dividers or compasses are unlikely to open as much as 18 inches.

One way to draw a curve of large radius is to improvise a *compass* with a strip of wood (Fig. 5-11). From one end measure the radius and push through an awl into the floor. Hold a pencil, knife, or scriber against the end to draw the curve (Fig. 5-11A).

If other curves have to be drawn about the same center, cut notches in the wood for the other positions of your pencil (Fig. 5-11B).

The method can be used for a very large radius if you nail strips of wood together. You might need a helper to prevent the "compass" bending as you pull it around.

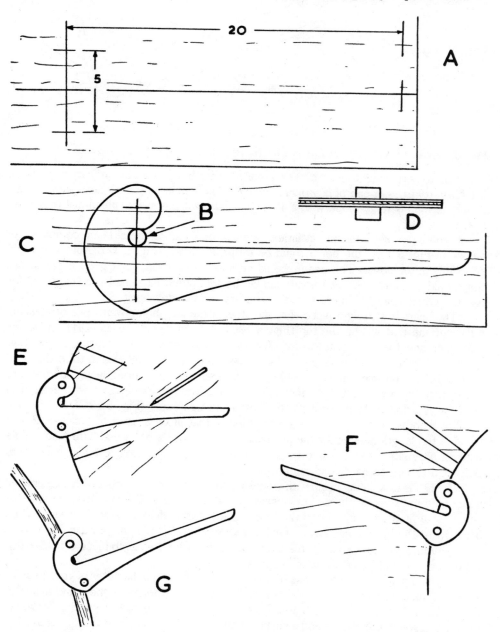

Fig. 5-10. *Setting out and using a round square.*

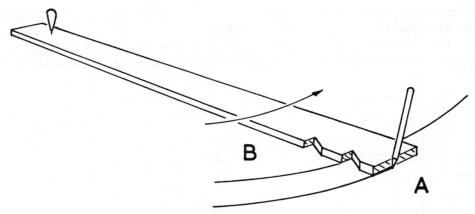

Fig. 5-11. A curve of large radius can be drawn with an improvised compass.

A more permanent tool for curves larger than can be spanned by ordinary compasses is a *beam compass* or pair of *trammel heads*. Radius is limited by the length of the beam. A light assembly might cope with a 48-inch radius, while a more substantial tool could reach 20 feet.

If you have metal turning facilities, you can make an all-metal beam compass. As shown in Fig. 5-12A, the beam could be up to 24 inches (Fig. 5-12B), but you could scale this up or down. The beam should be steel. The heads look good if brass, but they could be steel. The two points should be tool steel, hardened and tempered for use on metal; heat treatment is not necessary for woodworking.

The beam is a straight piece of round steel of the length you want. File or machine a flat surface that will be the top (Fig. 5-12C). Turn a pair of heads. Drill across for the beam, and drill and tap at top and bottom for the point and the securing screw (Fig. 5-12D). Make the steel point with a long taper and screw its other end to fit the head (Fig. 5-12E). You might have suitable screws with wing or knurled heads for the top. If not, turn them with knurled heads (Fig. 5-12F). You can use screws with hexagonal heads if you drill through for a pin to allow hand tightening (Fig. 5-12G).

For woodworking use, make a pair of heads that fit on a piece of 1-inch-×-2-inch wood of the length needed for the particular job. The heads are wood with steel points with an alternative pencil when required (Fig. 5-13A). Use close-grained hardwood. Softwood or coarse hardwood might not last for long.

The heads lock on the beam with wedges, and the steel points or pencil can be gripped at the bottom to change them after loosening two screws (Fig. 5-13B). Groove the heads squarely to fit them properly on the beam. Allow for wedges of moderate slope (Fig. 5-13C). At the bottom cut away to half thickness (Fig. 5-13D). If you use fine careful cuts, you might be able to keep the block cutout to make the clamp piece (Fig. 5-13E). If not, cut another piece to fit the recess.

The clamping arrangement has to hold a pencil. Check the diameter of your pencils. They are usually about 5/16 inch in diameter. Make steel points of the same diameter (Fig. 5-13F). For the clamp parts to grip, screw them together with a packing between, then drill through the clamps and a short distance into the solid wood (Fig. 5-13G). The packing could be a piece of card less than 1/16 inch thick. Discard the packing and test the grip. Wood screws are shown, and they should be satisfactory for normal use, but if you expect to frequently change points, bolts through into nuts will be better.

Well round both ends of the heads to make them more comfortable to use. A varnish finish will improve appearance. You might wish to use any available piece of wood as a beam, but a permanent hardwood beam about 48 inches long would suit most shop applications. If this has a hole in one end, the assembled beam compass can be hung on a nail.

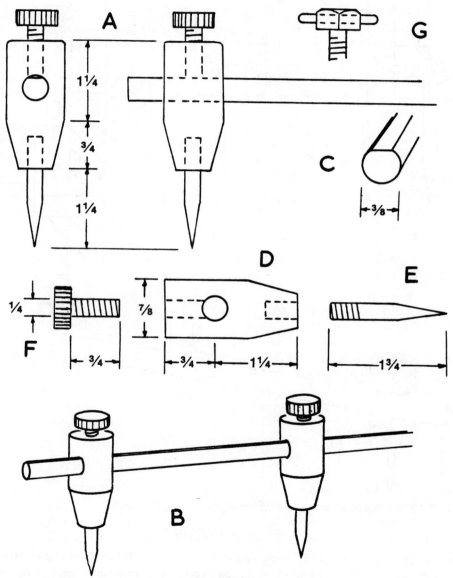

Fig. 5-12. *Details of metal compasses with turned parts.*

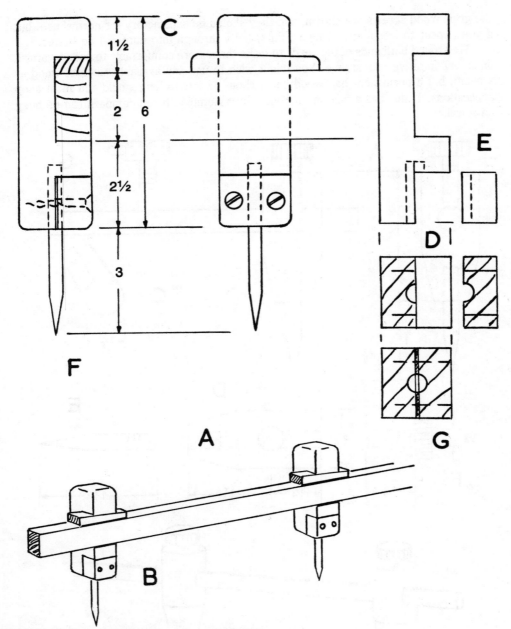

Fig. 5-13. Beam compasses made with wood parts.

ELLIPSOGRAPH

If you want to make an oval tabletop, how do you set about drawing the shape? Strictly speaking, *oval* is the wrong word. It means egg-shaped, with more curve at one end than the other. The correct word is *ellipse*, which is a symmetrical shape.

There are two ways of drawing a true ellipse. One uses string and nails and the other uses trammels (or ellipsograph). If the word *trammels* is used today, it is assumed to mean a beam compass. Originally though, trammels were a set consisting of a beam compass with three heads and a cross guide that were used to draw ellipses of various sizes.

An ellipse has a *major axis* (its length) and a *minor axis* (its width) and two *foci* on the major axis, about which the curve is drawn. The string-and-nail method shows you how these terms are used. It is a satisfactory method for a one-off ellipse, if you work carefully with string without stretch.

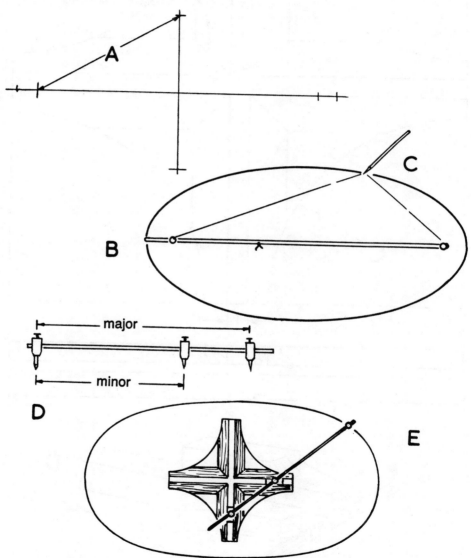

Fig. 5-14. *An ellipse can be drawn with beam compasses and a guide called an ellipsograph.*

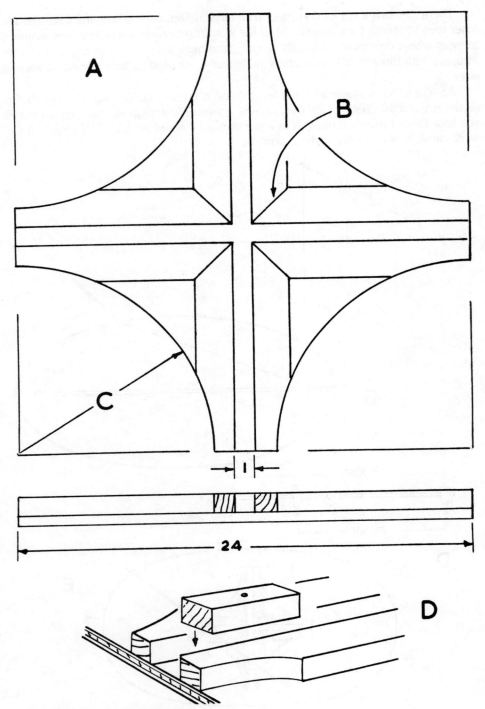

Fig. 5-15. *Details of the ellipsograph.*

Mark the length and width you want on the major and minor axes, which cross squarely. From the limit of the minor axis, measure a length equal to half the major axis to a point on the major axis line (Fig. 5-14A). Measure the same the other way. These are the foci, which are the places where you drive in nails. Knot a loop of string around the nails so its end, when stretched, reaches the end of the major axis (Fig. 5-14B). Put a pencil in the end of the loop and move around with a tension on the string to draw an ellipse (Fig. 5-14C). You can experiment with different distances between foci to draw ellipses in different proportions. Increasing the distance makes a longer and narrower ellipse. Reducing the distance gives a wider proportion until bringing the two foci together produces a circle.

For the ellipsograph you need a beam compass, as just described, but with three heads: two with points and one with pencil. The beam should be more than half as long as the major axis of any ellipse you want to draw. The size of the guide is not important as long as each arm is more than the difference between half of the major and minor axes of the ellipse you wish to draw. Making it 24 inches across will take care of most ellipses you are likely to need in furniture making, unless you are planning very long and narrow shapes.

The guide shown in Fig. 5-15A has a plywood base and troughs made with strips of 1-inch- × -2-inch wood. Start with a square base and glue and screw the pieces to it. Miter the meeting corners (Fig. 5-15B) and check that the grooves are parallel with a test piece. Cut away the corners of the base. The example shows hollows with centers at the original corners (Fig. 5-15C).

Two blocks slide in the troughs. Make them 3 inches long and round their corners so they will slide through the crossing without catching (Fig. 5-15D). At the center of each block, make a hollow into which the point of the beam compass can fit. This could be a hole made with a fine drill, then opened out with a punch having an acute taper.

To use the ellipsograph, set the pencil point near one end of the bar. Set one point a distance from it equal to half the minor axis and the other at a distance equal to half the major axis (Fig. 5-14D). Position the guide so the troughs are over the major and minor axes on the surface you wish to draw on. Put the points in the hollows in the blocks and adjust the length of the pencil. Keep the points pressing down in the blocks and move the pencil around to draw the ellipse (Fig. 5-14E). Wax in the grooves will ease the movement of the blocks in a new assembly.

PENCIL GAUGES

Designers of marking gauges appear to assume that what you always want is a scratched line parallel to an edge. In many cases that is so, but there are places where such a line would disfigure the wood when the job has been finished. It would be better to mark a pencil line, which can be planed, scraped, or sanded away later. You cannot buy a marking gauge to take a pencil, but there are several types of pencil gauges you can make.

A boatbuilder might have to fit plywood or other wood to make a deck or a top in another part of a boat. He usually makes that too wide and planes it level afterwards. He then needs a guideline on the top surface, for which he uses a simple pencil gauge that could have uses in other types of woodwork.

The pencil gauge in Fig. 5-16A is made from a block of wood up to 1½ inch thick.

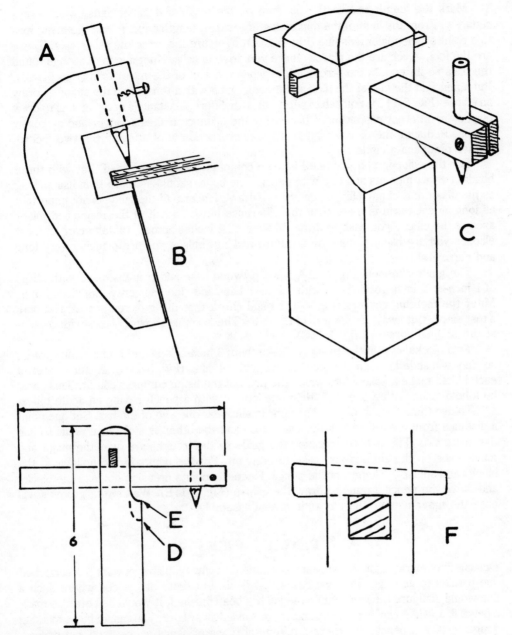

Fig. 5-16. *Two types of pencil marking gauges.*

For most purposes, it could be about 6 inches long, with the width depending on how you want to shape it. Make a long flat surface (Fig. 5-16B) to bear against the work and drill for a pencil point that will come in line with that part. How much you cut out depends on what thickness and overhang you want to clear. The gauge will give you

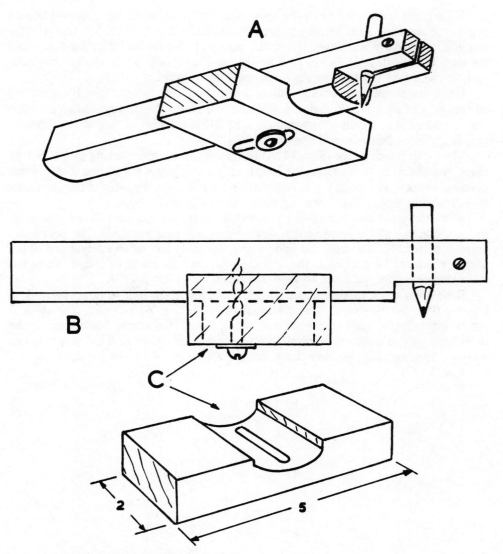

Fig. 5-17. *Another pencil marking gauge.*

the correct line on top no matter what angle you are dealing with. On a boat deck, the angle will vary considerably as you draw along the length of a gunwale. A simple screw is shown holding the pencil, but you could use one of the methods of gripping described for the new two gauges.

The second gauge (Fig. 5-16C) functions more like a standard marking gauge. It is a boatbuilding type for a similar purpose to the first one, although with its adjustment it can be used for marking pencil lines at various distances from the edge in general woodworking. Use hardwood. A 1¼-inch square stock could have a ⅝-inch square stem, but any reasonable size is possible.

If the gauge is intended for similar uses to the first example for marking overhanging edges, cut away the stock enough to provide clearance (Fig. 5-16D). For normal edge marking, particularly on thinner wood, the cutout can be smaller (Fig. 5-16E). Make the stem the length you require. Drill for the pencil and make a saw cut into the hole, so a screw across will pull the cut sides together to grip the pencil.

Leave the top of the stock too long until after you have cut it to take the stem and its wedge. Cut squarely through the stock for the stem, then cut across so a wedge can be pushed in to lock it at any position (Fig. 5-16F). Finish the top of the stock by rounding. Shape the bottom if you wish.

The other pencil gauge (Fig. 5-17A) is more like a normal marking gauge, but its range of adjustment depends on the length of the slot in the stock. In a 2-inch width of stock you can have about 1½ inches of movement. Use hardwood. Cut the stem from ⅞-inch square wood. The stock can be a 1-inch-×-2-inch section.

Make the stem with a moderately rounded lower surface. That allows you to tilt the gauge in use and is more natural than holding any gauge upright. The pencil also draws a better line. Cut back the end to give clearance for the sharpened end of the pencil, which can be gripped in the way described for the previous gauge. Make the stem long enough to hold and to allow for adjustment (Fig. 5-17B).

Hollow the stock to slide under the stem and put a slot in it to clear the neck of a screw (Fig. 5-17C), which could be about 12 gauge in a ³⁄₁₆-inch slot. The stock is shown with squared ends, but you could round them. Use a large washer under the screwhead. If you want more adjustment than can be obtained with the screw in one position, prepare other locations for it along the stem.

6

Hand Tool Accessories

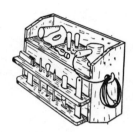

Although power tools are used more and more, and the well-equipped shop has machines to perform many operations, anyone tackling more ambitious woodworking follows machining with handwork. There are many things that can only be done with hand tools. Beginners and those with less equipment are more dependent on hand tools. In any case, skill with hand tools is important. If you understand a process or operation when performed by hand, you are better able to apply machined work to the best advantage. Anyone who wants to be called a craftsperson should be able to do things by hand, even if power tools are available. For some jobs, power tools take over some of the drudgery and heavy work of woodworking, though hand tools are needed for final work such as fitting joints.

Some hand tools can be made in your shop, and examples have been given already in earlier chapters. There are other things you can make to use with hand tools to make them more effective. There is a great satisfaction in making your own tools or accessories that are crafted to suit your needs. No one else will have anything exactly like them.

There are accessories that also have applications with power tools. Any tool or aid you make for a tool will increase the scope and efficiency of your workshop. If you are engaged in production work, it might increase your speed and accuracy and, therefore, your profitability.

SHOOTING BOARD

Shooting boards (sometimes spelled shuting) in various forms have been used by woodworkers for centuries as aids to hand planing edges and ends squarely. Even when you can rely on power planing to achieve accuracy, there are many occasions when you need to follow machining with hand planing. Sawn ends sometime need planing to get a smooth finish. A shooting board supports the wood and keeps the plane square to its edge or end.

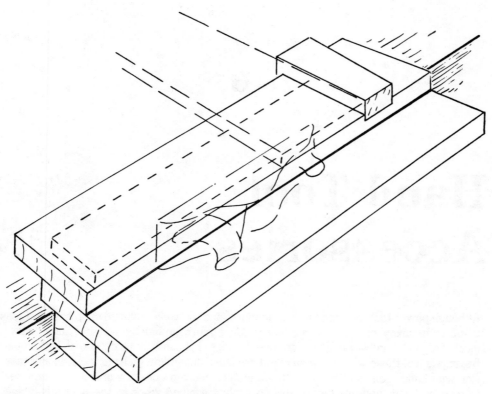

Fig. 6-1. *A shooting board is a guide for a plane to make square edges.*

Some traditional shooting boards were quite large, but a big one is hard to store. At the other extreme, a small board might be all you need for model work. The suggested board in Fig. 6-1 will suit average needs, or you can use the same construction for a board of any size. A close-grained hardwood throughout would be ideal, but you could use plywood or even particleboard. The part the plane slides on could be either one, while other parts are solid wood.

Flatness and squareness are important. Prepare the parts with square edges and check that they are without twist. Solid wood with end grain lines through the thickness of the wood will be less liable to warp than wood with curved end grain lines across the width.

Plane a small chamfer on the under edge of the top piece (Fig. 6-2B). This prevents the buildup of dust and wood particles in the angle, which might interfere with the smooth running of a plane. The stop might have to resist considerable thrust when planing hardwood, so it is better let into a dado about ¼ inch deep. To get the stop tight, give it a slight taper (Fig. 6-2C). Place the side of the dado towards the work square to the edge (Fig. 6-2D), but first cut the stop too long and with a slight taper, which can be marked on the other wood. If you drive the stop until it becomes tight, you can cut off

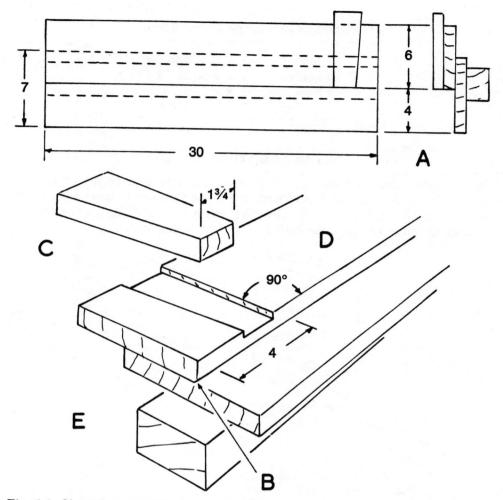

Fig. 6-2. *Size and construction of a shooting board.*

any surplus at its narrow end. It can be left long at the other end. This will give support to work put across for end planing and allow for knocking in further if you ever need to tighten the stop, which can be held in place by a screw driven from below. Screw the two boards together from below and add a strip for gripping in the vise (Fig. 6-2E).

Use a long plane on edge in your right hand while you hold the work against the stop with your left hand, keeping only a small amount of the work overhanging the edge. For planing end grain, you might prefer a shorter plane. To prevent grain breaking out, you can put a piece of scrap wood between the work and the stop; then you plane its end as well.

The instructions are for a right-handed shooting board. If you prefer to hold the plane in your left hand, you could make a board with its stop at the other end.

Materials List for Shooting Board

1 top	1 × 6 × 32
1 bottom	1 × 7 × 32
1 stop	1 × 2 × 9
1 vise grip	2 × 3 × 32

MITER SHOOTING BOARD

In some home shops, a guide for planing miters accurately might be at least as useful as an ordinary shooting board, particularly if you don't have an accurate miter sawing guide or an advanced type of miter trimming tool. A miter shooting board allows you to keep the plane square to the surfaces and plane angles accurately.

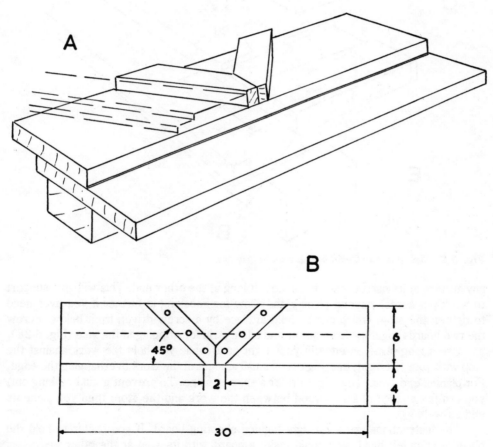

Fig. 6-3. This shooting board allows miters to be planed either way.

Because of the grain formation, a miter has to be planed from the short edge to the long edge. Arrange a double stop at the center of the shooting board (Fig. 6-3A) to keep one side of the wood up either way. This reduces the effective length of the shooting board by half. If you are only concerned with picture molding and other fairly narrow pieces, the length will not matter, providing there is enough length to support and guide a plane.

The suggested miter shooting board has the base part the same size and construction as the previous shooting board described (Fig. 6-3B). The double stops are made with two pieces of 1-inch- × -2-inch section doweled in place. Glue and three ¾-inch dowels should be satisfactory.

Mark the 45-degree lines on the top board. The stop pieces can be slightly too long at first, but make their edges that provide stops straight and square. Test the angles and clamp them in position while drilling for dowels. Level and smooth edges after the glue has set. Attach the lower board and the piece to be gripped in your vise to complete construction.

Materials List for Miter Shooting Board

1 top	1 × 6 × 32
1 bottom	1 × 7 × 32
2 stops	1 × 2 × 11
1 vise grip	2 × 3 × 32

FRETWORK TABLE

If you use a hand fretsaw, coping saw, jigsaw, or other fine saw for cutting curves, you need a firm support that keeps the parts on each side of the cut in shape with the minimum risk of breaking. Some of this work can be done with a power fretsaw, but if you are doing marquetry or some other fine pierced work, many cuts have to be done by hand.

For some work, sawing is best done while sitting with the work horizontal and the saw blade cutting on the downstroke. In some circumstances, experts prefer to stand and hold the work upright with the saw cutting on the push stroke.

The simple table described in Fig. 6-4 can be gripped in a vise with the working surface horizontal (Fig. 6-4A) or turned up the other way with the work held vertically (Fig. 6-4B). The suggested sizes (Fig. 6-5A) allow for two V cuts: one for general use and the other for very small work.

Use a close-grained hardwood. Keep the cuts square and avoid rounding edges, so there is good support close up to the veneer or other material being cut.

The vise block has to be fixed firmly to the table. You could use dowels, but mortises and tenons are shown (Fig. 6-5B). The grain of the block should be vertical for this joint, although it might be horizontal with dowels. Put saw cuts in the tenons so you can drive in wedges as you glue the joint (Fig. 6-5C). Plane the top surface level and sand it smooth to prevent things catching in the work as you move it around.

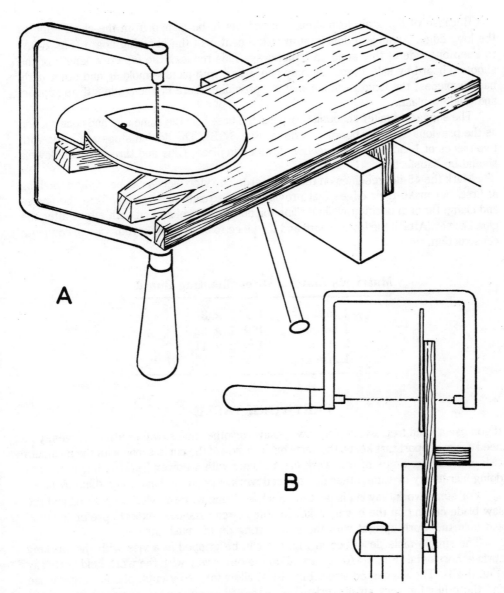

A

B

Fig. 6-4. *This fretwork table can be used for horizontal or vertical work.*

Materials List for Fretwork Table

| 1 table | ¾ × 5 × 13 |
| 1 block | 1 × 5 × 5 |

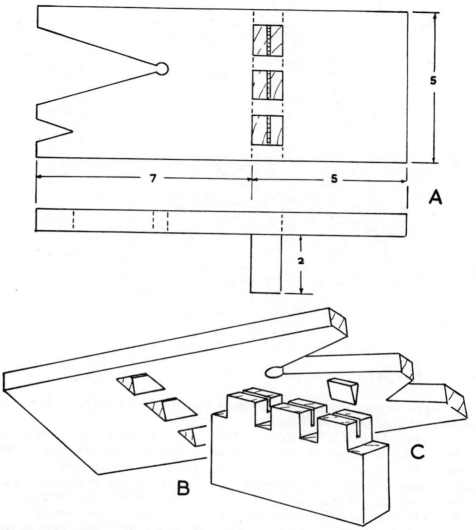

Fig. 6-5. *Size and construction of the fretwork table.*

OILSTONE BOX

To keep woodworking edge tools in good condition, you need more than one oilstone or whetstone and some slipstones if there are gouges or other curved tools to be sharpened. To get the best edge, you should follow sharpening on a coarse stone with a fine one. For carving or other precision woodworking, you might want to work through three grades of stone.

Sharpening stones should be kept clean. Clogging with dirt or thick oil will affect their efficiency. Always use a special oil—a thin lubricating oil or kerosene—never auto oil. Wipe a stone and keep it covered when out of use. Individual stones might have

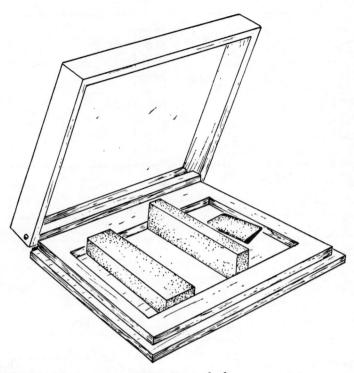

Fig. 6-6. *This box holds two or more oilstones ready for use.*

their own cases; but if you have several stones, keep them in a box that can also serve as a stand for sharpening most tools.

The box in Fig. 6-6 is intended to hold two or more stones 1 inch × 2 inches × 8 inches long. The stones can be moved about, so there is clearance around the one in use for tools of awkward shape or for a honing guide. You can also store slipstones and any other small sharpening equipment. The stone in use can lay flat or stand on edge between stops. The box is 14 inches square (Figs. 6-6 and 6-7A), but sizes can vary. It is made almost entirely of ½-inch plywood. Joints can be screwed or nailed and glued, which should be satisfactory, but you might prefer finger or other joints for the lid corners.

Your oilstone or waterstones provide the key sizes. Mark out a base with strips back and front (Fig. 6-7B) to allow the stones to drop in. Put narrower strips at the ends (Fig. 6-7C). Let the base extend ½ inch at the sides and front and 1 inch at the back, where there is a strip 1-inch square and cutback corners (Fig. 6-7D), to give clearance for the lid sides.

The lid is made like a box to rest on the projecting base. The sides extend over the 1-inch square back strip and pivots on central screws. Cut away the back of the lid to clear the square strip when the lid is swung back (Fig. 6-7E).

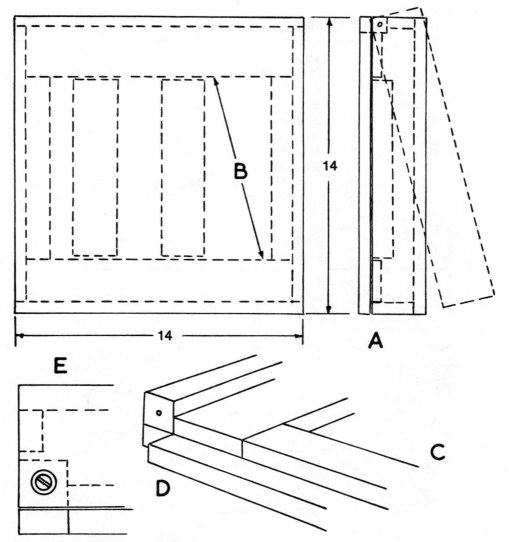

Fig. 6-7. *Details of the oilstone box.*

Drill through the lid and strip together. Roundhead screws, 1½ inch × 8 gauge, with washers under the heads are satisfactory.

To prevent oil and dirt penetrating the wood, paint it thoroughly or give it several coats of boat varnish. Clear varnish or a light-colored paint inside will encourage cleanliness and therefore better standards of sharpening.

You could put a handle at the front of the lid, but it will open easily without one. If the box will have a permanent position, screw it down to prevent movement; otherwise, it is a good idea to arrange a stop to push the box against.

Materials List for Oilstone Box

1 strip	1 × 1 × 14
½" plywood	
1 base	14 × 14
2 strips	2 × 14
2 strips	1 × 9
1 lid	14 × 14
2 lid ends	2 × 14
1 lid front	2 × 14
1 lid back	1 × 14

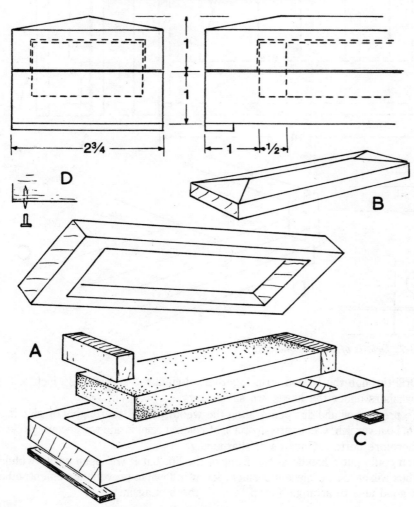

Fig. 6-8. This case for an individual oilstone is cut from solid wood.

OILSTONE CASE

You might prefer to store your oilstone in its individual case, which might be more convenient than the box just described if you need to take your sharpening stone elsewhere. Oilstones should never be left unprotected. They are brittle and could be damaged by dirt.

It is possible to make up a case in the form of a fitted box, but making the case from solid blocks is better, particularly if you have a router to cut the recesses. It is also possible to drill away most of the waste and finish with a chisel. The case in Fig. 6-8 has its base and lid cut from solid wood, preferably hardwood.

Sizes shown suit a stone 1 inch × 2 inches × 8 inches. If you have to fit a stone of another size, keep sides narrow but extend the ends. Narrow sides give clearance for awkward tools and for sharpening guides. The case could fit the stone directly, but it is shown with pieces of wood at each end (Fig. 6-8A). Little blocks of hardwood, with their end grain uppermost, provide pads for the tool being sharpened to run on. You can then use the whole length of the stone, and the tool edge will not be damaged if it is dropped over the end of the stone. You can replace the wood when it becomes worn.

The two blocks have matching hollows, except the lid needs a little clearance. After routing to size, square the corners with a chisel. The stone should fit tightly in the base to prevent movement, yet still lift out to turn it over or use its edge. The top of the lid could be chamfered all around the edges, but it looks better with a fully beveled top (Fig. 6-8B).

One way of preventing the case from sliding on the bench top when you are rubbing a tool on the stone is to glue strips of leather or rubber under the ends of the case (Fig. 6-8C). Another way is to provide small spikes near the corners that press into the bench or other surface. Make a spike by driving in a nail. Cut it off and file a point (Fig. 6-8D).

Give the wood several coats of varnish, including inside the hollows. This will prevent the absorption of oil and dirt.

GRINDING JIG

Probably the best way to grind a woodworking cutting tool is on a large, slowly turning sandstone wheel running in water. Overheating is avoided, and you can maintain the same grinding angle until completion. Most people grind their tools on a smaller diameter, dry grinding wheel turning at high speed. The risk of overheating can only be reduced by frequently removing the tool from the wheel and dipping it in water. There is a problem then in always returning the tool to the same position to obtain a uniform bevel. Usually the tool rest is a flat one, intended for metalworking tools, and that is little help in maintaining the tool angle.

It is possible to hold the tool with a finger resting against the tool rest and return to that position after quenching, but this lacks precision. A jig to clamp onto the tool that serves the same purpose as the finger will ensure more accuracy. This can be brought up to the edge of the tool rest in the same position every time (Fig. 6-9A).

A jig could be made of wood, but it would be neater in metal, preferably brass. If made ¾ inch thick to the sizes shown (Fig. 6-9B) the jig would suit any width chisel, and on a plane iron, it would allow sliding across the stone to deal with the whole width. The jig need not go fully onto narrower tools (Fig. 6-9C).

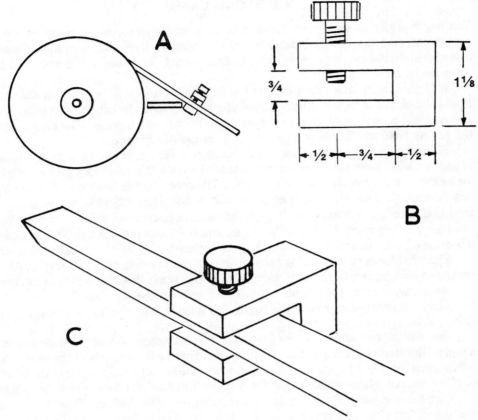

Fig. 6-9. *This grinding jig helps maintain the correct angle.*

Saw or machine the slot and drill into it for the screw, which can be ¼ inch with a knurled head, or use any other type available. Tap the hole to match.

Put the tool to be ground against the wheel to decide on the position of the jig. Set the jig squarely across the tool so that sideways movement across the rest and wheel will not affect the grinding angle.

SHARPENING GUIDES

A tool intended to cut wood needs a sharp edge, not so acute as a razor, which would soon crumble, and not so obtuse as a metalworking tool, which would not cut wood. The usual angle of a woodcutting tool edge is between 25 degrees and 35 degrees—the exact angle depending on experience rather than precise measuring.

A tool can be ground to remove excess metal, but that leaves a rough edge with many minute teeth that have to be removed. What is then left is an edge with serrations so small that they are negligible. This cutting edge is usually produced by rubbing it on one or more grades of flat oilstone or waterstone, which are both made of abrasive grits, and the difference is in the method of lubrication.

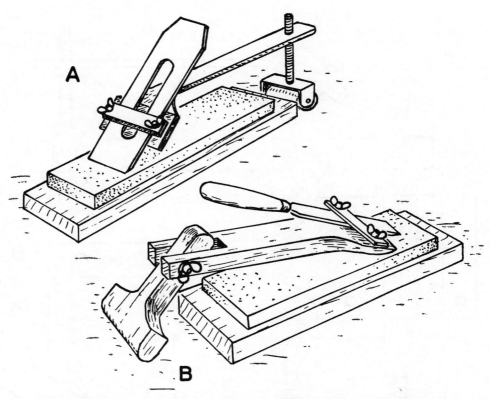

Fig. 6-10. *A metal or wood sharpening guide helps hold the blade being sharpened at a constant angle to the stone.*

An experienced woodworker holds the tool in his hands and maintains the same angle throughout the length of the stone by correctly using the joints in his wrists, elbows, and shoulders. Until you have gained experience, it is too easy to alter the angle as you move the tool along the stone. A guide that helps you maintain the correct angle all the way is valuable.

The fault with many sharpening aids is that they depend on a roller traveling on the surface of the stone behind the chisel or plane iron. This means that only about half the stone can be used for sharpening, and you have to be careful not to let the blade go over one end or the roller fall off the back of the stone.

The sharpening guides described here are supported on the surface of the bench, so you can move the tool edge over the whole area of the stone. You can also turn the guide askew to move the blade at an angle to the stone, which is sometimes an advantage. A roller could run on the bench top, although a rounded pad will be adequate. The guides are necessarily larger than some store-bought ones, but that is unavoidable if they are to be kept off the stone and give you the whole area to work on.

Two versions are described. One is entirely metal (Figs. 6-10A and 6-11), but the other is mainly wood (Figs. 6-10B and 6-12). Sizes are to suit a 1-inch-×-2-inch-×-8-inch stone in a wood box, and any width chisels or plane irons up to 2¼ inches wide.

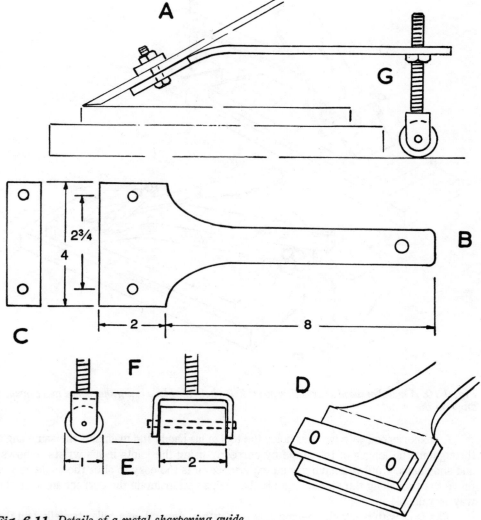

Fig. 6-11. *Details of a metal sharpening guide.*

Metal Sharpening Guide

The metal sharpening guide (Fig. 6-11A) has a roller and a screw adjustment that allows the tool to be at less than 25 degrees or anything up to more than 35 degrees to the stone. Check the maximum width blade you will want to sharpen and adjust the bolt spacing, if necessary.

Make the body from ³⁄₁₆-inch steel plate (Fig. 6-11B). Make the blade holder from ³⁄₁₆-inch-×-1-inch strip (Fig. 6-11C and D). You could drill both parts for ¼-inch bolts to be used with wing nuts. An alternative would be to use screws with knurled heads with clearance holes in the blade holder and tapped holes for the ends of the screws in the main part.

At the other end, drill and tap to take a ⅜-inch diameter screwed rod. Bend the body in an easy curve until the two faces make an angle of 30 degrees.

Turn a roller (Fig. 6-11E) with a hole through for a ³⁄₁₆-inch diameter axle. The roller could be metal or hardwood. Bend a piece of ⅛-inch-×-¾-inch strip to take the roller. Fix the screwed rod to the center of this piece (Fig. 6-11F). You could shoulder the end to go through a hole and be riveted. You could tap a hole and screw the rod in, then solder it.

Use a locknut on the screwed rod (Fig. 6-11G). When you have adjusted the combination of blade projection and height of screwed rod to get the angle of blade on the stone face that you want, tighten the locknut to prevent movement. If you set the guide askew so the blade travels diagonally to the stone and the roller has to move on the bench at the side of the stone, set the roller square to the direction of its intended travel.

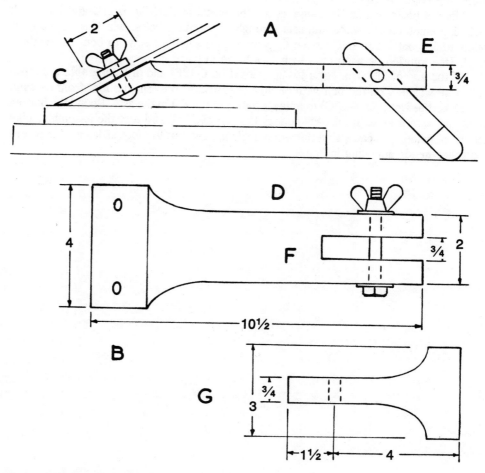

Fig. 6-12. *Details of a wood sharpening guide.*

Wood Sharpening Guide

If you prefer working in wood than in metal, most of a very similar sharpening guide can be fashioned from hardwood (Fig. 6-10B). The effect is the same, but you use a T-shaped piece instead of the screwed rod. You adjust the blade angle by altering the angle of this foot, which allows about the same range as that of the metal guide. Tool clamping is the same as in the metal guide, and capacity can be made the same.

The angle of wood at the tool blade is 30 degrees (Fig. 6-12A). Project about 1 inch of the blade and position the body of the guide parallel with the bench to form the sharpening angle. Moving the foot alters the angle. The body has to be made with a broad-bearing face. Start with a block of wood 4 inches wide and at least 1½ inches thick. Bevel the end face (Fig. 6-12B and C). Reduce the arm to width (Fig. 6-12D). Reduce the arm thickness (Fig. 6-12E). Blend the changes of section with curves and round the edges of the broad palm end.

Make a blade holder the same as for the metal guide (Fig. 6-11C and D). Mark matching holes on the wood and drill through for carriage bolts, which will have their heads underneath. You might have to counterbore slightly below to bed the heads in level. Use knurled or wing nuts to hold a blade in place.

At the end of the arm, cut a ¾-inch slot (Fig. 6-12F) and drill across for a ⅜-inch bolt. Use washers on the bolt with enough pressure to prevent the foot from moving.

Make the foot (Fig. 6-12G) to fit fairly tightly in the slot in the arm. Round the bottom edge and sand it smooth for easy action. Drill for the bolt and test the assembly. Like the metal guide, you can swing the wood guide askew, but the foot slides as it is where the roller needs adjusting in line.

7

Storage

Whatever size your workshop, you have to do something about storage. Even if you are not normally a tidy person, you will soon realize that there are so many tools, pieces of material, and assortments of hardware and fittings that there must be some order or the resulting chaos will mean that you cannot find anything. There also could be considerable risk of damage to equipment or harm to you.

Even a shop of moderate size that is used for limited activities can have equipment and materials that add up to more things than are normally handled in other situations. Coupled with that is the value of many things—in terms of their cost, or the difficulty of replacing them, or how vital they are to the job at hand. Searching for equipment or materials would hold up progress. For instance, to avoid frustration and loss of time, you should always know where to find the key to drill chucks. Or there might be a piece of wood of a certain size that you know you had somewhere, but you have to work your way through a muddle to discover that you must have cut it to make something else.

Storage is a very important part of the shop arrangement, particularly if you want to enjoy your work and get the most out of time spent in the shop. Store your tools in racks or other places where you can reach them. This applies to some of the less frequently used tools or accessories as well as the tools in regular use. It is no use having places for tools if you do not put your tools away. Allow time to pick up tools instead of letting them get lost in shavings. Put them back if you will not be needing them for some time.

Consider storage of materials. You might buy wood for a particular project, but most people accumulate pieces of wood that they know will be useful for something one day. It is this stock that is often the mainstay of the shop. There is certainly no point in going out to buy every piece of wood you need. For one thing, good wood can be very expensive. It is better to keep every piece you find that might be useful. Another advantage in storing wood is in seasoning. A piece of wood that has been in the shop for some time will probably be in a more stable condition than a piece bought recently.

It is no use keeping a lot of wood if you do not know what you have and where each size and species is, at least in a general way. Otherwise you might be turning over and sorting out when you could be occupied more productively.

Order is important with smaller items as well—screws, nails, hinges, plugs, nuts, washers, and the multiplicity of little things. Ideally, store all screws of one size together. Apply this to all the other little things. Use labeled containers and an index sheet that tells you where everything is. Most people do not achieve that ideal, but at least aim towards it, if only to get most small items organized. Then the box of unsorted bits you possess will not be very big!

Fortunately, storage is not an isolated problem. If it had to be treated independently, there might not be much space to work. Usually, many storage facilities can be incorporated in something else. Wall space that is not used to support machines or equipment can have racks or even deeper storage. Space under a bench can store something. When making, say, a support for a machine, you can include drawers or compartments to suit tools or other equipment. It is always helpful to store accessories near where they will be needed. Roof space has possibilities for storing long things.

Unless you have unlimited space, avoid making too many fitted racks and compartments because they take up room. For instance, screwdrivers or other tools unlikely to damage each other will take up much less room in a drawer or box than they would in individual racks, however attractive the racks might be. You might have to restrict limited rack space to chisels or other tools that would not store satisfactorily thrown together. Some tools store better flat than hung vertically. If a tool will hang on a nail, there is no need to provide anything more elaborate.

With wood, much of the storage problem is due to differing lengths. Store long pieces horizontally, but make sure there is plenty of support. Medium pieces might store better on end. Store short pieces in some sort of box. Sheet material takes up least space when standing on edge, but you still have to find wall or other space to take it.

Before rushing into making storage facilities, it might be advisable to make temporary storage arrangements to check if what you have in mind is best after all. You have to be able to move things around, use machines, and perform various operations at your bench or elsewhere. First ideas might not always be the best. Allow a little time to confirm or alter your plans.

Store tools you need frequently in a visible place and within reach. Other tools can be in drawers or compartments where they will be protected from dust. If tools are needed in different places, you might consider a mobile storage unit.

Storage of tools is an ongoing process. Plan space for new items. You might find a replacement for something worn out will not fit in its space, so as far as possible, allow for altering storage occasionally. If racks are fixed with screws, they can be moved and changed easier than if they are glued or nailed.

WALL TOOL RACKS

The obvious place to store tools is on a wall. If the wall is over your bench, your tools will be ready at hand and easy to return after use. Before rushing into fixing racks in place, lay out the tools you want to hang on a flat area of similar size and move them around until you have the best arrangement. Allow for putting some tools in front of others. If possible, make multiple units that will take up less room than separate racks. For instance, a single batten can take tools on hooks, others through holes in shelves, and some going into slotted racks.

Consider heights. Don't arrange a tool through a hole that is so high that you have to stand on something to get it. Tools in upper positions you can pull forward from an open-front rack. Some lower tools can go into holes.

Spring clips of many sizes are available and useful for holding tools like screwdrivers and chisels upright. You can use several clips for a shaped tool like a brace, but avoid the situation where it is a two-handed tricky job to hang the tool—you might not bother. Get plastic-covered springs, if possible, because they are not so rough on wood tools. Perforated hardboard and the wire clips to go with it have possibilities. They allow you to alter arrangements. The material is not very durable, though, and you should expect wear at some heavily laden holes.

In higher positions, you can put wider shelves, possibly with doors, to store wide items that are not so frequently needed. If above head height, these projections will not be in the way when you do normal work at the bench or machine below. Fairly high shelves could be extensive and would allow you to store many things out of the way, yet still have them accessible.

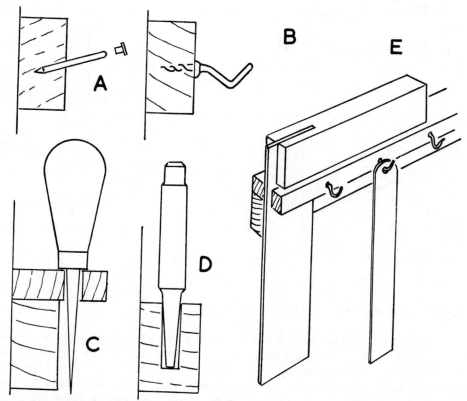

Fig. 7-1. *Simple wall tool racks based on battens.*

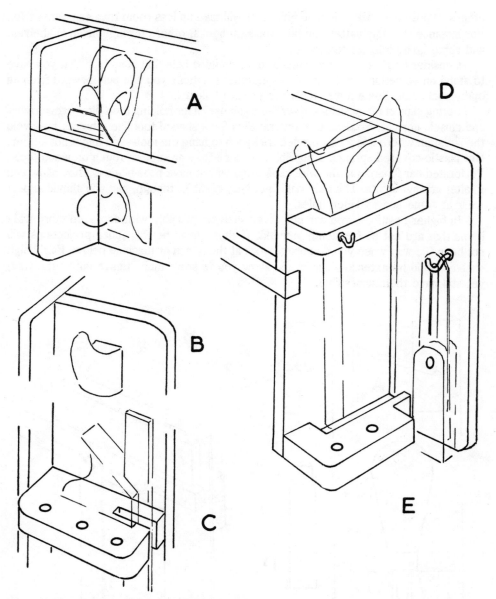

Fig. 7-2. *A rack can have multiple purposes.*

Horizontal battens on the wall will provide the bases for many racks. Even if you want to hang a tool on a nail, it is better to drive the nail into a batten (Fig. 7-1A). You can then get your hand around the tool. Cut the head off the nail and round its end. If you expect to be troubled by rust, you could use stout brass wire instead of a steel nail. If you feel that a nail is not sufficiently "professional," use a cup hook, either as it is or adapted to suit the tool (Fig. 7-1B).

For awls and similar things that will go through, drill holes in a little shelf to fit on a batten (Fig. 7-1C). Make the holes to suit the largest diameter and countersink on top, then you can put any tool in any hole. For such things as punches, which are better not taken through, drill blind holes in a block (Fig. 7-1D). Pencils, scribers, and marking knives can go in this sort of rack positioned just above bench level.

Experiment with tools that could be doubled up without projecting too far. A try square could hang in a slotted block, and other tools might go on hooks in front of it (Fig. 7-1E).

Some tools, such as planes, need a rack that projects more. You can arrange this as a combination unit that takes other tools as well. Many planes can be supported by a rail under their wedges (Fig. 7-2A). You might be able to get special planes, as well as the ordinary bench planes, into this type of rack. It might be wise to allow for at least one more plane than you have. Besides making it easier to put planes in, it allows for possible future purchases.

The end of a plane rack can take several other tools. A wood hook can hold pincers (Fig. 7-2B). A combination square could go into a slotted shelf, which might also have holes for awls (Fig. 7-2C). A backsaw can fit into a pair of shelves (Fig. 7-2D). One or both shelves might be widened to take other tools, and you could hang more on the backboard (Fig. 7-2E). By planning ahead, you can expand this unit to incorporate other racks without having to treat them as separate fittings.

Racks with open slots give easier access to tools than holes were the tool has to be lifted. Many tools with narrower tangs under the handles, such as files, can go into forward-facing slots. Marking gauges, hammers, and mallets also go into these slots, although their shelf might have to be wider.

Although a horizontal slotted shelf might seem satisfactory, vibration or knocks on the wall could make a tool fall out. It is better to let the shelf slope up slightly (Fig. 7-3A). Although a tool might fit fairly closely when in, open the entrance and round the corners for easy access (Fig. 7-3B). You might need to bracket the shelf for things like heavy bar clamps, and you might have to add a front ridge to prevent the clamp from falling (Fig. 7-3C).

Cutting tools require special storage treatment. It would be unwise to put a row of chisels on the wall with their cutting edges exposed. Besides the risk to you, the edges could be damaged. One way of supporting them with protection so you can still see the ends is to put the chisels through slots and screw a Plexiglas screen in front (Fig. 7-3D).

Not every tool is best screwed on the wall. For instance, you could put lathe tools in a rack on the wall behind a lathe, but do you want to reach over a revolving machine to get a tool? Faceplates and centers could go there because you would only reach for them when the lathe is stopped.

Shelves could be plywood or solid wood, but avoid deep slots or other cuts across the grain, which would be weak. Round the edges well. Paint or varnish the racks. A light color on the wall will show up the tools. Painting the outline of a tool will emphasize when a tool is not in its rack. That might be worthwhile if several people use the shop, but in your personal shop, you will know where everything goes. Include a bench brush on the rack. This will encourage you to sweep off the bench and put tools away!

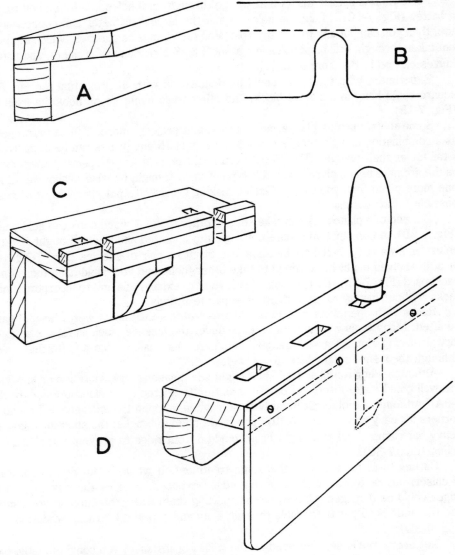

Fig. 7-3. *Some tools are best stored in slotted racks.*

BENCH-END TOOL RACK

Some woodworkers arrange a tool rack along the back of the bench. It is convenient to be able to reach for tools standing in slots there, but this is a problem when you are working on wood that is wider than the bench top. There can be a surprising number of occasions when you need a clear, level surface all over the bench. If there are tool handles projecting above the level, you have to remove them every time you need to spread things across the back of the bench. It might be better to arrange tool racks at one or both ends of the bench below the working level.

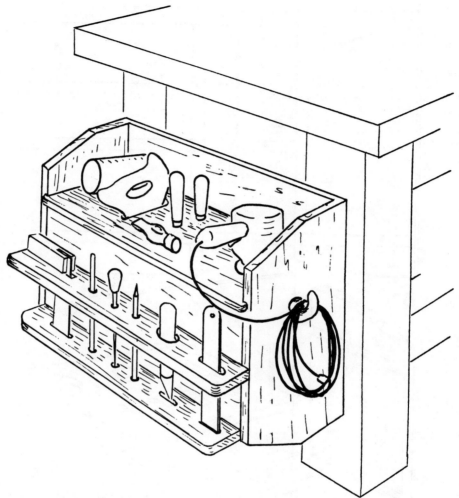

Fig. 7-4. A rack on the end of a bench keeps tools where you can reach them.

A bench-end rack is the place for the tools you regularly want. You can reach for them and know they are ready to use. Much depends on the type of work you do, but you will almost certainly want to have a hammer, mallet, saw, plane, chisels, and basic marking tools such as rule, square, knife, and pencil. You might include an electric drill or other portable power tool.

The size and details of a rack at the end of a bench will depend on available space and access, but in most circumstances you can attach it to the legs and probably to one or more rails. If there is not much overhang to the bench, you might have to fit the rack between the legs, but the rack will be wider, and therefore more accommodating, if you can put it on the surfaces of the legs and rails.

The suggested rack in Fig. 7-4 is intended to go on the outsides of the legs and might overlap one rail. Sizes are suggested (Fig. 7-5A) as a guide to construction, but

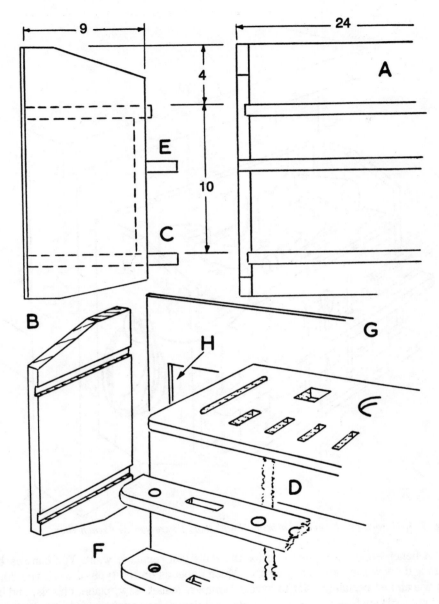

Fig. 7-5. *Details of a rack for the end of a bench.*

they will have to be adjusted to suit your bench and storage needs. As shown, tools such as saws, hammers, mallets, and other long items go through holes in the top and rest on the bottom shelf. Some other things, like chisels and screwdrivers, go through holes and are supported by their handles. Smaller tools fit in supports across the front. You can put spring clips or hooks on the ends for other tools.

Construction is with solid wood finished ¾ inch thick. Plywood could be used. Joints can be screwed or doweled, but dadoes are shown for the shelves.

Make the pair of ends (Fig. 7-5B), grooved to take the shelves. Arrange the shelf lengths to make the rack long enough to go across the bench legs. If you want to hang tools on a loop of cable on the end of the rack that will be at the front of the bench, set it back enough to keep whatever goes there away from the line of the front of the bench. Project the top shelf about ¼ inch, but project the bottom shelf 2 inches (Fig. 7-5C) to form the bottom part of the front rack.

Set out and pierce the top shelf to suit the tools that have to fit there. Allow ample clearance and round the edges so tools slip in and out easily. Leave the bottom shelf plain, unless you want to include a tool with a very long handle that has to go through.

Make a front to fit between the other parts (Fig. 7-5D) and screw the upper part of the front rack to it (Fig. 7-5E). Pierce this to suit the tools to be fitted and make matching hollows in the bottom shelf for those tools that go through and rest on it (Fig. 7-5F).

Assemble all these parts with glue and screws or dowels. The front should hold the assembly square, but test it against the bench end. You can make a plywood back (Fig. 7-5G), but if you make that solid, you will seal the inside of the rack; then if you drop anything through a slot, you cannot retrieve it. To give access for this emergency, cut away the middle of the plywood (Fig. 7-5H) to allow access from the back. Try all the tools in position before fitting the back and screwing to the bench legs and rail. A paint or varnish finish will keep the rack clean. A light color on the top surface will make it easy to see when putting tools away if the rack is in shadow.

Materials List for Bench-End Tool Rack

2 ends	¾ × 9 × 18
1 shelf	¾ × 9¼ × 25
1 shelf	¾ × 11 × 25
1 front	¾ × 9¼ × 24
1 rack	¾ × 2 × 25
1 back	17 × 25 × ¼ plywood

TILTING BENCH-END TOOL RACK

If the bench top overhangs the legs very much at the end, the bench-end tool rack just described might be difficult to get at. It also leaves the tools exposed, which might not matter. If you want to get at tools under an overhang or if you want to enclose them, you can make a tool rack that tilts out for access and closes to cover the tools. The number of tools it can hold is about the same as the bench-end rack.

The tilting rack has a frame attached to the bench legs and one or more rails. The actual rack is hinged inside this. Its movement is limited by pegs traveling in grooves. The rack will stay shut by its own weight but can be pulled open easily (Fig. 7-6). Most parts can be ½-inch plywood. Joints can be anything from nailing or screwing to dovetails or more advanced methods. Suggested sizes are given in Fig. 7-7A, but they will have to be adjusted to suit the leg arrangements on your bench and the tools you wish to fit in.

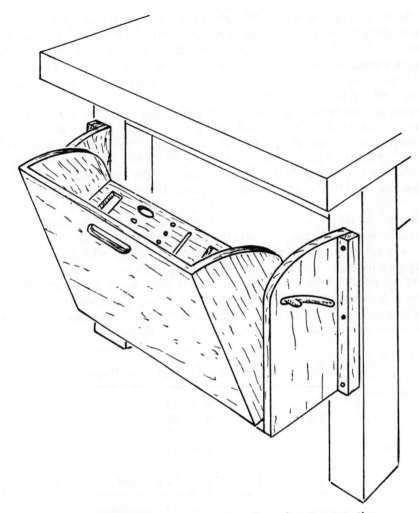

Fig. 7-6. *A tilting rack at the end of a bench gives the tools extra protection.*

Start with the actual rack (Fig. 7-8A). Its overall width must allow at least 1¾ inches each side for the frame on the bench legs. Use any joints you wish at the bottom, but the shelf should have dadoes. Cut the openings for tools before assembling the parts. Allow plenty of clearance and round the edges of the holes. Make the plywood front with a handhole about 1 inch × 5 inches (Figs. 7-7B and 7-8B). Fit the pegs later. Glue the joints between the solid parts and glue and screw on the plywood front to hold the assembly square.

The frame consists of a bottom and two sides with cleats for screwing to the bench legs (Figs. 7-7C and 7-8C). Prepare joints for the parts, leaving about ⅛-inch clearance around the rack assembly. With the joints ready, mark the curved grooves the same in each end (Fig. 7-7D). Draw a curved groove ½ inch wide; let one end come almost to the cleat and the other end to within ½ inch of the edge of the wood. Drill and saw

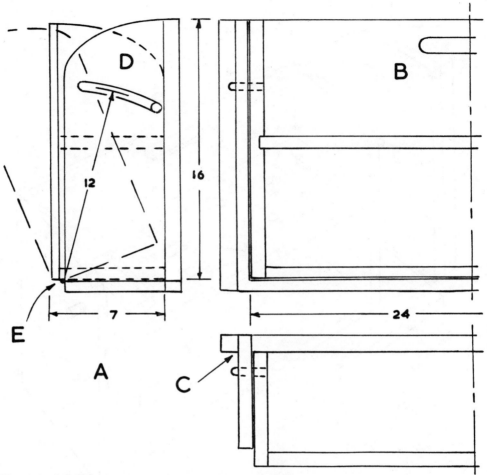

Fig. 7-7. *Suitable sizes for a tilting bench-end tool rack.*

the grooves to shape. See that they match and are smooth. Assemble the frame parts, including the cleats. Drill the cleats for screws into the bench legs.

When assembled, the bottom of the rack should project from the bottom of the frame by 1 inch (Fig. 7-7E). Fit 3-inch hinges under the ends of the assembly, with the knuckles 1 inch in from the outside surface of the front. Test the action. Mark through the positions of the pegs, which can be ½-inch hardwood dowels. At each end when the rack is upright, the peg should be against the inner end of the slot; then it follows around the curve and stops the rack at its outward position. You could experiment by driving screws temporarily where the pegs will come. If the action is satisfactory, drill for the dowels, which should project outside the slots. If you make them a push fit and do not use glue, they can be pulled out if you ever want to service or alter the rack.

The rack will stay closed under its own weight. If you want to be able to lock it open, use a carriage bolt with a washer and wing nut outside instead of one of the pegs. Finish the rack with varnish or paint.

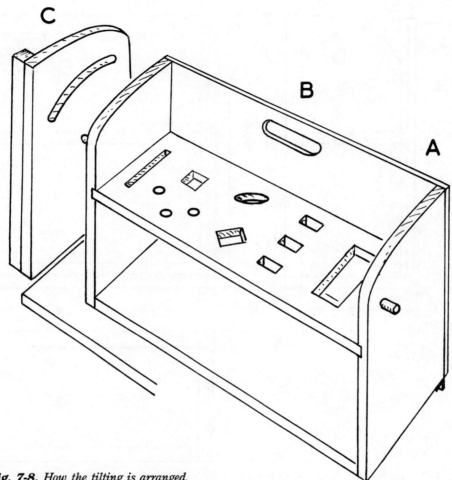

Fig. 7-8. *How the tilting is arranged.*

Materials List for Tilting Bench-End Tool Rack

2 rail ends	¾ × 7 × 18
2 frame ends	¾ × 7 × 19
1 rack bottom	¾ × 7 × 26
1 frame bottom	¾ × 7 × 29
1 rack shelf	¾ × 7 × 26
2 cleats	1 × 1 × 19
1 front	17 × 26 × ½ plywood

MATERIAL BOXES

Every worker in wood or metal accumulates a great many offcuts and short pieces that are too big to throw away. It is not easy to store these pieces so you know what you have and can sort through stock easily for something that will be useful in the next project. "Short" is a relative term. It depends on what you do. Maybe you consider 24 inches too short to be any further use to you, yet a wood turner might regard 6 inches as still useful. In metal you might have a stock of strips that will stand on end as well as pieces only an inch or so that will still have uses.

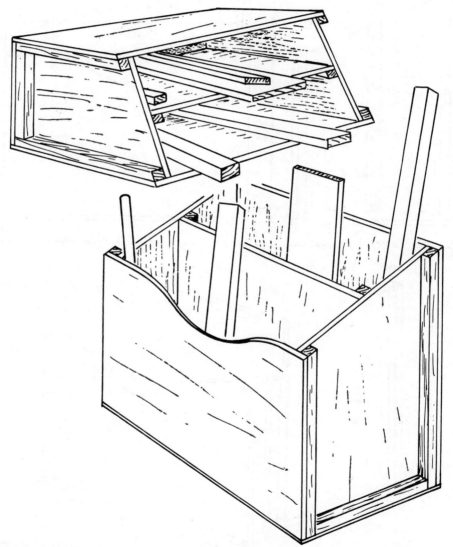

Fig. 7-9. *Short ends of wood can be stored in a horizontal box. Slightly longer pieces can go in an upright box.*

Tossing short ends into any available box is only possible when quantities are small. Strip wood or metal is usually identified by its end section. After seeing the size, you look to see if it is ash or oak, brass or steel, or whatever. This means that any storage arrangement should let you see the ends of material. Strips in the region of 36 inches long should stand on end, while anything up to about 15 inches could be horizontal. Two boxes are described in Fig. 7-9 that are made in the same way, but in different sizes to allow storage in both directions.

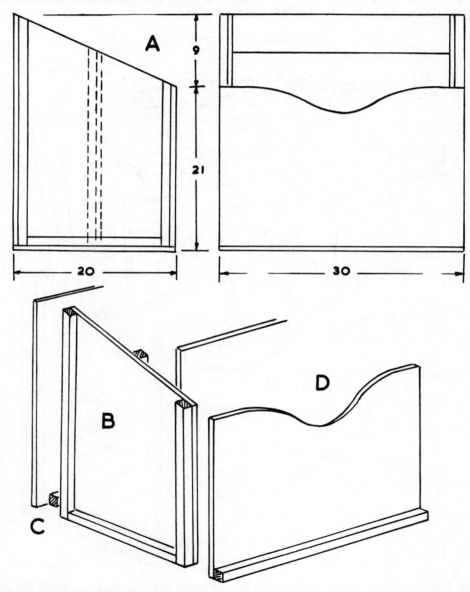

Fig. 7-10. *Sizes and construction of an upright storage box.*

Plywood is the best choice for box parts of large area, but you need some strips, possibly drawn from your stock of short pieces. It is too easy to settle for something knocked together quickly for use in the shop, but you will be happier with your boxes later if you use good construction and spare time to varnish or paint them.

For the upright box in Fig. 7-10A, make the pair of ends, framed outside on three edges (Fig. 7-10B) and with strips inside to hold the division. The back is shown with a strip inside to take the bottom (Fig. 7-10C), so you can push the box close to a wall or screw it there.

Make the front the same length as the back with a strip across the bottom edge. It is drawn with a hollowed top edge (Fig. 7-10D), allowing easier access to the contents. You could shape the division similarly, if you wish. All of the parts can be nailed, but the box will be more rigid and durable if you glue as well.

Smaller pieces are better stored horizontally. The box in Fig. 7-11A is intended to be put on a shelf, although it could be bracketed to a wall over your lathe or in whatever place you expect to use short pieces of wood or metal. It will also take short pieces of dowel rod or offcuts of sheet material.

Make the ends (Fig. 7-11B), framed outside on three edges and with strips inside for the shelf. The back (Fig. 7-11C) overlaps the ends and has strips inside to attach the top and bottom to. Plywood should be stiff enough, but if you think it needs reinforcing, put lips on the front edges of the lengthwise parts. Round the front edges.

In both boxes you could put divisions the other way. You might want to put softwood one side and hardwood the other side, or separate ferrous metals from nonferrous strips. However, it is probable that needs will change according to what offcuts you accumulate, and broad spaces give you a more flexible choice of storage arrangements. You might find it better to have two narrower storage boxes.

Materials List for Material Boxes

Upright box

2 ends	20 × 30 × ½ plywood
1 back	30 × 30 × ½ plywood
1 front	21 × 30 × ½ plywood
1 division	26 × 30 × ½ plywood
4 strips	1 × 1 × 30
6 strips	1 × 1 × 26

Horizontal box

2 ends	15 × 18 × ½ plywood
1 bottom	18 × 24 × ½ plywood
1 top	12 × 24 × ½ plywood
1 shelf	15 × 24 × ½ plywood
2 strips	1 × 1 × 25
6 strips	1 × 1 × 15
2 strips	1 × 1 × 19

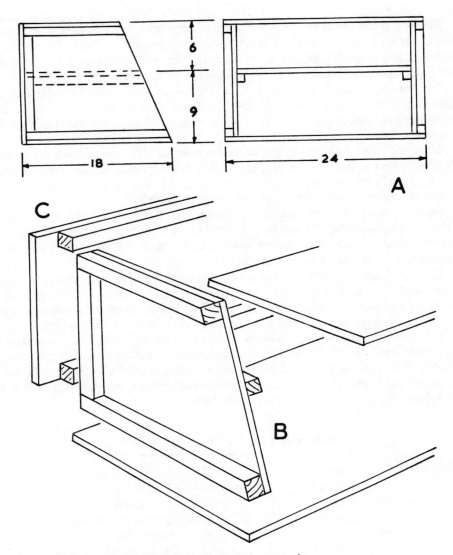

Fig. 7-11. *Sizes and construction of a horizontal storage box.*

VERTICAL RACK

Wood or metal too long to go in boxes and not long enough to justify horizontal storage is best kept standing on end. This makes selection easy and the wood unlikely to warp or twist. Vertical stacking is also one method of seasoning, so if you have wood that is not fully dried out, this is a good way to store it.

A vertical rack can go against a wall, with the wall becoming part of it. Putting the rack in a corner gives further support. You might be able to fit such a rack behind where a door swings open, using up space that might otherwise be wasted.

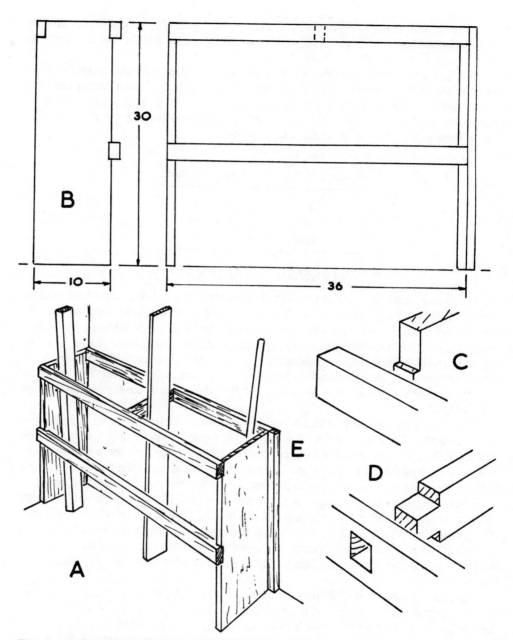

Fig. 7-12. A vertical storage rack to fit against a wall.

The rack in Fig. 7-12A is made with solid wood ends and rails across the front. If it is more than 18 inches long, there should be one or more front-to-back divisions at the top to keep strips from falling over very far if the rack is not full. Leaving the front almost wide open allows you to see your stock and makes cleaning out easy.

Make the pair of ends (Fig. 7-12B). Notch the back rail fully, but make only shallow notches in the front rails (Fig. 7-12C) to give maximum space inside. Any divisions can have dowels or tenons (Fig. 7-12D).

How you fix the rack depends on the situation. In a corner, one end screws directly to a wall, and more screws go through the top rail. An end away from a corner can have a cleat inside or outside (Fig. 7-12E) for screwing to the wall. You can use the shop floor as the bottom of the rack, but if you want to keep wood ends away from possible dirt or dampness, put a solid wood bottom across.

Materials List for Vertical Rack

2 ends	1 × 10 × 32
2 rails	1 × 2 × 38
1 cleat	1 × 1 × 32

HORIZONTAL RACKS

When planning racks for wood or metal too long to stand upright, it is important to allow ample supports. Thick wood or metal can span long supports without sagging, but thin sections need quite close supports. Very thin long material would be better on a full-length shelf. If you are careful to always put thin material over thicker pieces, you can use comparatively widely spaced supports. For average conditions, supports no more than 30 inches apart are a reasonable choice. The supports must be level with each other or they might induce curves in the wood, and the whole idea of the racks is an attempt to avoid that.

Sheet material is usually 48 inches wide, and it stores satisfactorily on edge leaning against a wall. There is no need to make a rack for it, unless you are storing large quantities. You will probably find it convenient to arrange space for sheets against a wall and racks for long material above that. The rack uprights can go to the floor. If you want to keep the sheets above dirty or damp floors, put a wide board down as a base.

For a wall rack, either full depth or above sheets (Fig. 7-13), assess the widest things you want to support and what space is available. Dividing the height to give a large number of supports allows easy removal of wood. At the other extreme, a wide spacing means you might have to move many pieces to get at the one you want near the bottom of the pile. Against that, the depth of each support takes up what might be valuable storage height.

This rack is made from 2-inch square wood (Fig. 7-14A), with the uprights securely screwed to the walls. Because it is important that the supports do not sag below 90 degrees, start by setting them out a few degrees higher (Fig. 7-14B). Joints could be halved (Fig. 7-14C), although it is better to use mortise-and-tenon joints (Fig. 7-14D). Wedge at the back to ensure maximum tightness. Reinforce the joints with plywood gussets at one or both sides (Fig. 7-14E) that are glued and screwed on.

An alternative, which uses up what might otherwise be empty roof space, is a rack above your head. Do not be tempted to bring it too low—allow at least 78 inches of clearance under the rack. How you arrange it depends on what you attach it to. The

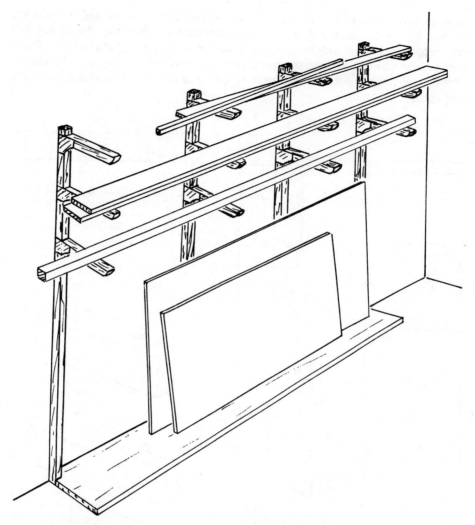

Fig. 7-13. *A horizontal rack stores long parts above sheet material.*

load can be considerable. If there are exposed rafters, you can bolt horizontally into them (Fig. 7-15A). If you have to attach between rafters, put supports along (Fig. 7-15B). If rafters are behind a ceiling, locate them and put long screws into them (Fig. 7-15C). Where the hanger has to change to a horizontal or sloping support, use a dovetail as well as plywood gussets (Fig. 7-15D).

Support the bottom of the rack level with dovetails and plywood gussets or strip metal straps taken around the joints (Fig. 7-15E). A second higher bar could be tenoned with gussets similar to the wall racks.

If you are working in a sloping roof, one hanger will be much longer than the other. If this, or both, tend to sway when you slide in wood, link the supports with one or more lengthwise strips screwed or bolted on (Fig. 7-15F).

Sliding wood over the bars of a rack can be rough on both the wood and the support. Round the edges of the horizontal parts to prevent wear and splintering. Round exposed corners. Supplement hanging racks by matching pieces across the end of a building. There is a limit to how you can arrange overhead storage, however, as you must be able to slide stored wood in and out. Experiment with the clearance you can arrange, possibly working through an opened door.

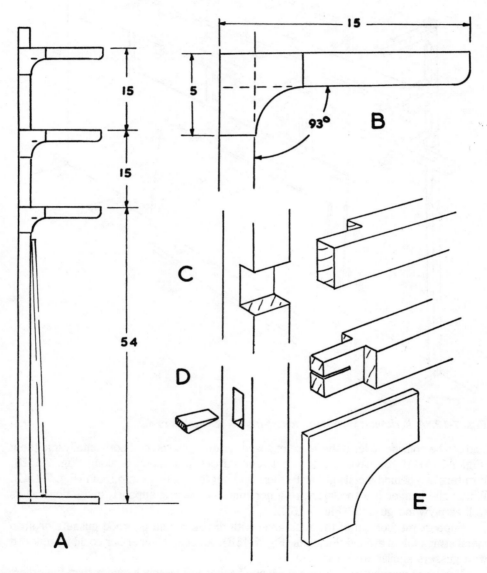

Fig. 7-14. *Constructional details of a horizontal storage rack.*

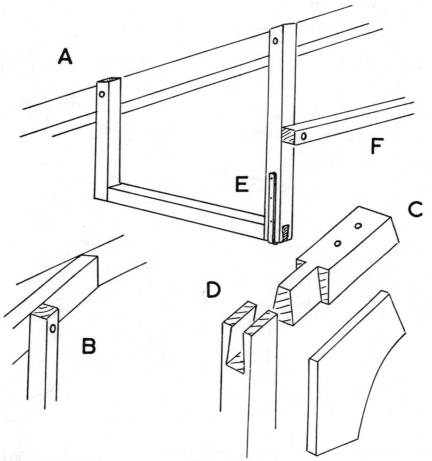

Fig. 7-15. *A horizontal rack can hang from rafters.*

ADD-ON DRAWERS

There are many things that are best kept in a drawer. Frequently used tools can be stored in a drawer under the bench. Accessories for power tools, with their screws and other attachments, need secure storage. Screws, nails, and similar things of assorted sizes can be in containers in drawers. A metalworker might want to keep precision tools in a drawer rather than a rack. Paperwork, such as working drawings and reference books, should be enclosed in a drawer for the sake of cleanliness.

It is not very difficult to add a drawer to an existing table or bench by screwing runners upwards and hanging the drawer from them. The simplest situation is where there is no rail under the tabletop. If there is a rail, you can hang the drawer below it or cut it away. If you cut it away, remember the rail is there to provide stiffness for the top, which you do not want to weaken too much. A shallow drawer that leaves a reasonable depth of rail below the opening should be satisfactory.

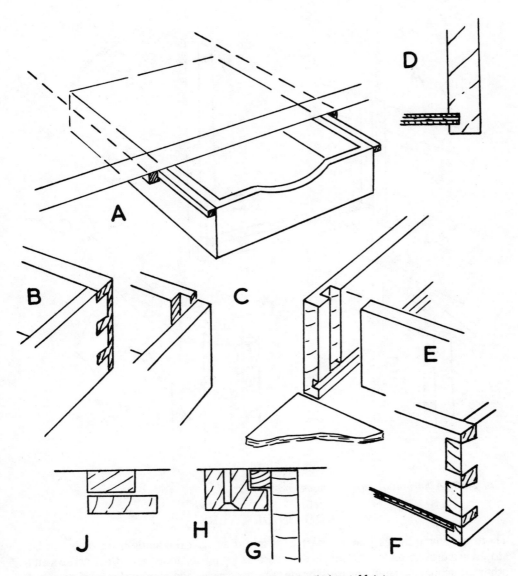

Fig. 7-16. *A drawer can be made to hang under an existing tabletop.*

For a drawer directly under the top (Fig. 7-16A), plan the width and back-to-front size as well as the depth. The drawer need not extend the full width of the tabletop, although the runners can. If the table is used on both sides, you could make the drawer to slide out from either side.

The drawer itself can be anything from a nailed box to a dovetailed construction of traditional form. End grain should not show at the front. If you use stopped dovetails, it will not (Fig. 7-16B). A rabbet (Fig. 7-16C) hides end grain if you screw or dowel. The bottom could be nailed on from below, but it is better let into plowed grooves (Fig. 7-16D). If the drawer is to slide both ways, make the back the same as the front.

Otherwise, the back can come above the bottom (Fig. 7-16E and F) so that you can slide the bottom in during assembly, then screw upwards into the back.

When making the drawer, be careful to square the corners. The plywood bottom should hold it in shape. An inaccurately made drawer might not slide correctly.

Glue and pin runners on the edges of the drawer (Fig. 7-16G). Make bearers to support the drawer by rabbeting solid wood (Fig. 7-16H) or building up (Fig. 7-16J). If the drawer is not to go back the full length of the bearers, put small stops in the rabbets. Use the drawer as a guide when screwing the bearers upwards into the tabletop. Allow enough clearance, but avoid excessive slackness or the drawer will wobble and stick when pushed in or out. Wax on the runners will help a new drawer settle into its bearers.

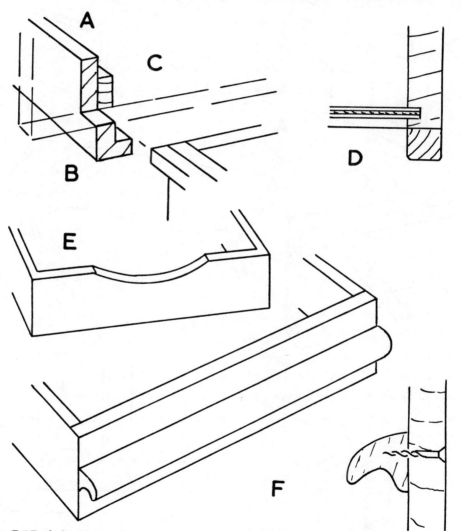

Fig. 7-17. A drawer can be made to fit through a table rail and can have a notch or a long wood handle.

In this case the tabletop acts as a kicker to prevent the drawer tilting when it is partly withdrawn. If you want to hang the drawer below the rails, incorporate kickers with the bearers to keep the drawer level, otherwise it could tilt or even fall out when partly open.

The drawer itself could be made in the way just described. Make the bearers to fit between the rails so that they extend upwards. They could go as high as the top, but that is unnecessary (Fig. 7-17A). Let each bearer extend below to make a rabbet (Fig. 7-17B) and notch it to come level at the front, but that would only be necessary

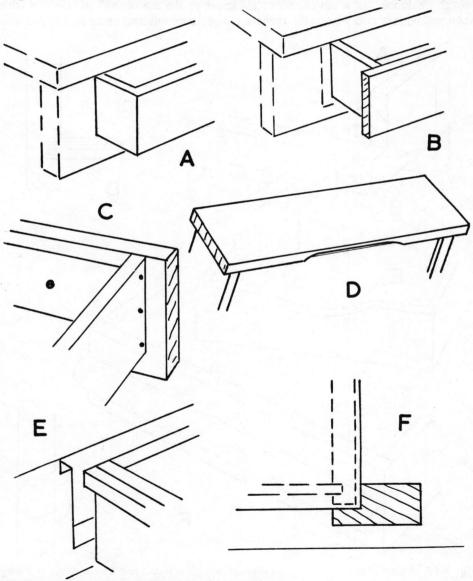

Fig. 7-18. *Several ways to fit a drawer through a rail.*

at the back if it is a two-way drawer. Fit kicker strips level with the lower edge of the front rail (Fig. 7-17C). Screw or dowel through the rails.

You need to be able to grip both of these drawers. You might be satisfied with just putting your fingers under the drawer front to pull it. You could add a thickening piece under to give a better grip (Fig. 7-17D). Hollowing the front gives you a better grip at the top (Fig. 7-17E). If a projection at the front does not matter, you could add a store-bought handle, possibly with a dropping bail, if you want to keep projection to a minimum. A long shaped piece of wood (Fig. 7-17F) allows you to pull the drawer open from whatever position you are working.

If the table has a deep rail or if it is a bench with a deep front apron, the drawer can go through it. Arrange the drawer depth to leave some rail depth below the opening—much depends on the size of the wood, but 1½ inches of table rail and 2 inches of bench front are suggested minimums. The top of the opening will come level with the underside of the bench or tabletop. The drawer width can be anything you decide, but a drawer always slides better if its depth back to front is less than the width across the front.

There are two possible ways of arranging the drawer front. You can make it in a way already described and fit it to finish level with the rail (Fig. 7-18A), or you can make a false front that overlaps the opening (Fig. 7-18B). If you need to avoid projections, as you should on the apron front of a woodworking bench, finish the drawer flush. If projection does not matter, the overlapping front means you do not have to cut the opening with such precision because it is hidden when the drawer is closed.

For an overlapping false front, make the drawer with dovetails or let the sides overlap the inner front, then screw or dowel, then screw the false front on from inside (Fig. 7-18C). If you want to avoid any further projection, put a finger hollow under the center of the front (Fig. 7-18D).

Support for the drawer can be the same as for the first drawer, with the runners passing through notched corners of the opening (Fig. 7-18E). Another way is to put bearers in a position to support the bottom edges of the drawer (Fig. 7-18F). If there is room, make the bearers wider to allow ample area for screwing through the rails.

Although the overlapping false front will stop the drawer from going too far back, slamming in a heavily loaded drawer will put a lot of strain on this. It might be advisable to also put stop blocks inside.

NEST OF DRAWERS

For very small items there are compact metal and plastic blocks of drawers that are worth having as they take up less space than anything you make of the same capacity in wood. For greater capacities, you might prefer to make wood containers. These are best arranged as drawers, either fitted into vacant floor space, mounted on a table, or fixed to a wall. The design in Fig. 7-19 is offered as a suggestion to show a method of construction, and you will have to vary the size and layout to suit your needs. Drawers could be fitted with divisions or made to take containers of standard sizes.

As shown (Fig. 7-20A), all drawers are the same size. This allows you to prepare wood to standard sizes and set up any jointing operations all at the same time. You could have drawers of different depths, preferably with the larger ones towards the bottom, for appearance and stability.

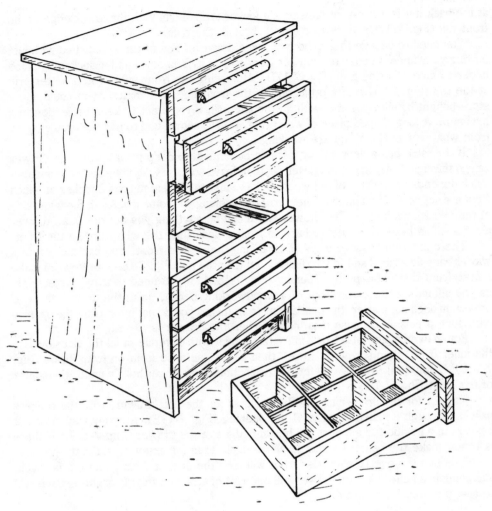

Fig. 7-19. *A nest of drawers provides plenty of storage space for small items.*

It would be possible to use metal or plastic drawer slides, but they need greater clearance at the sides, and drawer fronts would have to overhang more. Some parts could be made of plywood, which has the advantage of being unlikely to warp or twist, but properly seasoned hardwoods or softwoods should be satisfactory. To minimize wear after long use, the drawer sides and their guides are best made of hardwood.

Construction of the case is suggested with dado joints with the plywood back let into rabbets. The drawers might be dovetailed, but they could have rabbeted fronts and dadoed backs (Fig. 7-16C and E). This construction is suitable for quantity production with a table saw and router. Drawer bottoms should go into grooves (Fig. 7-16D).

Start by setting out the two sides, which can be ½-inch or thicker plywood or solid wood ⅝ inch thick with pieces glued together to make up the width (Fig. 7-20B). Rabbet the rear edges to take the plywood back (Fig. 7-20C). Allow for ¼ inch of a side going

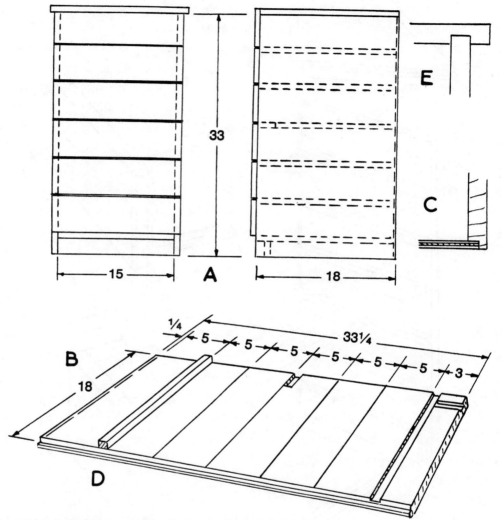

Fig. 7-20. *Sizes and side layout of a nest of drawers.*

into a dado at the top. Cut dadoes for the bottom and a plinth under it. Any distorting of the sides would affect the movement of drawers. The back will limit warping, but at the front, cut a dado for a rail at the midposition to prevent movement there. Mark the positions of the drawer guides and glue and pin on these strips (Fig. 7-20D).

Make the case top (Fig. 7-21A) to fit over the sides (Fig. 7-20E). Make the bottom and plinth (Fig. 7-21B) and the middle rail (Fig. 7-21C) to fit into their dadoes in the sides. Have the back ready to fit in, then pin and glue the parts together.

Make the drawers with the sides slightly too long at the back (Fig. 7-21D). Trim them off during assembly so that they stop against the case back when their fronts are fitting level. At the front of each drawer, make a false piece to overlap the case sides and reach almost to the tops of the guides above (Fig. 7-21E). The gaps at the sides

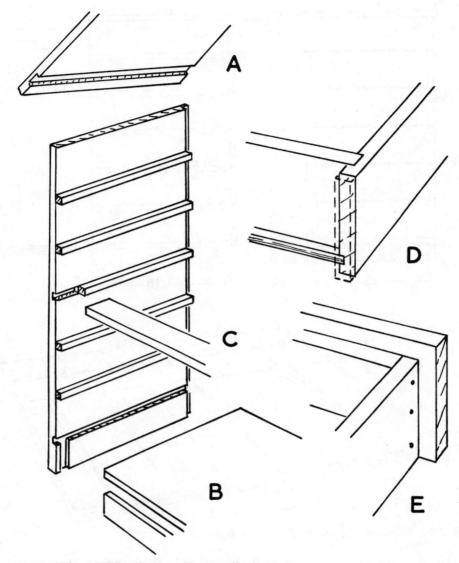

Fig. 7-21. *Assembly details of the nest of drawers.*

of the drawers will be hidden, and there will only be a small gap between the top of one drawer and the bottom of the next. The top drawer front can overlap the top of the case.

Try each drawer in several positions and trim the backs until a drawer closes level at the front. Several types of handle are possible. You could fit store-bought metal or plastic handles, turn a pair of knobs for each drawer, or make wood handles as already described (Fig. 7-17F) or to your own design.

Materials List for Nest of Drawers

2 case sides	$\frac{5}{8}$	×	18 × 34	
1 case top	$\frac{5}{8}$	×	18 × 18	
1 case bottom	$\frac{5}{8}$	×	18 × 18	
1 case plinth	$\frac{5}{8}$	×	$2\frac{3}{8}$ × 18	
1 case back	16	×	34 × $\frac{1}{4}$ plywood	
10 drawer guides	$\frac{5}{8}$	×	$\frac{5}{8}$ × 18	
12 drawer sides	$\frac{1}{2}$	×	$4\frac{3}{8}$ × 16	
6 drawer backs	$\frac{1}{2}$	×	4 × 16	
6 drawer fronts	$\frac{5}{8}$	×	$4\frac{3}{8}$ × 16	
6 false fronts	$\frac{5}{8}$	×	5 × 18	
6 drawer bottoms	15	×	18 × $\frac{1}{4}$ plywood	

BENCH WITH DRAWERS

An obvious place for storing tools and materials is under your bench. It could be an open space where you put boxes, portable power tools, or stacks of wood. There could be one or more shelves to provide more systematic storage. Drawers are probably the best way of making maximum use of the space, either filling all the volume or sharing it with open shelves or a part enclosed with a door. Making a bench with drawers underneath can involve a considerable amount of work, but this is the area where you do most of the important work in your shop, and anything done to improve conditions and efficiency there is worthwhile. It is possible to add drawers to an existing bench, but it is better to treat the whole concept as one project, if possible, and that is how it is assumed here.

Building in drawers and their framing helps to give rigidity to a bench. The weight of the contents of the drawers helps to ensure stability. However, it is unwise to consider these benefits as a reason for using a generally lighter construction, and you should build the bench so it is strong in itself. Any strength coming from the installation of drawers is an added benefit. Ideas for making strong benches are given in more detail in chapter 2.

The bench described in Fig. 7-22 is of moderate size, with an apron front suitable for woodworking. There can be a vise at the front and another at one end. The same bench could be used for metalworking or other crafts without alteration. The top is shown flush across, but it could have a well. It is assumed that the bench will be used from one side only. It could be put against a wall with racks above.

The drawing (Fig. 7-23A) shows a bench with two blocks of three drawers: all the same depth at one side and graduated in depth at the other side. The legs form two end frames, which are joined with the front apron and two bottom rails. There is no need for a rear top rail.

Start by making the two end frames, with legs and rails 3 inches square. The parts are best tenoned, but they could be halved or doweled. Notch the front legs ½ inch for the apron (Fig. 7-24A). Make the lower lengthwise rails (Fig. 7-24B). Fit 1-inch square strips to the front legs, notched to go a few inches above the apron edge (Figs. 7-23B and 7-24C). These form the edges of the drawer openings.

Fig. 7-22. *A bench with drawers puts storage space where you want it.*

For the back of the bench, make a plywood panel that reaches down to the lower rail. Frame it behind with 1-inch square strips (Fig. 7-24D), so it will fit between legs, rail, and top.

On each end fit a plywood side (Fig. 7-24E) that fits behind the front strip, goes against the plywood back, and can be screwed to the end frame rails. Mark on it where the drawers will come. Make a partition for the center. Put an upright at its front, notched under the apron (Fig. 7-24F), so its forward surface will be level with the strips on the legs. Behind it goes a piece of plywood against the back and with stiffeners along the top edge (Fig. 7-24G). At its lower positions, it will be supported by the divisions between drawers.

For each block of drawers, there are four, almost identical frames (Fig. 7-24H), which are tenoned or doweled together. Be careful to keep surfaces level as the drawers slide on them. Put guide strips on the three lower frames each side (Fig. 7-24J), keeping their inner surfaces level with the pieces that form the sides of the drawer openings. The frames that come above the top drawers do not need these and have to be made to fit behind the apron.

There could be a drawer fitted through the apron (Fig. 7-23C). If you wish to do this, cut away the apron and deal with the drawer as previously described (Fig. 7-18). Leave 2 inches of the apron below the drawer opening.

Assemble the bench parts. Fit the apron to the legs with counterbored screws and glue. Plug the holes. See that the assembly is upright and square. Fit the plywood inside the ends and mount the partition temporarily in position. Try the division frames in position. Fit by screwing into them through the plywood at the back as well as at their ends. Use plenty of glue. Check that the divisions are parallel and square, otherwise the movement of drawers will be affected.

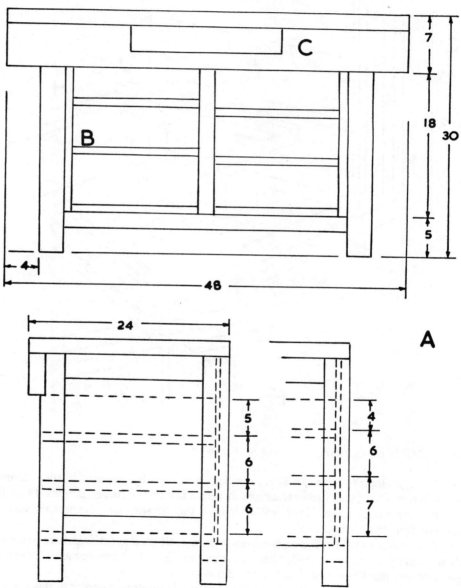

Fig. 7-23. *Main sizes of a bench with drawers.*

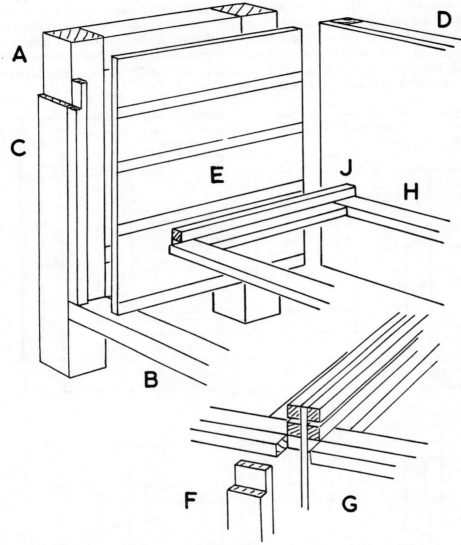

Fig. 7-24. *Assembly details of a bench with drawers.*

Make the top. You can glue several wide boards together or make it from narrower strips in a butcher block manner. Try its fit with a few counterbored screws, but fitting the drawers will be easier if you wait until after the drawers have been made and you are satisfied with their action.

The drawers have to slide on the division frames, which also act as kickers to prevent them from tilting, then the guides keep the sides straight. Remove any unevenness and see that the parts that bear against the drawers are smooth.

The drawers can be made by any of the methods described earlier in this chapter. Make each drawer to fit level within its opening, so all fronts are flush when the drawers reach the bench back. The apron front is about 1 inch forward of the drawer fronts. You can fit handles up to this thickness without interfering with wide boards being worked on and being held against the apron with a vise or other means.

When you are satisfied with the drawers and their fit, fix the bench top down with counterbored and plugged screws into the end frames and apron. Screw upwards through the strip behind the back plywood.

Materials List for Bench with Drawers

4 legs	3	×	3	×	30	
4 rails	3	×	3	×	24	
2 rails	2	×	3	×	40	
1 back	23	×	26	×	½	plywood
2 back frames	1	×	1	×	23	
2 back frames	1	×	1	×	36	
1 apron	1½	×	5	×	50	
1 top	2	×	24	×	50	
3 panels	23	×	23	×	½	plywood
16 drawer divisions	1	×	2	×	18	
16 drawer divisions	1	×	2	×	24	
14 drawer guides	1	×	1	×	24	
2 front strips	1	×	1	×	22	
1 front strip	1	×	2	×	22	
4 drawer fronts	¾	×	5	×	17	
4 drawer backs	⅝	×	4½	×	17	
8 drawer sides	⅝	×	5	×	24	
1 drawer front	¾	×	4	×	17	
1 drawer back	⅝	×	3½	×	17	
2 drawer sides	⅝	×	4	×	24	
1 drawer front	¾	×	6	×	17	
1 drawer back	⅝	×	5½	×	17	
2 drawer sides	⅝	×	6	×	24	
6 drawer bottoms	17	×	24	×	¼	plywood
1 top drawer front	¾	×	3	×	20	
1 top drawer back	⅝	×	2½	×	20	
2 top drawer sides	⅝	×	3	×	24	
1 top drawer bottom	20	×	24	×	½	plywood

NAIL BOX

Not everything you make for use in the shop must be complicated, but if you are to be happy with it, it should be functional and well made. Most of you have nailed together a box to take nails to a job. A crude box can serve the purpose, but any visitor might not be impressed by the example of your workmanship. For your own satisfaction and for long-term use, a better quality box would be worth making. The suggested box in

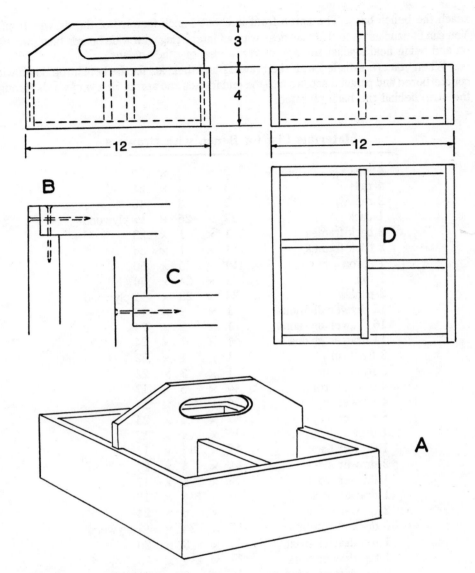

Fig. 7-25. *A box with a handle is useful for transporting nails.*

Fig. 7-25A takes the popular form, but there are a few points about the construction that show an appreciation of good-quality work.

You could use solid wood, but ½-inch plywood would be satisfactory. If you use solid wood, dovetail the corners if you wish. Dovetails are inappropriate for plywood. Simple nailing or screwing might do, but it is better to rabbet the corners, then you can use glue and fine nails both ways (Fig. 7-25B).

Nailing the bottom on from below is weak construction. It is better, although slightly more difficult, to enclose it within the sides, again with glue and plenty of fine nails through the sides. Fit the central division and handle into dadoes (Fig. 7-25C). A suitable handhole is 1¼ inches wide and 5 inches long. Drill the ends and saw away the waste. Well round the edges of the hole and the top of the division.

Compartments in this type of box are often made with halving joints across the center. In this box, it is suggested that they be staggered, which will suit different sizes and quantities of nails and allow nailing in without having to cut joints (Fig. 7-25D).

Although this is a utilitarian item, it will benefit from a varnish or paint finish, which will keep it clean and improve appearance.

Materials List for Nail Box

4 sides	½	×	4	×	13
1 bottom	½	×	11	×	11
1 division	½	×	6½	×	12
2 divisions	½	×	3½	×	6

TOOL CARRIER

It is helpful to have a box or other means of carrying a number of tools to a job in the home, yard, or elsewhere. Some tools could be carried in the nail box just described, but many of them are too long for a box of the size suggested. A longer box is advisable. Two versions of this box are shown (Fig. 7-26A and B). The one with the central division is made in almost the same way as the nail box. The other has raised sides instead of the central division. Both use a piece of dowel rod as a handle.

Sizes for the first type are suggested (Fig. 7-26C). Make this in the same way as the nail box using ½-inch or ⅝-inch solid wood or plywood. Drill squarely for a ½-inch or thicker length of dowel rod (Fig. 7-26D), which will be glued in.

At one side fix a strip to the ends and leave a gap for tools to fit in (Fig. 7-26E). You could do the same on the other side, but a shelf with holes in it will hold screwdrivers, chisels, and other tools of that form (Fig. 7-26F). Larger and longer tools can go in the two compartments.

If you prefer to have the tools more enclosed or if your tools are too wide to fit into the first type of compartments, make the box with higher sides and no division (Fig. 7-26G). Fit a dowel handle through holes drilled to match. Arrange tool racks on opposite sides, similar to those on the division of the other box.

Materials List for Tool Carrier

2 sides	½	×	5	×	22
2 ends	½	×	5	×	16
1 bottom	½	×	14	×	20
1 division	½	×	10	×	22
1 strip	½	×	1	×	22
1 shelf	½	×	1½	×	22

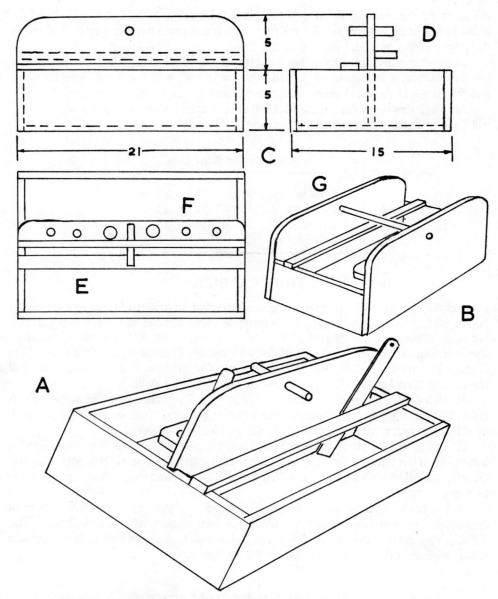

Fig. 7-26. *A carrier can be made to carry the particular tools you need for a job.*

TOOL CABINET

The wall is the best place to store many tools so they are accessible, but there might be reasons why you cannot spread racks on an open wall. The place might be used for other purposes. You might need to secure your tools from unauthorized use or protect the tools from the atmosphere. You might just feel it is tidier not to have tools spread

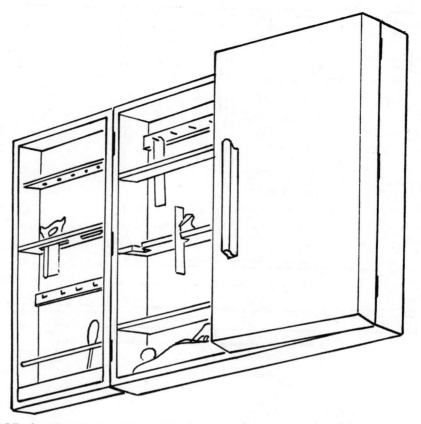

Fig. 7-27. *A tool cabinet on the wall provides protection for the tools when not in use.*

on the wall when not in use. The answer is one or more wall cabinets that can be closed and locked, if necessary.

The cabinet in Fig. 7-27 has a deep pair of doors that hold racks. When the doors are swung back on each side, the total effect is very similar to having tool racks directly on the wall. The tools are all accessible, but when you finish work, you can close the doors and there is just a simple cabinet without any evidence of the tools.

Size will depend on available space. The open cabinet will be twice as wide as when it is closed, so check the width you wish to use and halve it for the basic width. The example is assumed to be 36 inches. Height also depends on available space, but if you want to be able to reach all tools easily, do not make it more than 48 inches. More will mean you want to use all available space and are prepared to stand on something to get at the highest part. Front-to-back sizes will depend on the tools you wish to store. In the example (Fig. 7-28A), the back part has a depth of about 4 inches, and the doors have a depth of about 3 inches inside. This is probably more than the depth of any single tool you wish to store, but to make the best use of available space, some thinner tools can be arranged in front of others.

A full load in the cabinet can be quite heavy; therefore the structure should be

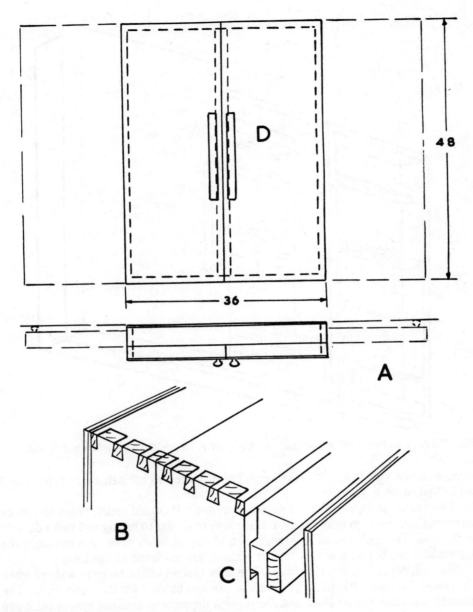

Fig. 7-28. *Tool cabinet sizes and corner construction.*

strong—½-inch plywood and 1-inch boards are specified. For the corners, you could use any of the usual joints, but dovetails are strongest.

To ensure matching parts, make the doors and the back part together first as one unit, then separate them. Mark out and join the boards. Draw a line around to mark the cut and arrange dovetails to come through a tail (Fig. 7-28B) on each corner. For the strongest joints, have the tails on the upright parts.

The plywood back and front could be let into rabbets, but it is simpler and satisfactory to glue and screw them on. You will hang the cabinet on the wall with screws through the back. That load should not be taken only by the plywood. Before attaching the back, let in a strip near the top (Fig. 7-28C). This could be there just for strength to take screws, but you can make it part of a tool rack. If you can arrange the backs of other tool racks in a similar way lower down, they will give you other strong points for screwing to the wall.

Work out where you want to fit racks in the back and doors before fitting the plywood. You need not fit them now, except for those that ought to be notched into the boards. You might find it worthwhile allowing for a shelf in the back part about 9 inches from the bottom. Leave the space below open for tools that are only temporarily stored or boxes of screws and similar things. Such bulky tools as planes and electric drills also can go there.

Details of racks can be similar to those described earlier in this chapter and will have to be arranged to suit your needs. With a little ingenuity, however, you can arrange ways of using the full depth available for putting some tools in front of others. It is possible to let a rack extend forward of the cut edges, providing you arrange for clearance in the other part when the doors are closed.

When the unit has been glued, level all joints and edges, than saw the doors from the back and separate the doors from each other. Clean the cut edges with the minimum amount of planing. Put identity marks on adjoining edges, so you assemble them in the same way. Use 3-inch hinges at each side. At the cut edges of the doors, fill in with uprights to stiffen the edges and provide support for racks.

Make the door handles thick enough to hold the doors parallel with the wall when they are swung open. Check the actual clearance; it should be a little more than 1 inch. You could fit store-bought handles, but vertical wood handles are probably preferable (Fig. 7-28D). They could be simple blocks with hollowed edges, screwed from inside. Use spring or magnetic catches to keep the doors closed, but if you want to lock the doors, arrange bolts inside one door and fit a lock to hold the other door to it.

Almost certainly you will have further thoughts about the arrangements of some tool racks. You might choose to leave the interior unpainted until you arrive at a final solution. The outside can be painted a dark color. A light color inside will be pleasant and make it easier to see tools.

Materials List for Tool Cabinet

2 sides	1	×	7	×	50	
1 top	1	×	7	×	38	
1 bottom	1	×	7	×	38	
1 back rail	1	×	2	×	38	
2 door uprights	1	×	2½	×	48	
1 back	36	×	48	×	½	plywood
1 front	36	×	48	×	½	plywood

8

Lathe Accessories

A lathe is a fascinating machine tool, with the accent on the word "tool" because the user has far more control over what is produced than with most other power tools. The use of a wood-turning lathe, in particular, might be described as almost more of an art than a craft. In metalworking, especially engineering type of work, the lathe can be the principal power tool in a shop. In a professional woodworking shop, a lathe might not feature so prominently, but it has many uses. In a woodworking hobby shop, a lathe is more popular because of its scope for doing attractive work.

Once you have a lathe, there are many things you can make for use with it to help you with your work. These projects can increase the accuracy and effectiveness of the machine, add to the range of work that can be done, and generally add to your enjoyment of lathework.

Some of the additions and accessories can be made on the lathe. If you have the use of a metalworking lathe, there are many things that can be made for use on a woodworking lathe. There are many items of basic lathe equipment that are better bought, unless you have extensive engineering equipment at your disposal. It would be unwise to make and use anything that could only be described as an improvisation, particularly if it is intended to rotate at the high speed of the lathe. As with any power tool, safety should be an overriding consideration. Even so, there are many accessories you can make and safely use on your lathe.

TOOL TRAY

If you put a tool on the bed of the lathe, it might become damaged. If you put it on the stand, it could get lost amidst shavings or swarf. For most turning, the end of the bed furthest from the headstock is not used. A tray mounted there will be out of the way and provide a safe place to put tools, including gauges and calipers, as well as small items if you are engaged in turning a run of objects. The tray must be removable, so the end of the lathe can be cleared when you want to use its full length for turning. How the tray is mounted depends on the lathe bed, but several methods are suggested.

The tray in Fig. 8-1A can be a piece of plywood with strips framing the edge. A suitable size would be 12 inches square, but make it to match your lathe—12 inches would look out of proportion on a small modelmaker's lathe but would be right for a lathe that takes 30 inches or more between centers.

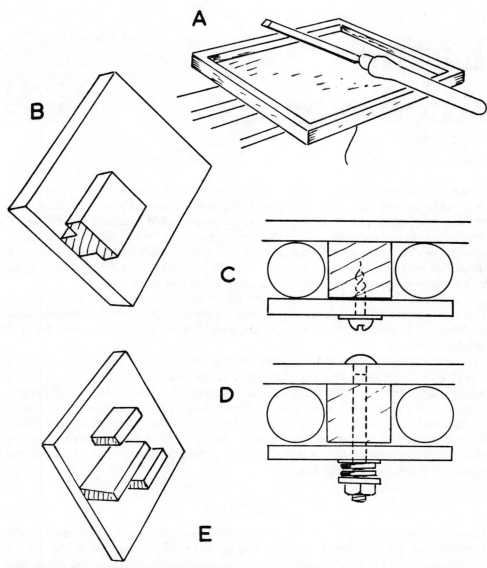

Fig. 8-1. *A tray that fits at the end of lathe is a place for tools and other equipment.*

For flat parallel ways add a block underneath to slide in (Fig. 8-1B). If you arrange this at one end, you get the benefit of the tray going past the end of the bed, and you can allow greater movement of the tailstock.

If the bed is made of two parallel rods, make a block to pass between them and a turnbutton below (Fig. 8-1C). A wood screw through the turnbutton might be sufficient, but you could use a bolt through with a spring to tighten the turnbutton (Fig. 8-1D).

For the split tubular bed of a Myford or similar lathe, you can make a block to push in the slot and two steadying pieces at the sides (Fig. 8-1E). For lathe beds of other forms, adapt one of these methods.

TOOL RESTS

Most woodworking lathes are supplied with one tool rest, which is straight and usually about 6 inches long. This is satisfactory for most turning. When dealing with long work, however, you have to move the tool rest frequently; when turning hollowed work, such as bowls, it does not conform as closely as you might wish to the shape being turned. It is worthwhile making extra rests to allow you to do better work on a greater variety of turned objects.

On most lathes the tool rest has a base that fits across and clamps to the bed. It has a hole into which a rod on the rest can be locked with a thumbscrew. Any new rest needs a matching rod (Fig. 8-2A).

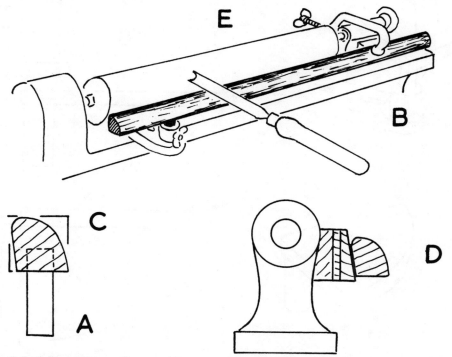

Fig. 8-2. *A long tool rest allows you to turn long cylinders without having to move a standard rest many times.*

The capacity of many lathes is enough to take a table leg. You can make a tool rest long enough to use at this size, then you do not have to move a short rest. It also allows you to do any long curves in one sweep, making it easier to get a smooth flow to its outline. The rod to fit in the tool rest base should be metal, if possible, but a hardwood dowel should have a reasonable life. Make the rest long enough to overlap the tailstock (Fig. 8-2B). Use a hardwood stiff enough to resist bending. Starting with 1½ inches square will suit many lathes (Fig. 8-2C).

Glue the rod into the strip—epoxy will hold metal to wood. Try the rest in position. At the tailstock there will have to be a packing. Its shape will depend on the section of the tailstock. You can include fillers of different thicknesses to allow for adjustments of the rest (Fig. 8-2D). In use, put a C clamp over the tailstock (Fig. 8-2E).

When turning a disc, you have to use a tool on the face and on the edge, which involves moving a straight tool rest several times. This can be avoided by having an L-shaped rest (Fig. 8-3A). Work on the edge can be done with a shorter rest than is required on the face. Cutting on discs is mostly done with a scraping tool, so a flat top to the rest is better than the usual slope intended to suit spindle turning.

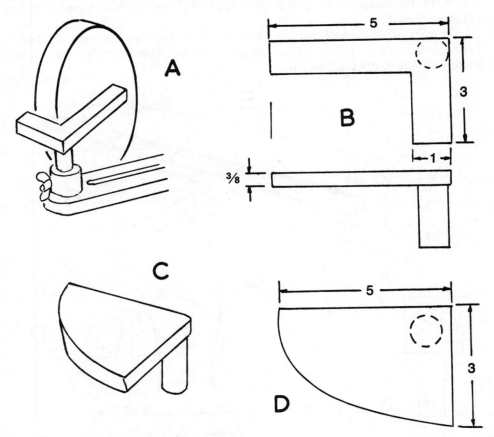

Fig. 8-3. *Special tool rests let you get closer to the work.*

Prepare a metal rod to suit the base, with its top turned square. What you use for the top depends on the size you require, but the example should suit many lathes (Fig. 8-3B). Cut it from sheet steel and weld it to the top of the rod. If you do not have welding facilities, you can braze it or drill and tap for a screw.

For cutting inside a hollow, a flat-topped rest is best, but it needs some clearance below if it is to be taken close to the wood. It does not have to conform to the curve you are turning, but if you give it an edge with an uneven curve, such as part of an ellipse, you can move it about so that your tool works close with little risk of chatter. A long extension would be useful, but vibration could then be a problem. The rest shown (Fig. 8-3C and D) should suit most bowls and similar hollow turning. Join the top to its rod in one of the ways suggested for the L-shaped rest.

BOWL DEPTH GAUGE

When turning the inside of a bowl or similar hollow article, you have to check depths of cut, so you do not cut so far that you weaken the bowl or stop before you have gone as deep as you want. One way is to put a straightedge across the rim and measure from it with a rule, but you have to stop the lathe and use two hands to do that. Store-bought depth gauges only have short stocks and are intended for engineering measurements. What is needed is a gauge with a long stock, which can be set and held to the work while it is rotating, if you wish.

This depth gauge has a stock long enough to bridge your largest bowl and a probe held to it with a wedge (Fig. 8-4A). Use close-grained hardwood for stock and wedge. The probe could be turned from hardwood dowel rod.

Mark out the stock (Fig. 8-4B) and drill for the probe before doing any shaping. If you are doubtful about being able to drill through squarely from one side, drill part way from both sides.

Make the wedge (Fig. 8-4C). With that as a guide, cut the groove for it through the stock until the wedge is clear of the probe hole when pushed back but still closes on the probe when about three-quarters of the way in. Turn the probe with a slight taper to a rounded end (Fig. 8-4D).

When you are satisfied with the action, cut the shaped part of the stock and well round those parts. A waxed finish is appropriate for this tool.

Materials List for
Bowl Depth Gauge

1 stock	1	×	1¼	×	12
1 wedge	⅜	×	⅝	×	4
1 probe	6	×	5/16 diameter		

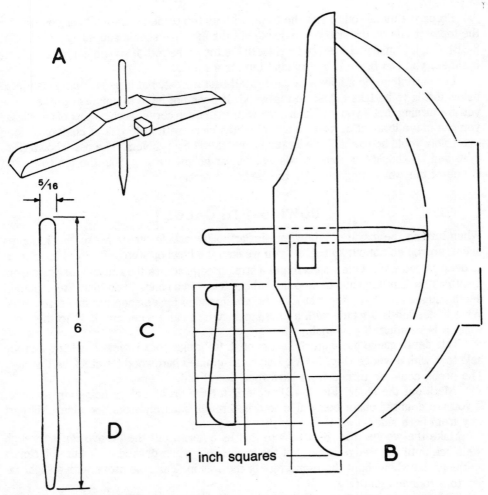

Fig. 8-4. *This wide depth gauge helps you check the depth of a bowl being turned.*

DOWEL GAUGE

Many things you have to turn have ends that have to fit in holes. A tool handle might have to fit a ferrule. Chair rails might have to fit holes in the chair legs. When the dowel end is next to the tailstock center, you can often try what you have turned in the actual other part or in a hole of the same size drilled in scrap wood, but if the dowel comes next to the wood being driven at the headstock end, you are dependent on measurements for accuracy. This usually means checking with calipers that you will probably have to set and reset many times, unless you have many pairs, making small errors inevitable.

In practice, you will probably find you only use a few drills of different sizes for the things you make, so the dowels you turn have to be made to these few sizes. A gauge with these sizes, to be used at either end of a turning, would obviously be useful, and this split hole gauge (Fig. 8-5A) might be the answer.

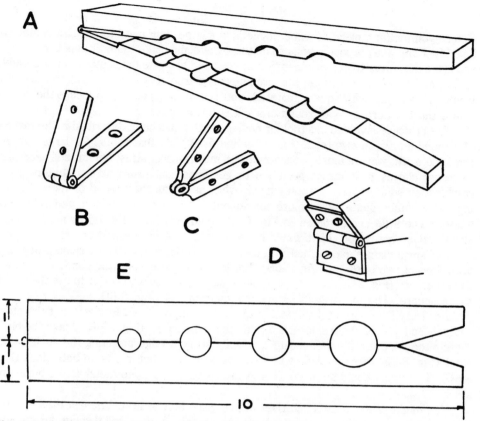

Fig. 8-5. A hinged gauge lets you check dowel ends turned on a lathe.

You need a reliable narrow hinge. There are small strap hinges intended for jewelry boxes and similar things (Fig. 8-5B). Another suitable type is flat (Fig. 8-5C). You might be able to cut down an ordinary hinge (Fig. 8-5D), but allow for the gauge being no more than ½ inch thick.

Make the gauge of a really hard, close-grained wood. If you use the gauge without stopping the lathe, it has to stand up to wear. Sizes are suggested (Fig. 8-5E), but make the parts to suit the holes you adopt as standard.

If possible, make the holes with a drill press to ensure squareness. Have the parts clamped together, preferably in a table vise. Round the external edges and ends. Fit the hinges and try some test pieces against holes in scrap wood to see that the gauge tests correctly. From this you will see what tolerances you might need to allow for particular jobs. When the dowel gauge is out of use, protect it from damage by holding the ends together with a rubber band.

This gauge will stand up to plenty of use, but you might be glad to have a second one in reserve. The two can be made easily at the same time. Use a piece of wood twice as thick as each gauge is to be. After drilling, saw through the middle and finish both sets of parts.

CENTER FINDER

Before you mount a piece of wood or metal in a lathe, you need to find the centers of its ends. For some purposes, you can do this by eye and make a center punch dot where you judge the center to be; for other pieces, you need to locate the center more accurately at first and not rely on turning the circumference true about your estimated centers. If you are starting with square material, you can draw diagonals to locate the center where the lines cross. With round stock it is not so easy.

The principle involved in a tool for finding centers has been described in the making of a round square in chapter 5 (Figs. 5-9 and 5-10), but that tool is for large curves. For lathe work, you are mostly concerned with much smaller sizes, but it is still necessary to bisect chords in different positions to get lines that cross at the center. Some combination squares have a center head, which is useful for a wood or metal turner, but a less cumbersome tool is more convenient for the sizes of stock in general use on a lathe. The little center finder in Fig. 8-6A could be made of wood or metal. Use a close-grained hardwood, or it would be very attractive in polished brass.

For small diameter rods, use the tool with a scriber or finely sharpened pencil to draw lines at two positions (Fig. 8-6B). For larger diameters, let the points rest on the circumference (Fig. 8-6C), but for really large curves, it would be better to use the earlier round square. The tool will also work on square stock (Fig. 8-6D).

Accuracy is important if the tool is to work with precision. In metal, cut the stock squarely and see that both sides are exactly the same length (Fig. 8-6E). Make the blade slightly too long at first, then locate it with its straight edge bisecting the angle of the stock (Fig. 8-6F). Fix the blade with two rivets lightly countersunk on both sides (Fig. 8-6G). The rivets could be made with 1/8-inch wire of the same metal as the blade and stock.

You might prefer to drill and rivet at one place only at first. You can then test the tool and move the blade slightly, if it has to be corrected, then drill through for the second rivet. Let the rivets heads stand a little high, so you can file them level. If you follow with abrasive and polish, you should not be able to see the rivet heads.

In wood, the tool can be slightly more bulky (Fig. 8-6H). Position the grain diagonally across. Pare the inner surfaces of the stock carefully with a very sharp chisel, then there might be no need to sand these surfaces. Trim the leg lengths the same. The outer edges are not so important and could be rounded (Fig. 8-6J). Pick a straight-grained piece of wood for the blade and make it as thin as seems reasonable for the particular wood. It should be under 1/8 inch thick. Bevel the marking edge.

It might be satisfactory to just glue the blade in place, but you can get more accuracy by following a similar procedure to that on the metal square. Screw on in one place, then check accuracy and drill for a second screw (Fig. 8-6K).

SHAPING OCTAGONS

For most wood turning between centers, you can mount a square piece of wood and turn off the angles. If the wood is liable to splinter or crack, or if the wood is very hard or if the lathe is underpowered, it is advisable to remove the angles to make the wood

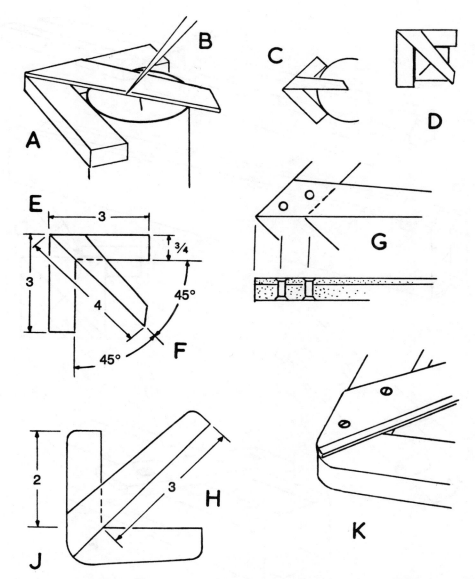

Fig. 8-6. *A wood or metal center finder helps you mark wood or metal to be turned on a lathe.*

octagonal before you start turning. In some instances you might want part of the work to remain octagonal, as in the attractive nonroll chisel handles.

You might remove the angles with a table saw or power planer, but with the comparatively short pieces usually turned, it is safer and quicker to use a hand plane. To do this you need a trough to support the wood.

The first trough is intended to be used on the bench top against a stop (Fig. 8-7A). If you make a second length without a built-in stop, it might support longer work. It is usual to make the built-in angle 90 degrees, but a slight error will not matter, providing

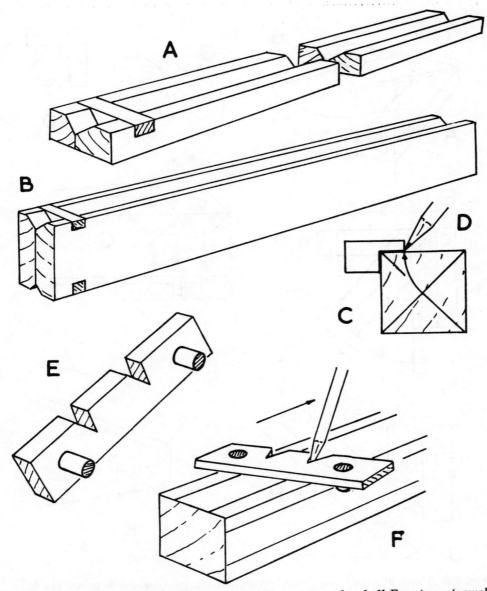

Fig. 8-7. *A trough (A, B) will hold square wood while corners are planed off. For a true octagonal section, use a notched block (C, D) or a special gauge (E, F).*

both sides are the same. Prepare a length suitable for both sides, then cut and glue the parts together. Softwood will do, but the inserted stop is better made of hardwood to take the thrust. If it is a push fit without glue, it can be replaced when worn.

A deeper trough can be held in the vise. The one in Fig. 8-7B is long enough at 18 inches for most things you turn and is double-sided with hollows of different sizes. Make it in the same way as the first trough.

To prepare wood for ordinary round turning, it will be sufficiently accurate to plane off the corners by eye until you see the shape is an approximate octagon. If the octagon is to remain as part of the finished turning, it has to be more accurate. Start with the wood planed truly square. At one end, draw two crossing diagonal lines, or do this on a piece of paper with a square of the same size. Measure half a diagonal and transfer this to one surface (Fig. 8-7C) to show where one edge of the octagon will be. Notch a piece of scrap wood to this line and use it with a pencil to draw along both ways from each corner (Fig. 8-7D) on all surfaces. If you plane off the corners to these lines, the result will be a regular octagon section.

If you expect to want to mark square wood for making octagons frequently, you can make a tool to do it without measurements even if the square wood is tapered. Decide on the biggest square you expect to have to mark. Make the tool to that size, and it can be used for smaller squares as well. Set out this size to get the positions of the lines to be drawn along wood of the maximum size, as just described. Mark on the centerline of a piece of wood the holes for dowels with the distance between the edges of the holes the same as the wood size. Between these holes mark where the drawn lines have to come. Cut notches into these points (Fig. 8-7E) for inserting a pencil.

To use on any size wood, put the tool over the side to be marked and slope it until the dowels bear against the other sides, put a pencil in each notch and draw the tool along (Fig. 8-7F). If you keep the dowels tight against the wood, the lines will be correct even if the wood tapers.

Make the tool of hardwood. For sizes to 3 inches square, you could ⅜-inch-×-1-inch section and ⅜-inch dowels.

SPECIAL TOOLS

When you have been using a lathe for some time, you will find the need for special tools, different from the standard ones, that might make your work easier or more accurate. Many of these you can make yourself. For metal turning, you can grind tools from blanks to suit particular needs, then perhaps grind them again for another purpose. Wood turning is done with more standard tools, but there are cutting tools you can make. In particular, the many scrapers needed in bowl and other hollow turning can be ground and reground to suit needs. It is possible to grind old files to make wood-turning scraper tools, but care is needed. Files are almost fully hardened, and this makes them brittle, increasing the risk of a tool breaking unless you reharden and temper it to a slightly softer state.

Faceplate Lever

Some tools you can make are quite simple. A faceplate lever is one. After the loads in use, a faceplate can be screwed extremely tightly on the mandrel nose. Gripping its edge might not allow you to unscrew it, and you need more leverage. A metal lever can be made with a bar about ½-inch-×-¾-inch section. Turn two metal dowels with shouldered ends to rivet through (Fig. 8-8A). If the faceplate has round holes only, you must space the dowels to suit, but if there are slots, spacing is not so crucial. If you

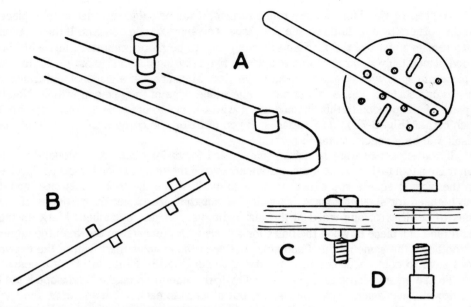

Fig. 8-8. *A lever will unscrew a stubborn faceplate.*

have two faceplates of different sizes, add a second set of dowels on the other side (Fig. 8-8B).

A similar lever could be made with a strip of wood of ½-inch-×-1-inch section. Use nuts and bolts instead of dowels (Fig. 8-8C) if you do not have facilities for turning metal dowels to fasten in with nuts (Fig. 8-8D).

Bumper-outer

On many lathes, the centers fit into the headstock mandrel and the tailstock with tapers at the ends of holes. To get a center out, you have to knock it with something through the hole. Instead of searching for an odd piece of rod to go through the hole, it is better to make a special tool—for want of a better name, call it a "bumper-outer" (Fig. 8-9A). Use a metal rod that fits easily through the headstock spindle, probably a ⅜-inch diameter and a few inches longer than the hole it has to pass through. Turn a knob handle that will allow you to give a comfortable thump (Fig. 8-9B) and fit it with a ferrule.

Graver

A tool that you might find more uses for than you expected is a graver (Fig. 8-9C). It can be used as an awl for marking centers of wood or plastic rods. It will serve as a scriber. It will scratch lines on the rotating wood or metal to mark locations of cuts. Its main function, however, is turning brass or other nonferrous ferrules on handles. If you put a tube ferrule on a handle and bring the triangular end of the graver up to

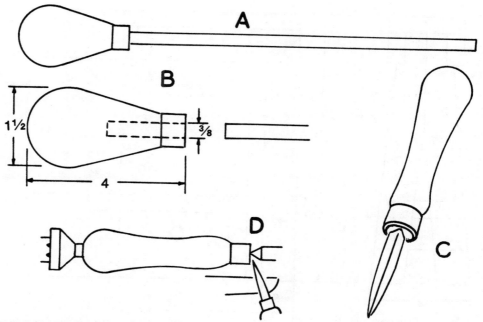

Fig. 8-9. *A handled rod (A, B) will knock out lathe centers. A graver will true the ends of metal ferrules (C, D).*

it, you can rotate it on the tool rest until it cuts and use it to true the end or put a bevel on it (Fig.8-9D).

A graver should be kept short and can be made from an end broken or ground off an old triangular file. Grind the teeth off and take the end to a point. You can get better cutting edges by rubbing the surfaces on an oilstone. Mount the tool in a wood handle. It need only project a few inches, but the handle could be 6 inches or more.

BASIC LATHE STAND

You can mount a lathe on a bench, but then it might be in the way when you want to use the bench and not the lathe. Most makers of lathes will sell you a metal stand, but these tend to accentuate noise and are hard on edge tools that come into contact with them. Stands made from sheet metal can vibrate and might not be heavy enough for adequate stability. A wood bench made from pieces of a reasonably large section is quieter, presents no hazard to tools, and should be more rigid than a light metal stand. This applies to lathes used for metal or wood.

The stand in Fig. 8-10A is made completely from planed 2-inch- × -4-inch softwood, and the suggested sizes suit many popular lathes. Turners have their own preferences for working heights, and you might want to adjust the height of this stand to suit your height and that of the lathe centers.

Set out a pair of ends (Fig. 8-10B) with the outsides tapering from a 12-inch spread at the feet to 7 inches at the top. Cut the legs to fit against each other. Notch the tops for the lengthwise rails (Fig. 8-10C), which are inset ½ inch at the top.

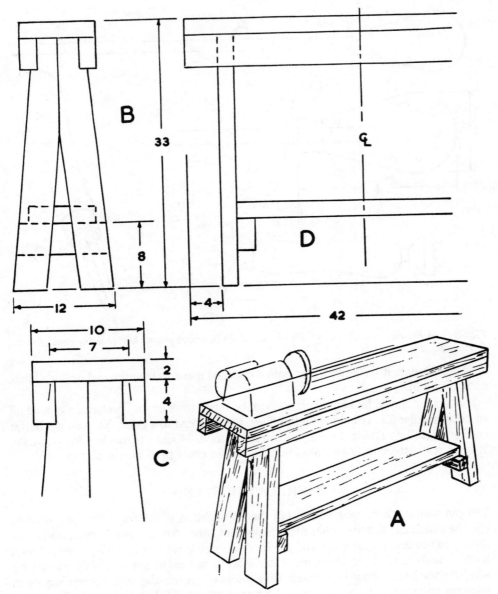

Fig. 8-10. A stout bench makes a lathe stand.

Glue the two pairs of legs together and add lower rails, glued and nailed or screwed on (Fig. 8-10D). Glue two pieces to make the shelf and join this and the top rails to the legs. It should be satisfactory to use 3-inch-×-12-gauge screws, or larger, counterbored and plugged. Check that the stand is upright and that the legs stand level. Sight over the top to check that there is no twist. If necessary, plane top surfaces true. It is important that a precision metalworking lathe is mounted on a surface without twist. This is desirable for a woodworking lathe, but not quite as crucial.

Join boards to make up the top to either finish flush with the rails, as shown, or to overhang a little. Much depends on your lathe or personal requirements.

You could use metal brackets to fasten the legs to the shop floor. If you do not want to fix the stand in one position, load the bottom shelf well to make it more stable. You will probably do this by storing equipment and materials, or you could use stones or bags of sand.

Materials List for Basic Lathe Stand

4 legs	2 × 4 × 33
2 rails	2 × 4 × 12
2 top rails	2 × 4 × 44
2 shelf parts	2 × 4 × 36
3 top parts	2 × 4 × 44

STAND WITH STORAGE

There are a large number of accessories and tools with any lathe, whether it is for turning wood or metal, and the obvious place to store them is within the stand or bench under the lathe. With many lathes, the motor has to go under the bench, which means mounting also has to be arranged there.

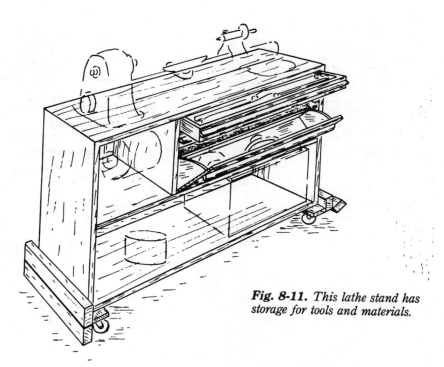

Fig. 8-11. This lathe stand has storage for tools and materials.

The layout under the lathe will have to be arranged to suit your needs, but the example in Fig. 8-11 has a space under the headstock for the motor and its adjustable mounting, two shallow drawers for wood-turning tools, and a tilt bin for chucks, centers, and similar things. The bottom space will take any large accessories as well as some of your stock of turning wood. The back of the stand is closed.

As you might not use a lathe constantly, you might want to move it out of the way when you need the space for other work. This stand is shown on large casters; to prevent

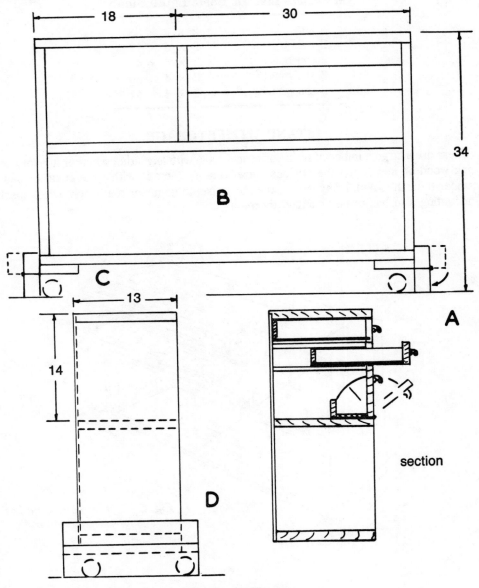

Fig. 8-12. *Suggested sizes for a lathe stand with storage.*

the stand from moving in use, there are blocks hinged at each end to turn down and rest on the floor (Fig. 8-12A).

As drawn (Fig. 8-12B), the stand is intended for a fairly large and heavy lathe. The wood used can be softwood, but it should finish 1¼ inches thick. Hardwood might be thinner, and you could scale the design down for a smaller and lighter lathe. Check the height of centers you prefer to work at, however, and adjust the stand to suit. If you do not need the casters, extend the stand ends to the floor. The plywood back could be merely nailed or screwed on, or it could be let into rabbets in the top and ends.

For the best construction, use dovetails at all the outer corners (Fig. 8-13A). Alternatively, you could rabbet the corners and nail or screw both ways. Set the shelf

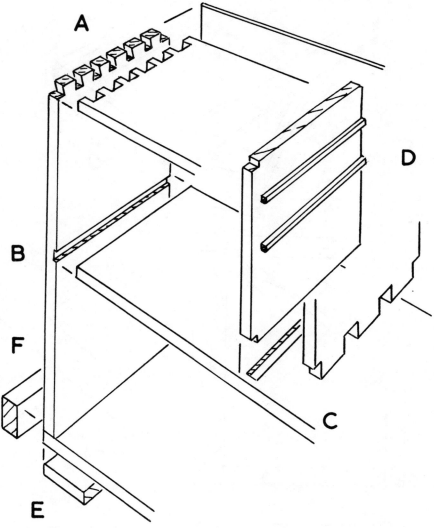

Fig. 8-13. Method of construction of a lathe stand with storage.

into dadoes (Fig. 8-13B) and the division into dadoes or tenons (Fig. 8-13C). Fit drawer runners, set back by the thickness of the drawer fronts (Fig. 8-13D). Add the back to keep the assembly in shape.

There will have to be pads under the bottom corners to take the casters (Figs. 8-12C and 8-13E). Outside these put 2-inch-×-3-inch strips across, projecting 2 inches back and front for stability (Figs. 8-12D and 8-13F). They form the base on which the support blocks are hinged. These also be from 2-inch-×-3-inch wood, but position the casters

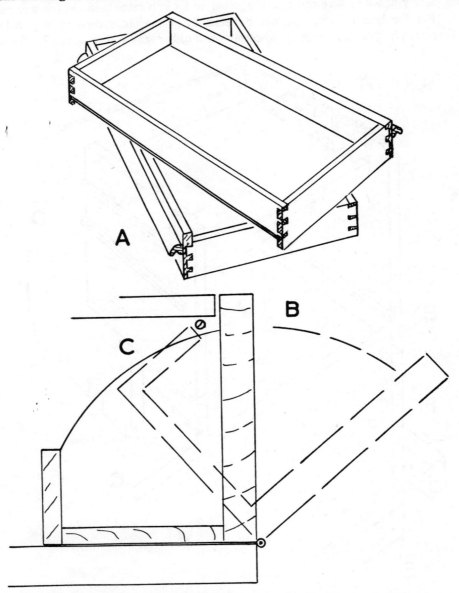

Fig. 8-14. *Details of drawers and bin for the lathe stand with storage.*

and adjust the blocks so, when they are lowered, they take the weight from the wheels and rest directly on the floor.

Position the motor and try the lathe in position, so you can cut away the top for the driving belt. You will also have to position the motor switch, which can probably go on a block of wood at a corner of the opening. You might find it convenient to have the back cut away behind the motor compartment. This will aid cooling and allow easier cleaning. You can coil the cable, when out of use, on a large hook at the back of the compartment. There might also be room for hooks to take faceplates and other things, but do not crowd the motor or have anything that might touch the belt.

Make drawers 3 inches deep. Position the front of the top one under the stand top. The front of the second drawer overlaps the runners (Fig. 8-14A). For the best construction, use dovetails. The bin fills the remaining space over the shelf. It has hinges at the front of the shelf, and its own front fits over the drawer runners like a drawer front (Fig. 8-14B). Measure the gap it has to fit and arrange the curve of the end so it can be stopped by a screw as the bin back comes up (Fig. 8-14C). Assemble the bin like a drawer. You might wish to fit divisions to take chucks and other parts.

Fit handles to the drawers and the bin front. Full-length handles allow you to grip easily from whatever position you are standing. To fit the bin, screw hinges to it, then tilt it downwards while you screw the hinges to the front of the shelf. Check that it will open and close properly, then tilt it to what will be the open position and drive screws into the uprights to act as stops. The weight of the contents will keep the bin closed.

The stand will look smart if given several coats of paint, preferably a dark color, but the drawers and bin can be varnished inside and out. If you need more drawer space, put a drawer under the shelf. You could make fitted boxes for equipment and wood to fit in the bottom space.

Materials List for Stand with Storage

2 uprights	1½	×	13	×	32	
1 division	1¼	×	13	×	18	
3 lengthwise parts	1¼	×	13	×	50	
4 feet	2	×	3	×	18	
2 pads	1¼	×	4	×	18	
1 back	32	×	48	×	¼	plywood
4 drawer runners	¾	×	¾	×	14	
1 drawer front	¾	×	3	×	30	
1 drawer front	¾	×	3¾	×	30	
2 drawer backs	⅝	×	3	×	30	
4 drawer sides	⅝	×	3	×	14	
2 drawer bottoms	13	×	30	×	¼	plywood
1 bin front	¾	×	8	×	30	
1 bin back	⅝	×	3	×	30	
1 bin bottom	⅝	×	7	×	30	
2 bin ends	⅝	×	7	×	8	

WORKING HELPS

There are many things, simple in themselves, that turners make to help in their work. Some are made to suit a particular job and then discarded, but other helpful items can be used many times. Some might have to be scrapped after a few uses, but they save time and increase your efficiency. These are the sort of auxiliary tools or accessories to make when you are between jobs or want to do something on your lathe but have no particular project in minds.

Many of these devices are well-known to experienced turners, but the following notes will serve to remind old hands and help newcomers on the way to becoming old hands. The ideas are aimed at wood turners, but a metalworker will see ways of adapting some of them to his needs. With a metal-turning lathe it is possible to make more sophisticated versions of some of them, which could then be used for wood turning as well.

Packings

If you want to mount wood on a screw center, it is advisable to put a packing between the two so your tool is not damaged by hitting the metal pad (Fig. 8-15A). The packing also effectively shortens the screw if you want to hold something shallow. A set of discs from ⅛ inch thickness upwards will take care of whatever length you wish to make the screw projection. Make the disc diameters larger than the pad. You can screw a disc on and turn it true. This is a way of using up odd pieces of hardboard or plywood. For thin packings, you could use plastic.

In a similar way, you need discs to go on the faceplate, usually to allow screws through into the job and provide a safety barrier to prevent a tool touching the metal faceplate (Fig. 8-15B). Plywood ½ inch thick is enough to take holding screws, yet permit other screws of reasonable length to go through into the work.

Make at least two discs, slightly larger than the diameter of the faceplate. Have one with fixing screws at inner positions of holes or slots in the faceplate, then large work can benefit from the hold of screws through outer positions (Fig. 8-15C). Let another disc have fixing screws at outer positions, then you can hold smaller work with long screws nearer the center.

With a three-jaw or four-jaw chuck, it helps to have packings if the work does not have to go fully into the jaws, otherwise you might not get it to run true. Fortunately, the steps in the jaws are fairly wide, and a packing disc can suit a wide range of work sizes (Fig. 8-15D). Packings could be wood or metal and in thicknesses to almost reach the total depth of the jaws, then quite thin work can be held without wobble.

Square Holder

If you have to turn a run of things like table legs with square tops, it helps to have a holder to drive the wood mounted on the faceplate. This provides more accurate centering and is quicker and easier to load than using a spur center. The arrangement is allied to the faceplate packing just described, but is better thicker—¾ inch should suit most work (Fig. 8-15E). Legs are commonly 1½-inch or 2-inches square, so one or two holders should suit your needs.

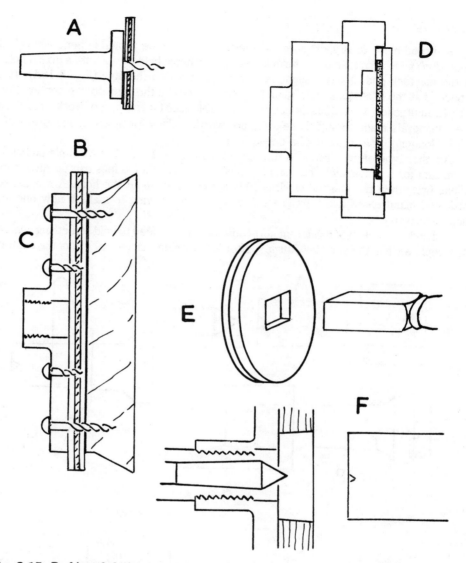

Fig. 8-15. *Packings help in mounting work on the screw center, chuck, and faceplate.*

Cut a square hole at the center of the disc with a slight taper (Fig. 8-15F) so that the wood tightens as it is pushed in. To get the holder accurately centered, carefully mark the center on the end of a sample piece of square wood and drill or center punch there. Loosely screw the holder to the faceplate. Mount the sample piece on the headstock center, while the other end is supported on the tailstock center, so it fits into the holder. This positions the holder on the faceplate; tighten the screws through the faceplate at this setting. Remove the headstock center. Subsequent pieces can merely be pushed into the holder ready for turning.

Mandrels

A turned piece to support something else that has to be turned is generally called a *mandrel*, which can take many forms. A simple example holds work with a drilled hole. At the tailstock end, it has a slight taper that pushes into the hole (Fig. 8-16A). If it is needed at the headstock end, it can be enlarged to take the spur driving center (Fig. 8-16B). In practice, most of us do not use many drill sizes for this sort of work, therefore a few mandrels made to suit these sizes are worth making for stock. A mandrel's life will be longer if you make it of a dense hardwood.

Another type of mandrel goes through a hole (Fig. 8-16C). The example shown is a drip ring for a candlestick, but napkin rings and many other things can be turned by drilling first, then the finished work is truly symmetrical about the hole. A few dense hardwood mandrels of this type in stock will save you having to make a new one for each particular job.

A mandrel problem of a different sort comes when you need to hold something against the faceplate while the outside is turned, after first turning a large part out of the center.

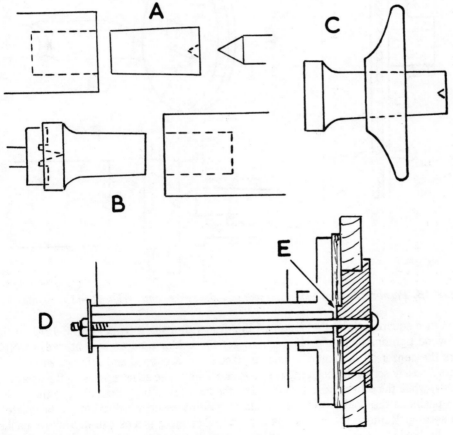

Fig. 8-16. *Mandrels will secure hollow work on a lathe.*

Usually, screw holes into the work have to be avoided. If the headstock has a hollow spindle, you can tighten a wood mandrel into the work with a bolt right through. Have a long bolt ready, with a nut and a washer large enough to go over the end of the spindle (Fig. 8-16D). Turn a hollow at the center of the pad. Turn a mandrel to go into the work and with a lug to fit into the hole in the pad (Fig. 8-16E). The outside of the mandrel can have a slight taper to go into the work and a rim to secure it. With the bolt tightened, you can turn the outside of the work knowing that it will be concentric with the inside. You might have to turn a wood mandrel for each job, but keep the bolt, nut, and washer as you will find them useful for pulling many pieces of work onto the faceplate.

Repetition Guides

It is easy enough to make a single turning between centers, but it is not so easy to make a matching set. Things such as stools and tables need parts made in sets of four and eight. Measuring or using calipers might suffice, but small errors can creep in. Quite often a rule is too long to put against the work.

If several pieces have to be made with beads and shaped parts at the same positions, a strip of scrap wood penciled on the edge is better than a rule (Fig. 8-17A). Even better

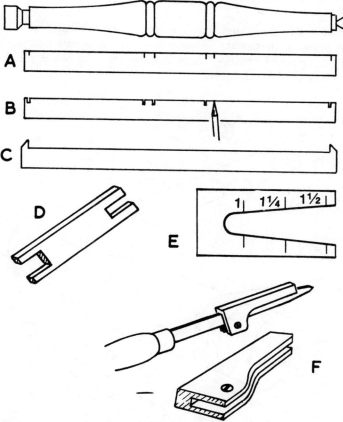

Fig. 8-17. *Gauges can be used when you have to duplicate lengths or diameters (A-E). A stop on a parting tool limits its depth of cut.*

is a saw cut in the edge at each point (Fig. 8-17B), then you can put the point of a pencil in each notch and draw lines round the rotating work. For a long run of parts that need to be the same length, your stick can be given ends to make it into a lengthwise caliper (Fig. 8-17C).

With these aids you can get the pattern right lengthwise and still finish with one piece thicker than another. Careful use of calipers on a few key diameters might be the best way to avoid this, but for a long run, it might be worthwhile making gauges for diameters at main test points (Fig. 8-17D). Alternatively, a tapered slot can be marked with diameters at particular points (Fig. 8-17E).

On some work, a good way of getting shapes to the correct depth is to cut in to mark the depths at important points with a parting tool, after you have turned a cylinder. Without the means of stopping the tool, you still have to work to a gauge or calipers. To avoid this, clamp a stop to the parting tool. A simple wood one is shown (Fig. 8-17F), but a metalworker could make a neat one in brass, with a tapped screw for tightening. On the usual waisted parting tool, make the stop long enough for the tightening part to grip on the parallel part further back.

Burning In

Turnings are often decorated with lines cut in the revolving work with the point of a chisel. A group of these lines will also provide a grip on a handle. The lines can be made more prominent by burning them. It sounds drastic, but all you do is char each line to show black against the lighter wood.

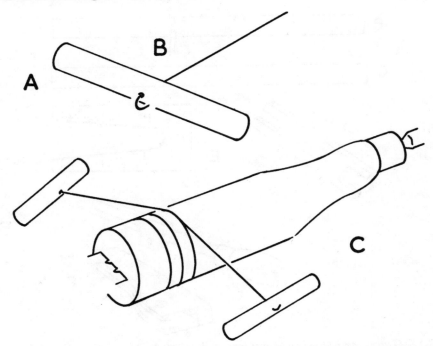

Fig. 8-18. *Cut lines around turned work can be burnt in by the friction of a wire.*

Use iron or mild steel wire about 18 gauge. High carbon steel wire could be used, but as it gets hot it loses any temper, making it no better than the other wire. Either turn two handles or use pieces of dowel rod (Fig. 8-18A). Take each end of the wire through a hole and drive the end back into the wood to secure it (Fig. 8-18B).

To use the tool, cut in the lines with a chisel, then while the wood is still rotating, press the wire onto a line. Keep up the pressure until you see smoke. The groove should be nicely blackened (Fig. 8-18C).

DRAWING STAND

When turning wood or metal, you are usually working to a drawing, which can be a sketch you have made, a published sheet, or a picture in a magazine. Because you often need to look at it while working, the best place for the drawing is in front of you. A stand mounted behind the lathe can hold a drawing where you can see it without moving your eyes far from the work mounted in the lathe. How you arrange the drawing stand depends on the type of lathe and whether it is on a stand, has its own legs, or is on a bench.

The stand shown in Fig. 8-19 has a board area 12 inches square and is sloped 15 degrees to vertical. This will take a folded magazine—most sketches are done on paper

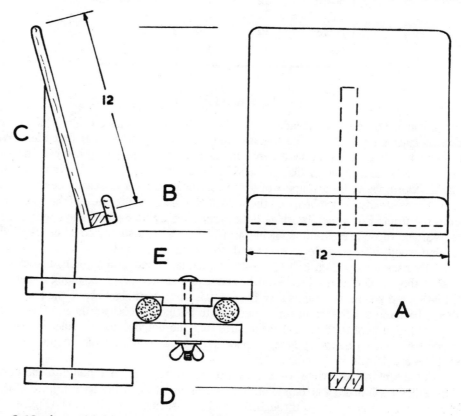

Fig. 8-19. A stand behind the lathe can hold a drawing where you need it.

no bigger than that—but you could make the board any size you wish. This board is on a single 1-inch- × -2-inch leg (Fig. 8-19A). A bigger board would be complicated because it would need two legs or a much stouter single one.

Make the board from ½-inch plywood with a built-up ledge at the bottom (Fig. 8-19B). Round all exposed edges and corners. Cut the leg to a suitable angle and screw through (Fig. 8-19C).

Two methods of mounting are suggested. In both, the leg is tenoned into a flat base. If the lathe is on a bench or a separate stand, you can let the base extend onto it and screw or clamp it on (Fig. 8-19D). You could arrange the base to go on the lathe bed, if it has parallel ways. Round rods are shown (Fig. 8-19E). You could slot the stand base, but it will probably be satisfactory to drill for the bolt at a position that keeps the board well clear of the largest size turning you will handle. You can fit the board stand across the ways below the work, but much turning is done shorter than the ways. Because you rarely move the tailstock to the far end clamping the board towards the end of the bed can be almost permanent.

Materials List for Drawing Stand

1 board	12	×	14	×	½ plywood
1 ledge	¾	×	1	×	13
1 ledge	½	×	1½	×	13
1 leg	1	×	2	×	18

BACK STEADY

When you are turning long slender pieces between centers, there is a risk of vibration causing inaccuracy and poor finish unless the work is supported near its center. What is slender is relative. Something 1 inch in diameter and 6 feet long has just the same problems as a piece ¼ inch in diameter and 9 inches long. To prevent vibration and chatter marks, there has to be a support of some sort built in. This is usually described as a backstay or steady, which bears on the work and resists the pressure of the tool cutting from the front. For a metalworking lathe, there are elaborate backstays with pairs of rollers, and these are essential for metal. Although such a steady could be used when turning wood, it is possible to make and use something simpler.

This back steady (Fig. 8-20A) mounts on the lathe bed, and a notched block bears against the slender work (Fig. 8-20B). The size and method of mounting depends on the lathe, but you must arrange it so the notch is at center height above the bed. There should be enough adjustment for the steady to be moved backwards and forwards as required. Use hardwood for the main parts, but the notched piece could be softwood to reduce wear on the work being supported. For an average lathe, suggested wood sections are 1 inch × 2 inches.

Cut the notch to a wide V—it is drawn at 120 degrees. A tenon into the upright (Fig. 8-20C) will make a strong joint. Tenon the upright into the base (Fig. 8-20D). A ⅜-inch carriage bolt can go through the bed to a securing block below (Fig. 8-20E).

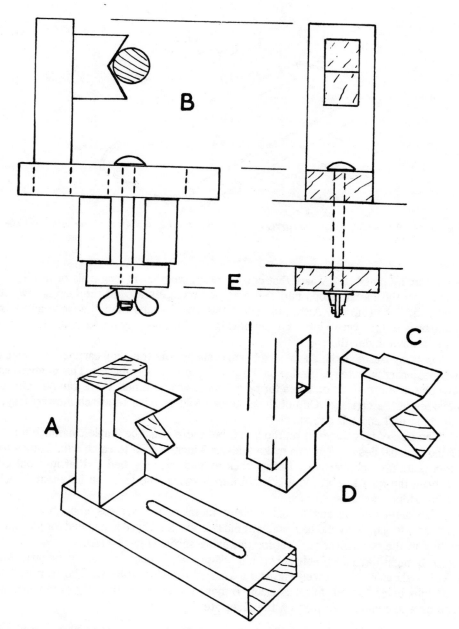

Fig. 8-20. *A back steady mounts on the lathe bed and supports slender work.*

To use the back steady, turn the work roughly to near the finished size, even if this causes vibration marks. Bring the steady tight to the work near its center, then turn the length of the wood on each side of it smoothly to size. Move the steady along a little way and finish the part where it was bearing.

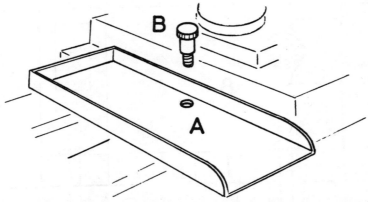

Fig. 8-21. A swarf tray on the carriage of a metalworking lathe keeps the lathe bed clean.

SWARF TRAY

When turning metal, the waste that comes away, whether in long coils or as chips depending on the metal, drops into the lathe bed and gets around the lead screw. It is often difficult to remove. A tray to collect this swarf keeps the lathe clean and allows you to brush all the waste into a container (Fig. 8-21). This tray travels with the carriage and is always under the tool.

On many lathes of the sizes used in small shops, the traveling carriage fits over the bed with a narrow extending ledge on the side towards the headstock. This might already have one or more screwed holes for taking accessories. If not, there can be holes into the sides of the carriage. One of these holes could be used to attach a swarf tray, or you could drill and tap one specially.

The size of tray depends on the lathe, but there could be ample clearance for it on a lathe of usual design. You can make it about 3 inches wide to catch what comes from a tool at its normal overhang. Let its back extend over the bed and let its front edge overhang the lead screw. On a lathe of 8-inch swing, the tray can be about 9 inches across. Depth could be ¾ inch.

Use aluminum or any available sheet metal of a thickness enough to provide stiffness—16 gauge should be suitable. Fold it to shape. There is no need for any special jointing at the rear corners. Drill for the fixing screw (Fig. 8-21A).

You might have a suitable screw but will probably choose to turn your own. Make it with a shouldered screwed end and a knurled top (Fig. 8-21B). The tray will clear most jobs being turned, but it is easily removed if it gets in the way of a special job, such as a maximum-size part on the faceplate.

TILT BIN

A wood turner accumulates a large number of short ends of wood, mostly of square section. He can use up pieces that are too short for most other types of woodworking. This brings a storage problem. A way of storing short pieces is to make one or more

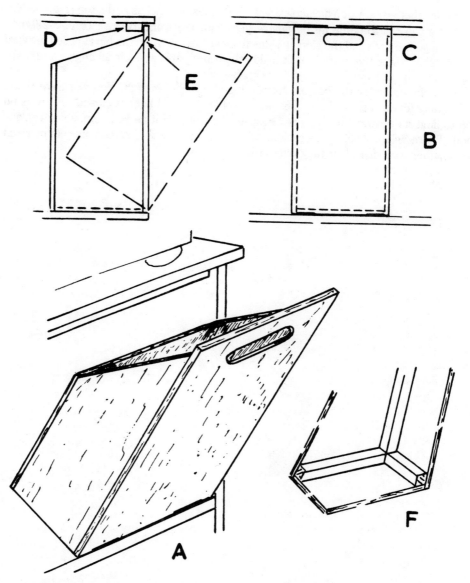

Fig. 8-22. *A tilt bin under a lathe will hold short ends of wood.*

tilt bins to fit under the lathe stand or bench. A *tilt bin* is a box that stands upright but can be pulled forward when you want to get at its contents (Fig. 8-22A). Its size and method of mounting will depend on the bench or stand, but if there are lower rails or a shelf, the bottom can be hinged there. At the top the bin closes against a rail, which can be under the bench top.

Size of the example is assumed to be about 12 inches square and 24 inches high (Fig. 8-22B). Use ½-inch plywood and ¾-inch square strips. Make the front first, as it controls other sizes. Cut a handhole about 1¼ inches × 6 inches at the top (Fig. 8-22C). Arrange a top rail to come inside where you want the front to close (Fig. 8-22D).

Arrange the back and the sloping sides to clear the rail when the bin is pulled forward (Fig. 8-22E). Make the bottom to fit inside the other parts and join all angles with nails or screws and glue into strips inside (Fig. 8-22F).

Two hinges under the bottom front edge should be enough. You will have to tilt the bin fully forward to fit them. The weight of the bin will keep it closed. There is no stop to limit its outward movement because you will hold it as you remove or replace wood. There will probably be occasions when you want to tip out the contents or clean the bin, then you can tilt it fully outward.

9

Drilling Accessories and Equipment

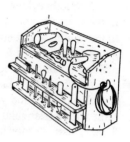

One of the most popular small portable power tools is the electric drill. In many simpler tool kits, it might be the only source of power. An assortment of accessories are available to do other things besides drilling with it. Some additions are effective, but others that are offered should be regarded as gadgets that appeal to the beginner rather than as serious tools. However, an electric drill does include a compact motor that can power other things besides drills, if you appreciate its limitations.

The efficiency of the tool as a drill is improved if it is mounted in a stand. It then becomes a drill press. The holes it makes will be square to the table and more easily controlled in depth. A better-equipped shop will have a drill press, built as such, as well as portable drills.

Care is needed to avoid overloading a portable electric drill. Most motors are sufficiently powerful to cope with drilling holes of the size specified by the makers. Attempting to drill larger holes with drills with reduced ends to fit the chuck can damage the motor. The revolutions per minute of the drill suit drilling, although the load can reduce the actual revolutions considerably. If you want to drive something else, you must allow for the revolution per minute (rpm). For instance, a small grinding wheel might not reach a sufficient peripheral speed for efficient working. You can still grind with it, but expect the stone to wear rapidly. A little circular saw suffers from the same problem and will stall if you try to cut anything but the thinnest wood. If you compare the rpm of a drill with that of a router, you will find that the router is about twice the speed of the drill, therefore do not expect to get satisfactory results with any but the smallest router cutter in a drill chuck.

If you remember its limitations, you can make full use of a portable electric drill or use a drill press for other things besides drilling. The drill is primarily for drilling however, and you should not do anything that impairs its efficiency for that purpose.

CENTER MARKING

Before using a drill, you must center it accurately on the work. In metal, it is usual to mark the position with a center punch with its end ground at about 60 degrees (Fig. 9-1A). The end of a metalworking drill is at a flatter angle than that, so as it enters, it is located by the rim of the hollow. Because of this, make sure the point is ground circular because with a very badly shaped end, the drill might not settle exactly over where the punch point entered.

A metalworking center punch is not the best tool for marking hole centers in wood. In most woods you can make a dent with an awl (Fig. 9-1B). In harder woods it is better to use a punch, but sharpen it more steeply—30 degrees is reasonable (Fig. 9-1C). That gives a good entry for the central spur of a woodworking bit or a good guide if you are making small holes for screws or nails with a metalworking bit.

A different problem comes with plastic, such as Plexiglas. It would crack if you hit it with a punch, and you cannot push in a plain awl. You can make a satisfactory locating dent with a triangular point, such as the ground end of an old triangular file (Fig. 9-1D). This is also another use for the graver (Fig. 8-9C), described as a lathe tool. You could grind the end of an awl (Fig. 9-1E). In both cases, press hard and twist the tool backwards and forwards through about 90 degrees.

For precision drilling in wood, particularly in an awkward grain or through a knot, it is advisable to follow metalworking practice and start with a pilot hole, either right through or far enough to ensure the full-size drill will be on course. Make the pilot drill about the same diameter as the spur on the large drill. The center of any drill does not cut, and the pilot hole not only guides the larger drill but removes the part that can only be penetrated by force.

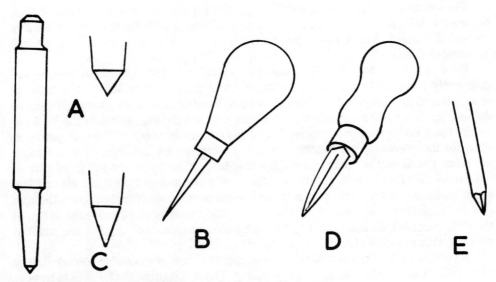

Fig. 9-1. *The center for drilling can be marked with a punch or awl.*

DEPTH GAUGES

One problem in drilling is dealing with *blind holes*—those that do not go right through. On a drill press or a stand for a portable drill, there is some means of limiting advance, but if you are drilling freehand, you only estimate how far the drill has entered, which might not be accurate enough. It might not matter if a screw hole is deeper than necessary, but if you are removing waste in a mortise that should not go through, control is important.

A simple depth stop can be a piece of drilled dowel rod, slid on the drill (Fig. 9-2A). You can cut it to suit the particular job. There are small collars available with setscrews to hold them on the drill, but because of the flutes, they might not grip very well in exactly the position you want them. It is better to make them a little longer, then they are less likely to twist and slip. If made of hardwood, secure it with a wood screw. Drive it once to cut the thread, then remove it and file off the point for a better grip on the drill (Fig. 9-2B).

A neat collar for wood or metal drills is held with a small setscrew (Fig. 9-2C). It is possible to make one collar lock on a slightly smaller drill than the one it is intended for, but you should make a set for all your commonly-used drills.

Another metal depth stop can be made from $\frac{1}{8}$-inch wire and some sheet metal about $\frac{1}{16}$ inch thick. Make the sheet metal into a little clamp, with one end to grip the wire and the other end to go around the drill (Fig. 9-2D). A hollow that will grip a $\frac{1}{4}$-inch drill will hold on a $\frac{3}{4}$-inch one. Experiment with the shape. Put a bolt and wing nut through the parts. Bend the wire so that the lower end can be moved alongside the drill (Fig. 9-2E).

All of the depth gauges described so far revolve with the drill. To avoid the end marking the surface of the work if it is brought down too hard, it is better to attach it to the drill casing to provide a stop without it moving. How it is arranged depends on the drill casing, but many drills have a parallel part behind the chuck. You clamp the depth stop to that.

For a stop with a wood clamp, use a close-grained hardwood or plywood as thick as the parallel part of the casing will allow. Use $\frac{1}{8}$-inch or $\frac{3}{16}$-inch rod for the stop

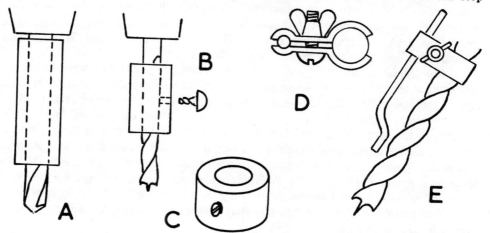

Fig. 9-2. The depth of a hole can be limited by a stop on the drill.

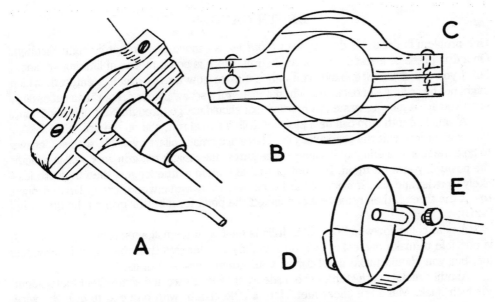

Fig. 9-3. A depth stop can be mounted on a portable electric drill.

(Fig.9-3A). Cut the wood to fit (Fig. 9-3B). Allow for a screw to tighten the grip and another screw with a flattened point to hold the gauge (Fig. 9-3C).

A neater stop of the same type can be made of metal. Use a pipe clip, preferably of the worm-drive type, to fit around the casing (Fig. 9-3D). Braze a block to this and drill in it for the gauge rod and a locking screw (Fig. 9-3E).

DRILLING IN THE LATHE

If you have a lathe, you have a precision drilling machine, if it is equipped with the usual accessories. You are familiar with drilling rotating work with a drill held in the tailstock chuck (Fig. 9-4A), but many things can be drilled the other way around. This achieves a squareness only possible otherwise with a drill press.

If the drill bit is driven by a chuck in the headstock spindle, the work has to be supported at the tailstock end. Quite small work might be drilled directly on scrap wood against the end of the tailstock mandrel, which is square to the line of drilling. Most work however, requires a broader bearing surface, although the drill will be pressing in line with the center of the tailstock mandrel whatever the shape or size of wood.

It is possible to buy a pad to fit the tailstock of many lathes, but you have a suitable part in the screw center. Turn a pad, maybe 6 inches in diameter and 1 inch thick to fit on the screw center (Fig. 9-4B). With this behind your work, you can feed the wood to the drill with the tailstock handwheel. Control the depth of drilling by noting how much tailstock mandrel is projecting when you start drilling. Most tailstocks will give you up to 2 inches of movement.

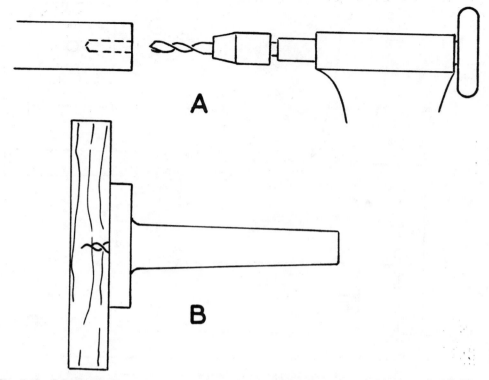

Fig. 9-4. *A lathe can be used for drilling rotating work (A), or the drill can be used towards a pad held in the tailstock (B).*

Most lathes have the power to drill larger holes than you can manage with a portable electric drill. The only limitation is the distance from the edge of the wood, which is governed by the height of the lathe centers above the bed.

HORIZONTAL DRILL STAND

With a portable electric drill mounted horizontally on the bench, you can use it to drive such things as a grinding wheel, sanding disc, and wire brush, all mounted on arbors to fit in the chuck. The practice of gripping a drill in the vise for this purpose is unwise as you could damage the casing and the motor inside.

A stand made from wood cannot harm the drill and will hold it at whatever height you decide above the bench top. You can arrange the stand so the drill is easily removed for normal use. Because portable electric drills do not conform to matching sizes between makes, it is impossible to design a stand that will suit all drills. However, many ⅜-inch drills have a cylindrical part just behind the chuck and a locating hollow at the opposite end in line with the chuck (Fig. 9-5A). These arrangements suit stands available for using portable drills as drill presses, but they also can be used for your horizontal stand.

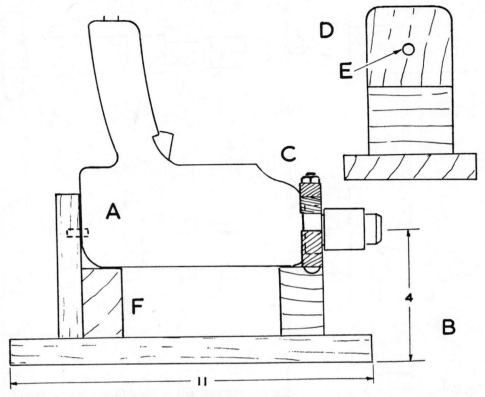

Fig. 9-5. A wood stand holds a portable electric drill.

The proportions of the stand drawn (Fig. 9-5B) would suit many ⅜-inch drills, but the arrangement can be modified easily to suit drills with bodies of different shapes. The important thing is to settle on the height you want above the bench and make this the center of the circular clamp for the cylindrical collar (Fig. 9-6A) and to ensure that the peg in the other end comes at the same level. Other shaping depends on what support the shaped drill body needs. The drill is drawn with the handle upwards. It might be more convenient to let it project to the back. This need not affect the arrangement of the front clamp, but you might have to modify the support at the back.

Start by making the front clamp assembly (Fig. 9-5C). The clamping bars (Fig. 9-6B and C) cannot be very thick, but make them ½ inch wide at least, even if the collar is narrower than that. If the collar is narrow, you might have to do some shaping to fit the rear edges over curves of the casing. Make these two strips of dense hardwood, even if the other parts are softwood. Hollow the lower one and make a pad under the upper one to grip the drill collar. Drill both for 3⁄16-inch bolts with plain or wing nuts and try them on the collar. Because security of the drill in use depends largely on this clamping arrangement, see that it fits well.

Make the base of this part 1¼ inches thick or more (Fig. 9-6D), with its grain crosswise. Glue the lower clamping piece to it, but you might have to do some shaping to the rear part to accommodate the shape of the drill casing.

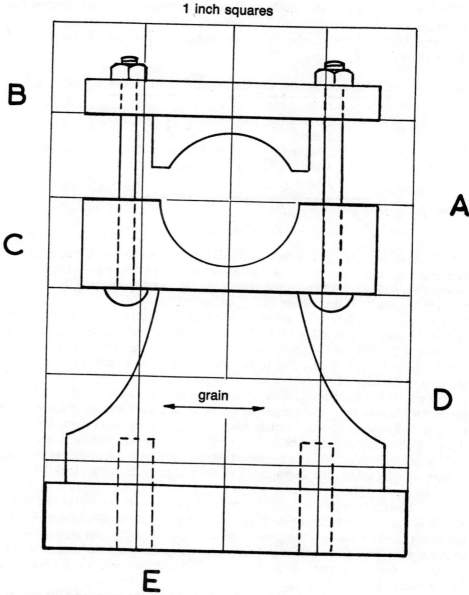

1 inch squares

B

A

C

D

grain

E

Fig. 9-6. *Details of the holder for an electric drill.*

The support for the other end on the drill is simpler. Make an upright about the same width as the thickness of the drill casing and ¾ inch thick (Fig. 9-5D). Mark the peg position on it (Fig. 9-5E). On many drills the locating hollow is fairly shallow, and it would be unwise to depend on a wood peg. Instead, cut a suitable piece of metal rod (probably ¼ inch in diameter) and fit it in a hole in the upright. Put a 1¼-inch block below the drill casing, with its top flat or shaped to suit (Fig. 9-5F).

Try the two parts you have made on the drill and measure the spacing they have to be on the base. How you make the base depends on how it is to be mounted. It could be screwed down, clamped to a bench top, or gripped in a vise. Join the parts with ⅜-inch dowels (Fig. 9-6E).

Materials List for Horizontal Drill Stand

1 clamp bar	½	×	½	×	5
1 clamp bar	½	×	1	×	5
1 stand	1¼	×	2½	×	4
1 upright	¾	×	2½	×	5
1 pad	1¼	×	3	×	3
1 base	¾	×	4	×	12

DISC SANDER

A disc of abrasive paper or cloth on a rigid backing can remove wood, true miters and other joints, and sharpen tools. For accurate work, it needs a table square to its surface. You can then slide an end to be trued against the rotating disc knowing that the cut it gives will be square to the surface sliding on the table.

A portable drill will drive a disc of about a 6-inch diameter, so the horizontal drill stand can be used to make a disc sanding assembly. The table should be at or just below the center of the drill and disc, then you bring the work to the side of the disc and cut towards the table (Fig. 9-7A). The table could be on its own stand or be part of an extension of the base of the horizontal drill stand.

It is possible to buy suitable discs on arbors to mount in a drill chuck, but you can make one if you have the use of a metal-turning lathe. There is some advantage in weight as this has a flywheel effect to maintain speed when you press work hard. The disc is 6 inches in diameter and could be ½-inch plywood (Fig. 9-7B). Behind it is a disc of steel 3/16 inch thick (Fig. 9-7C) on a spindle (Fig. 9-7D) as large a diameter as the chuck will take and of a length that keeps the disc only just away from the chuck when it is pushed in.

Turn the spindle with a shouldered end to fit in a hole at the center of the disc. Braze it in place. Mount the spindle in the lathe and true the surface of the disc. It is important that the whole assembly rotate without wobbling. Join the plywood disc to the metal parts with screws through four holes and again mount the assembly in the lathe so it is rotated by the spindle. True the edge and surface of the plywood disc. Try the sander in the drill chuck.

Attach abrasive sheets with rubber adhesive or one of the specified adhesives sold for the purpose. You will be able to peel off a sheet when you wish to change it.

The table is made adjustable (Fig. 9-7E) to set at the distance you want in relation to the rotating disc, and it can be withdrawn far enough when you want to remove the disc and its arbor from the chuck. As drawn, the table is 6 inches square at spindle height, and the amount of movement is about 1¾ inches (Fig. 9-8A). You may prefer a larger area. Anything much smaller is inadvisable for general woodwork, although it would be suitable for modelmaking, jewelry, or small work in plastics.

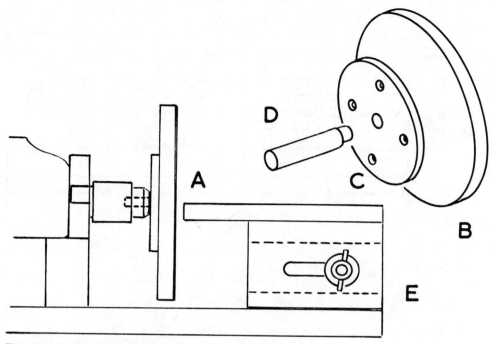

Fig. 9-7. A drill in a stand can make a disc sander.

The table has two pieces projecting below with strips to engage with rabbets in a supporting block (Fig. 9-8B). A bolt goes through the slot to lock the parts together with a wing nut over a washer. The table is drawn with its own base, but this and the base of the horizontal drill stand could be a single piece.

Cut the block with two ½-inch square rabbets (Fig. 9-8C). Make the outer pieces with strips glued on to mate with the rabbets (Fig. 9-8D). Drill the block for the bolt and arrange the slots in the outer pieces so that the table will be fully forward at one end of the slot and can be drawn clear when the bolt is at the other end.

Glue and screw the table to the outer pieces and the base to the block. Put the bolt through and test the action. When setting up the table in relation to the sanding disc, it does not have to be symmetrical as most work is done on the part of the disc running downwards. Most of the table area can be arranged opposite the forward half of the disc.

Materials List for Disc Sander

1 disc	7	×	7	×	½ plywood		
1 table	7	×	7	×	½		
1 base	¾	×	4	×	7		
1 block	2	×	2½	×	5		
2 sides	¾	×	2½	×	5		
2 strips	½	×	½	×	5		

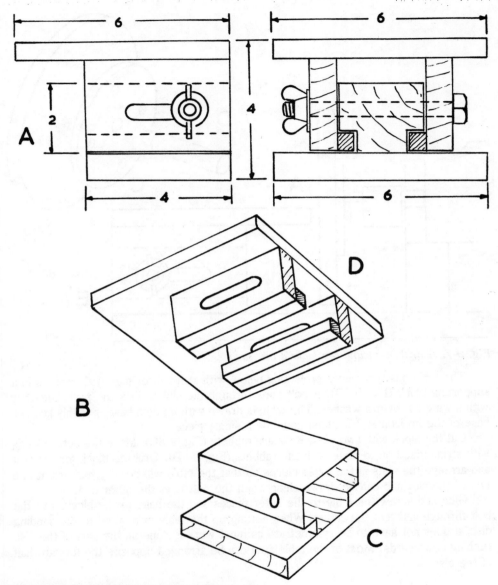

Fig. 9-8. *Details of the table of the disc sander.*

DRILL AS A LATHE

It is tempting to consider using a portable electric drill as the power head for a lathe, particularly if you do not have the use of a lathe and the idea of being able to produce turned work appeals to you. It is possible, but you have to accept some limitations. Do not expect to turn metal as the bearings of most drills do not run with the precision required. You might file or polish a rod held in the chuck, but that is about as far as work in metal goes.

Wood turning of quite good quality is possible, providing you limit your work to such things as spindles, tool handles, and other things of small diameter that can be held between centers. The largest work of this type normally feasible is a stool leg. Do not expect to do faceplate or screw-center work without the support of a tail center. This still leaves a lot of interesting and valuable work that can be done on a lathe in which the drive comes from a portable electric drill. Be careful not to overload the drill motor by trying to take heavy cuts off very hard wood of large diameter. Plane the corners off square wood before mounting it, so you do not have to impose the loads of a tool hitting the square corners before the work runs smoothly nearer round. Mounting eccentric wood puts a heavy load on the comparatively small motor, and it might not cope in the way the headstock and motor of a regular lathe could.

If you want to make a lathe to use your portable electric drill, keep its sizes reasonable, then you will not be tempted to load it with oversize work. The lathe in Fig. 9-9 has the centers 2 inches above the bed and 1¼ inches above the tool rest,

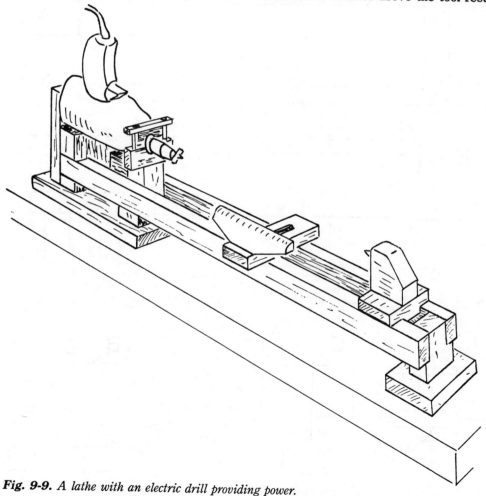

Fig. 9-9. *A lathe with an electric drill providing power.*

which lets you turn up to 2½ inches in diameter. The length is what you wish, but 16 inches between centers might be maximum, which allows stool or chair legs to be made. Hardwood is advisable throughout if you intend to do much turning and expect the lathe to last.

Prepare the two strips for the bed first (Fig. 9-10A and B). They should be straight-grained to match each other. They will overlap the drill support and a short post at the

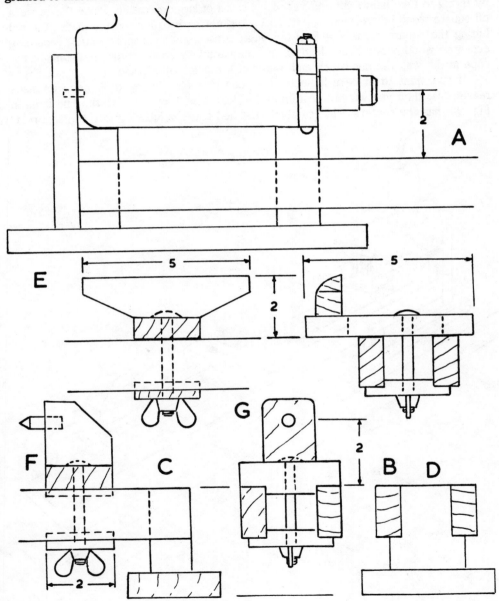

Fig. 9-10. *Details of parts of the lathe.*

other end. Measure your drill and allow for a driving center in the chuck when you settle the overall length of these pieces to give you the distance you want between centers.

At the head end of the lathe, the supports are very similar to the horizontal drill support described earlier in the chapter, but the height is increased (Fig. 9-11A). Allow for the bed pieces to fit in (Fig. 9-11B). Put the bolts in place before assembling as there will not be space to insert them when the beds have been attached.

Make the support at the other end of the drill similar to that on the horizontal stand, but at the increased height and with the block notched to take the bed pieces. Mount the support parts on a short base with dowels. A base the full length of the lathe is not suggested as that would make turning the wing nuts under the bed difficult.

At the other end of the bed, make a support to fit between the strips (Fig. 9-10C and D) and join it to its own base with a tenon or dowels. When the lathe is finished, screw the bases down to a bench to keep the assembly firm and minimize vibration, but the bed strips should keep the lathe in shape.

The tool rest consists of a horizontal piece mounted on a slotted strip (Figs. 9-10E and 9-12A). Make the total height above the bed the same as the centerline of the drill, or very slightly lower. Round the top edge. You might want to adjust the amount of curve when you start using the lathe. Make a slot to clear a ¼-inch carriage bolt square neck, long enough for the rest to be taken in to the centerline and out to rather more than the largest diameter you expect to turn. There is no adjustment for height or angle, but the whole rest can be swung on its bolt when you wish to conform to shaped work.

The tailstock is simple. Make a block to rest across the bed and notched to slide along it (Figs. 9-10F and 9-12B). Fit a carriage bolt through its center before adding the block above.

Glue and screw the top block (Fig. 9-10G) from below. The center can be a piece of ⅜-inch diameter steel rod with a 60-degree point on it. Turn the point if possible, but you might still do good work with a carefully filed center. Fix the center in a hole with epoxy adhesive.

For locking the tool rest and tailstock, make blocks to slide underneath and notch to hold them parallel under the bed (Fig. 9-12C). Use thin washers under the wing nuts.

A driving center might be bought, but you can make one to fit in the drill chuck. Use a piece of steel rod of as large a diameter as the chuck will hold. Make the driving part from steel about 1⁄16 inch thick (Fig. 9-12D). Let the central spur project and file the two side pieces almost to knife edges. Braze or solder this piece into a sawn cut in the end of the bar. Cut the bar so that it goes fully into the chuck, but project no more than is necessary.

Materials List for Drill as a Lathe

2 beds	¾	×	1½	×	24
2 stands	1¼	×	2¼	×	6
1 base	¾	×	4	×	12
1 back	¾	×	2¼	×	8
1 end	1¼	×	2½	×	6
1 end base	¾	×	3	×	6
2 tool rests	¾	×	2	×	8

1 inch squares

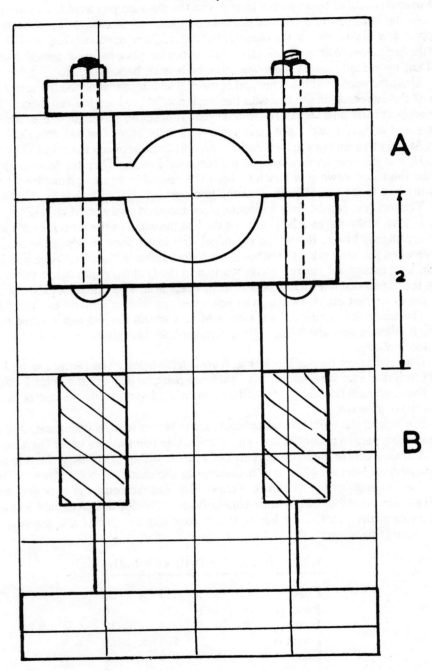

Fig. 9-11. *Sizes for the drill holder on the lathe.*

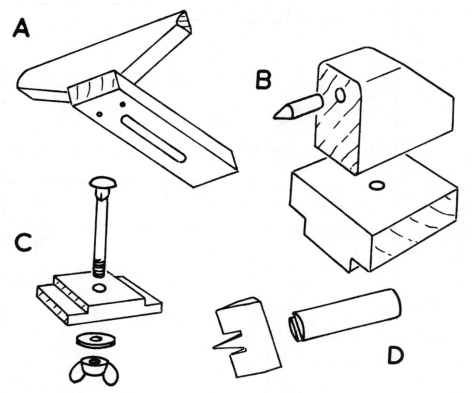

Fig. 9-12. *Details of the tool rest and tailstock for the drill lathe.*

V BLOCKS

Those who do machinist's type of metal work are used to having V blocks to support round rods when they have to be drilled across on a drill press. A woodworker might often try to hold a wood rod by hand and estimate the direction of the drill. It is more accurate and more convenient to have V blocks that can be made of wood. A trough, as suggested for use in preparing wood for a lathe in chapter 8 (Fig. 8-7), has some applications, but you do not want to drill into it. Something deeper is preferable, so it is better to make a matching pair of V blocks (Fig. 9-13A). You can position them to drill in the space between them.

Use hardwood. Because it is important that the two blocks match, whichever way they are used, make all four angled blocks at the same time. On some jobs there is a use for a third block, and you might wish to prepare parts for this as well. The angle is 45 degrees, but as long as all angles are the same, it does not matter if they are not exactly that for holding round rods. However, you might wish to use the V blocks for holding square stock to be drilled diagonally, then an exact 45 degrees is necessary (Fig. 9-13B).

The base is shown extended (Fig. 9-13C). This allows clamping, or you can bolt through if the drill press table is suitably slotted. Glue the parts and screw from below.

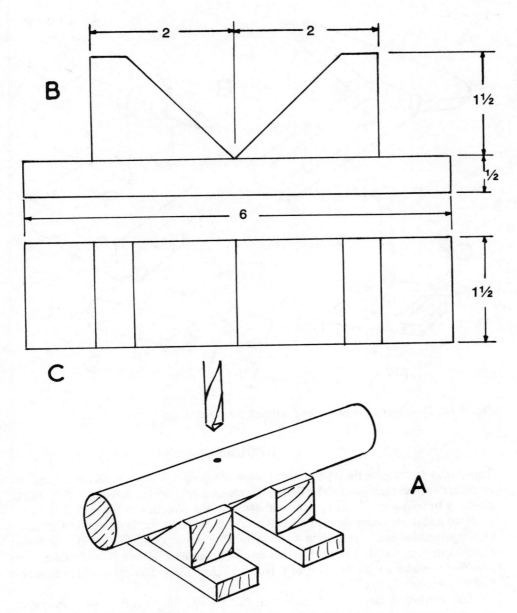

Fig. 9-13. *Wood V blocks will support cylinders being drilled.*

Materials List for V Blocks (two)

4 pieces	1½	×	1½	×	3
2 pieces	½	×	1½	×	7

DRILL TABLE VISE

If you need to hold wood, particularly of small section, on the table of a drill press or under a portable electric drill mounted in a stand, some means of securing the wood in place will ensure accuracy. To merely hold the wood with your hand is inadvisable as it might kick and rotate so that it is damaged or you are harmed. You could buy a machinist's steel vise to hold the wood, but you can make one from wood. Wood holding wood always seems kinder to the material than using steel against wood.

It would be possible to provide a screw action if you can obtain a suitable vise screw and its mounting nut, but the vise suggested (Fig. 9-14A) uses a wedge action for tightening. With the wedges shown (Fig. 9-14B), there is about ½ inch of movement

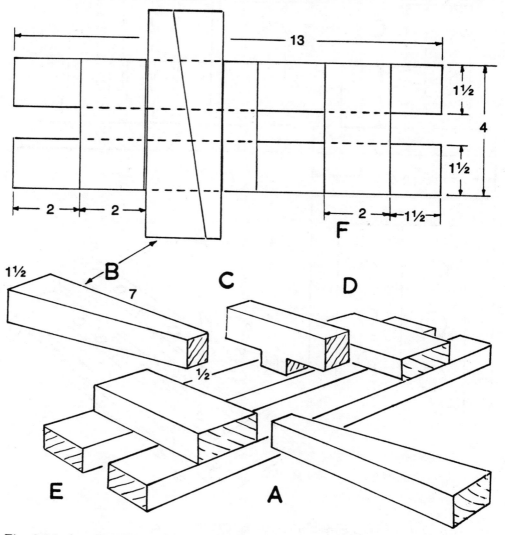

Fig. 9-14. A wedge-action table vise will hold work on a drill press.

possible. The wedges press against a packing (Fig. 9-14C). You could make several packings of different thicknesses or have just one packing and fill any space that has to be made up with scrap wood. The two-part base extends so that you can clamp the vise down or drill through for bolts to a slotted table.

Use hardwood. Cut two crosspieces (Fig. 9-14D) and make two strips for the base (Fig. 9-14E), then join these parts squarely (Fig. 9-14F). They have to take the pressure, so glue and screw strongly from below.

Make one or more packings, notched to fit easily between the sides of the base. The projection stops the packing from moving sideways when the wedges are driven opposite ways to tighten.

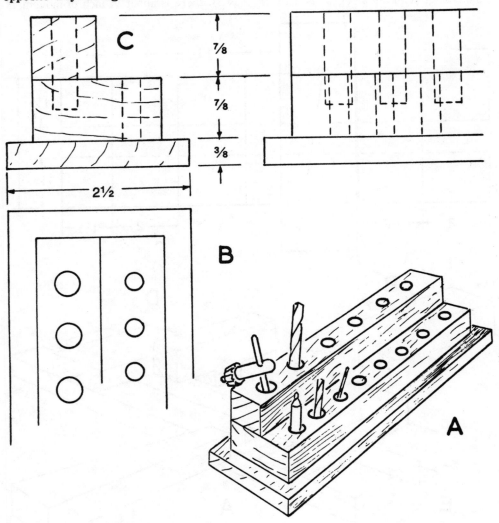

Fig. 9-15. *Drills and keys in regular use can have their own stand.*

Make the wedges identical; then the pressure they apply when driven will be parallel. Make the top surfaces of all parts on the base the same—1 inch would be satisfactory.

Materials List for Drill Table Vise

2 bases	1	×	1½	×	8
2 blocks	1	×	2	×	5
1 packing	¾	×	1½	×	5
2 wedges	1	×	1½	×	8

DRILL HOLDER

Metal stands to hold metalworking drills in holes of exact sizes are convenient for sorting and identifying exact sizes, particularly the smaller drills. General work, particularly woodworking, requires just a few of these drills for screw holes and similar purposes. There are also special drills for countersinking, counterboring, plug cutting, and centering as well as chuck keys. All of these have no places in a standard drill rack.

You can make a holder to store these similar things. The holder in Fig. 9-15A is shown with ⅜-inch holes along the back and ¼-inch holes at the front (Fig. 9-15B). Drills and keys can be dropped in without any attempt at a precision fit.

Use a planed 1-inch-×-1-inch strip over a 1-inch-×-2-inch strip, for whatever length will suit your requirements. For stability, make the holder at least 6 inches long. The rear holes are ¾ inch apart and those in front ⅝ inch apart, but if you want to fit special keys or other items, allow for them.

Glue these parts and drill through at the front; the rear holes should stop at half thickness (Fig. 9-15C). Fit an overlapping bottom.

Rubber or cloth glued to the bottom will prevent the holder from sliding on the bench when you reach for a drill. Varnish or paint in a light color will keep the holder clean and make its contents easier to see.

10

Circular Saw Aids

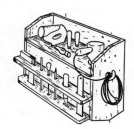

Putting teeth around the edge of a steel disc is the most direct way of providing a cut from a power source, with the saw axle on or in the same plane as the motor spindle. In modern power tools, this principle is applied mainly in three ways: table saw, radial arm saw, and portable circular saw. All have their uses, but the table saw is used mostly in a small shop for converting lumber to size, cutting joints, and general cutting that would otherwise have to be done with handsaws. The actual cutting is done in the same way with radial arm saws and portable circular saws, but the application is different.

A circular saw rotating at high speed is a great cutter—not only will it slice through wood, it will harm you if you do not take precautions. Even when it is freewheeling to a stop after switching off, it can be dangerous. All types of circular saws have guards. For the saw to do its job, a guard might have to swing aside or lift away, but safety devices are intended to provide maximum protection while allowing the saw to do its job. Never remove safety devices, even if that allows you to watch a cut more closely. Keep your hands and body well away from the saw. Avoid loose clothing. If anything goes wrong, do not do anything until the power is switched off and the saw has stopped rotating. Many aids for use with circular saws are concerned with safe usage of this valuable power tool.

PUSH STICKS

Many woodworkers tend to pick up any odd piece of wood to push the work the last few inches through a table saw. There is not always a suitable piece within reach, however, and fingers might get too close to the saw. You should make a few push sticks to hang within reach for such times.

Use hardwood. You do not want to risk softwood splitting when pushing hard. Cut a notch slightly wider than 90 degrees and round the other end for a comfortable grip.

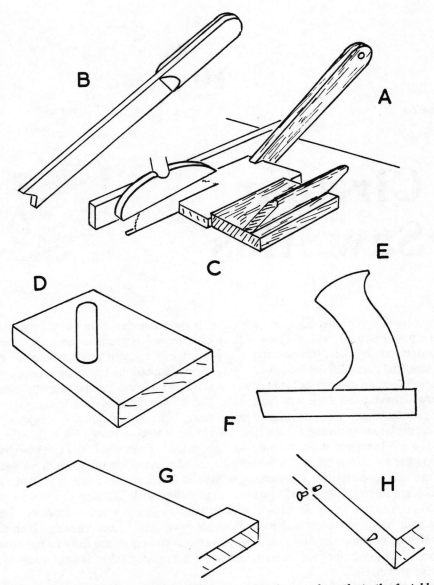

Fig. 10-1. *Push sticks of various kinds will keep your hands away from the teeth of a table saw.*

Drill a hole for hanging (Fig. 10-1A). Make a few push sticks of different thicknesses. Keep the length enough to allow for the notched end being recut several times before you discard the stick.

For a cut very close to the fence, you might allow the saw to cut into a wider push stick, but you could keep a stick about ¼ inch thick for this purpose. For comfort, thicken the top end (Fig. 10-1B).

As well as pushing wood forward through the saw, you have to hold it against the fence to keep the cut parallel to it. This is more important with smaller pieces, which might wander out of true, and you do not want to bring your fingers too close. The side push stick has to be flat on the table and needs some sort of handle. A piece with a rounded top can be glued and screwed on (Fig. 10-1C). You could use a piece of 1-inch dowel rod in a hole (Fig. 10-1D), or you could shape it more like a plane handle (Fig. 10-1E). If you tilt the thrusting edge slightly more than square, the effect will be to keep thinner wood flat (Fig. 10-1F).

For some small pieces of wood, it is an advantage to combine the two functions in one stick. If you notch the end of a side stick, it can be used to move the wood forward as well as hold it in (Fig. 10-1G).

If you are dealing with smooth and slippery wood, it will help to provide the side push stick with teeth. Drive in two or three nails, cut them off, and file points on them (Fig. 10-1H).

STRAIGHTENING JIG

Before you can rip a board to width, you need a straightedge to run against the rip fence. A board that is slightly uneven along one edge can be put through a jointer a few times to straighten it. You could draw a straight line near the edge and saw it freehand. A better way of making a straight sawn edge is to use a jig.

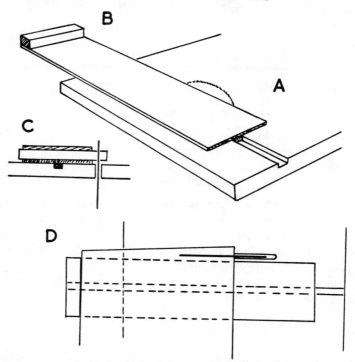

Fig. 10-2. This straightening jig helps you cut away a ragged edge.

This is a long thin board (¼-inch plywood is suitable) with a strip underneath to slide in the miter guide slot on the saw table. Make the width so that the edge comes fairly close to the saw slot (Fig. 10-2A). At the far end, put a stop across, square to the edge (Fig. 10-2B). If you put your board with the uneven edge on this jig and feed it forward (Fig. 10-2C), the saw will cut a true edge, which can then be used against the fence in the usual way when you cut the board to width.

The jig might also be used to cut square corners, from sheet material for instance (Fig. 10-2D), or to square the end of a board.

CORNER BLOCK JIG

Reinforcing blocks are glued inside some joints and corners (Fig. 10-3A). Larger pieces are sometimes cut diagonally from square stock (Fig. 10-3B) for rails. On most table saws, the rip fence will not tilt to 45 degrees, and if it does, you cannot bring it close enough to the saw to bisect the square. You might have to cut away from the diagonal, making one piece wider than the other (Fig. 10-3C).

One way to cut on the diagonal and get two equal pieces is to use a jig (Fig. 10-3D). The suggested sizes suit squares up to the capacity if a 3-inch saw cut (Fig. 10-3E). The end of the jig is slit to fit around the saw exactly on the line of the stock edge. In use, clamp the jig to the saw table. Try the wood to be cut in the jig and adjust the rip fence until the wood bears against it (Fig. 10-3F), if possible, to keep the wood straight as it is fed through. For very small squares, you will have to rely on the jig keeping the wood straight.

Materials List for Corner Block Jig

1 base	4	× 20	×	¼ plywood
1 side	1½	× 2	×	20
1 side	1	× 1	×	20
1 stop	1	× 1	×	6

TAPER JIGS

If you want to make a single tapered cut on a board, you can draw a line and cut it freehand, then true the edge by planing. If you have to make several pieces with the same taper, however, it is better to use a jig to get them all the same. The jig can be made for the particular job, or you can have a more permanent jig that can be adjusted to suit various taper cuts. Both types are used to push the wood being cut at an angle to the line of the saw cut. These jigs are described to be used on a table saw, but they could be used on a radial arm saw.

Notched Jig

A simple jig is a notched piece of wood with one step cut to provide thrust and another step inside it to control the amount of taper (Fig. 10-4A). The jig slides against the ripping fence, which is set to position the saw at the start of the taper, then the

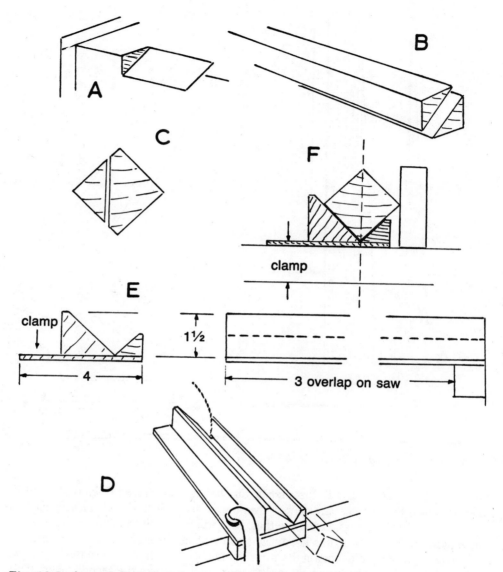

Fig. 10-3. *A corner block jig helps you cut square pieces diagonally.*

jig is pushed through. You should use a side push stick to keep the wood tight in the jig and the jig against the fence. Push the end of the jig with a push stick or provide it with a handle (Fig. 10-4B).

Quite often tapers are needed on opposite sides of a piece of wood, or on all four sides in the case of a table leg (Fig. 10-4C). You cannot use a jig with only one notch or the second side would have a different taper from the first. In this case, make the effective length of the jig to match the length of the taper (Fig. 10-4D). Cut the widths

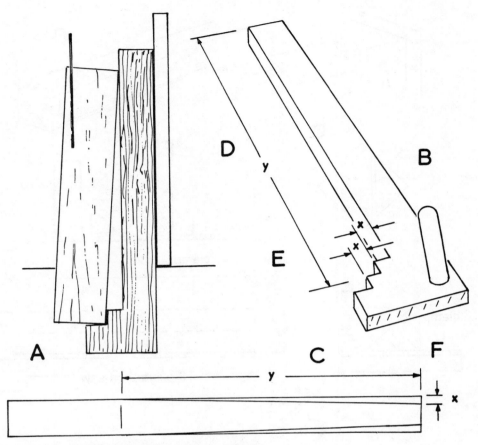

Fig. 10-4. *A notched jig guides wood for taper cuts.*

of two notches each equal to the amount that has to be removed (Fig. 10-4E and F). Do not make the notches any deeper than necessary to hold the wood. Anyone concerned with utmost precision will see that there will be a slight error due to differences in length, but in practice, this is so slight as to be negligible in furniture making.

To use the jig, cut a taper in the wood in the upper notch, then turn the board over and hold the side you have just cut in the lower notch to make the second taper. If you are tapering the four sides of a table or stool leg, cut the taper on one side with the wood in the upper notch, then do the same on an adjoining side. Change to the lower notch and cut the tapers on the remaining sides.

Adjustable Jig

A more permanent jig can be made to adjust to any amount of taper, so it can be used for anything from a slight taper on a leg to several inches in 36 inches, or whatever size you make the jig. The one shown in Fig.10-5A is made of two pieces of 1-inch- $\times$ -3-inch section hinged together and adjusted by a slotted piece of ½-inch plywood

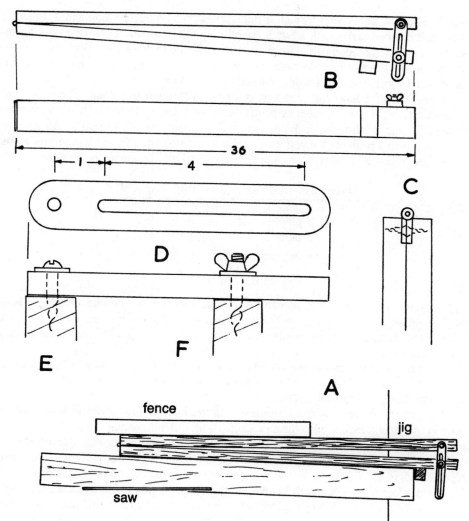

Fig. 10-5. *This jig can be adjusted to suit different taper cuts.*

or solid wood. This is more than long enough to deal with table legs and can handle wider slopes, such as might be used in a desk top. The 3-inch width is as high as the table saw fence is likely to be and is made for stability to keep thick wood being cut from tilting out of square to the saw table.

Prepare two identical pieces—square, straight, and parallel. Put a stop on one, 4 inches from the end (Fig. 10-5B). Let a stout 3-inch hinge into the ends (Fig. 10-5C). Pick a hinge with no slackness in the knuckle pin. Because some cheap hinges will wobble, get a cast brass hinge, if possible. Let in the leaves of the hinge so that the wood strips close against each other.

The slotted piece (Fig. 10-5D) gives 4 inches of movement, but you can make it any length you wish. At one end put a screw through a washer to form a pivot (Fig.

10-5E). The slot slides on a ¼-inch hanger screw (a wood screw end and a thread for a nut on the other end). Drill an undersized hole in the wood. Lock two nuts against each other on the threaded part. Use them with a wrench to drive the screw, then remove the nuts. Make the slot to slide easily on the hanger screw. Provide a large washer and a wing nut to lock the parts where needed (Fig. 10-5F).

In use, stop feeding when the saw has passed through the wood. There is plenty of clearance, but if you let the saw protrude through the table more than 3 inches and the push jig and work right through, you could damage the slotted strip. As with any other work, use a push stick if you would otherwise bring your fingers dangerously close to the saw blade. A side push stick will keep wood and jig close to the fence.

Materials List for Adjustable Taper Jig

2 pieces	1	×	3	×	38	
1 piece	½	×	1	×	8	

WEDGE JIG

A jig related to the first taper jig can be used to turn scrap wood into wedges. Make the jig from wood about as thick as the wood that will make the wedges and long enough to keep your hand away from the saw blade. It could have a handle, or you could move it with a push stick.

Cut a notch in the end of the jig at the angle you want the wedges to be and almost their length (Fig. 10-6A). Make the wedges from wood with the grain across, so they finish with the grain in their length.

To produce wedges, adjust the fence until the jig is just clear of the saw. Hold the wood in the jig and feed it onto the saw (Fig. 10-6B). After cutting the first wedge, turn the wood over to cut the next one (Fig. 10-6C). Continue doing this alternately until you have cut enough wedges. A wedge taken to a fine edge is weak; if you do not need a feather edge, set the jig back a little to produce wedges with ends ⅛ inch or so thick.

A stock of wedges is worth keeping in the shop for tightening any assembly work as well as for holding doors open, stopping windows from rattling, and other jobs about the home.

OUTFEED ROLLER

In a large busy shop where the table saw is in fairly constant use, there will be at least one strongly mounted outfeed roller to support long pieces coming off the saw. In a small shop, however, there are times when such a piece of equipment would be very welcome. At other times it would be in the way, taking up valuable space that could be used for other purposes.

If you do not have a helper to support the long wood as you cut it, it can break or you might risk damage to yourself in trying to feed and take off at the same time. A roller support is a near-essential piece of equipment to complement your table saw. One way of reducing its bulk so that it does not waste space when out of use is to mount it on something else. You will heed a trestle at about knee height that can be used to

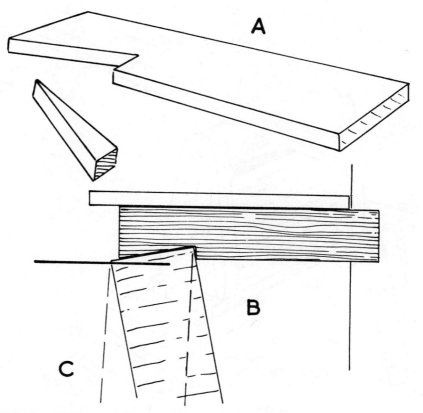

Fig. 10-6. *A notched board guides wood being cut into wedges.*

form the base of an outfeed roller (Fig. 10-7). Check what extra height you need to build up, but the suggested design assumes it is 14 inches (Fig. 10-8A). The stand can be clamped to your trestle, or you could drill the stand and trestle for bolts.

The important part is the roller. This is assumed to be 2½ inches in diameter and 10 inches long with a ½-inch steel rod as axle (Fig. 10-8B). You can turn it to that size on a lathe, preferably from hardwood. It might be possible to use a domestic pastry roller and adapt the size of the stand to suit. A piece of round wood rod could be drilled. If you have to drill wood without the aid of a lathe, work from the opposite ends. Although a perfect cylinder is best, absolute perfection is not essential, and a slightly eccentric cylinder will still support the wood as it is cut. You could convert wood of square section to octagonal, then take the angles off and smooth the wood with abrasive paper worked round the curve.

Use the roller size as a guide when setting out other parts. The base has to be wide enough to clamp or bolt onto the trestle top, but do not make it much less than 6 inches (Fig. 10-8C). Construction is shown doweled (Fig. 10-8D), but you could use mortise-and-tenon joints. Check that the overall height when on the trestle matches the normal height of your table saw when ripping and make the ends (Fig. 10-8E) to suit. In practice,

Fig. 10-7. *An outfeed roller for a table saw can be mounted on a trestle.*

differences of an inch or so in height, due to different setting of the saw table, will not matter. Make the spacer (Fig. 10-8F) long enough to give clearance at the end of the roller and cut it high enough to allow clamps to hook over the base.

Put wax or graphite in the roller hole as you fit the axle for final assembly. The spacer should keep the parts square, but check before the glue has set.

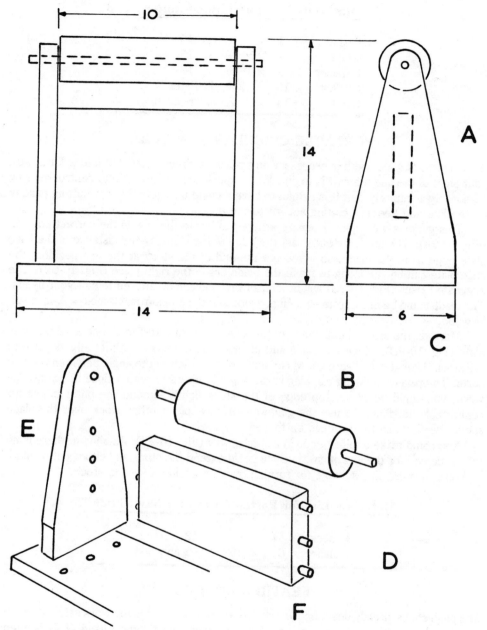

Fig. 10-8. *Details of the outfeed roller.*

Materials List for Outfeed Roller

1 base	1	×	6	× 15
2 ends	1	×	6	× 15
1 spacer	1	×	6	× 12
1 roller	10	×	2½	diameter
1 rod	14	×	½	diameter steel

PORTABLE CIRCULAR SAW GUIDE

A base plate of good width is necessary on a portable circular saw, but it interferes with your sight of the line the saw is to cut. With experience you are able to control the saw reasonably accurately, but it is helpful to have a guide that gets the saw cutting exactly on the line and keeps it cutting square to the edge.

This guide is a compact T square adapted to locate the saw in the correct position (Fig. 10-9A). The stock extends past the edge of the blade by the distance of the base plate edge from the blade, so if you put the end of the stock at the line position, the base plate can be run along to make the blade cut in the right place (Fig. 10-9B). The suggested sizes (Fig. 10-9C) will fit a small saw and can be altered to suit your needs. The blade could be made from ½-inch plywood and the stock from ¾-inch-×-2-inch solid wood.

Mark on the stock the distance of the side of the saw kerf to the edge of the base plate (Fig. 10-9D). Make the blade and mount it on the stock with its edge square to the stock. Use glue and screws. Make sure no glue is left in the angle between the two parts. To prevent anything catching in the angle to interfere with a close fit against the work, you could bevel the top edge of the stock lightly. Round the outer edges for comfortable handling. To use the guide either way, put another stock over the blade above the first, so the tool can be turned over.

You could make a miter guide in a similar way (Fig. 10-9E). As shown, there is no reference end for the line of cut, but you could extend the stock and either cut or mark it. You can make this suitable for turning over by adding a second stock.

Materials List for Portable Circular Saw Guide

1 stock	¾	×	2	× 12
1 blade	6	×	15	× ½ plywood

FEATHER BOARDS

The push sticks already described are all that are needed for guiding work safely through a table saw, but there are occasions when you might need a third hand. This is even more so with a radial arm saw, where you can often use a means of holding the work against a fence that leaves you free to do other things with your hands. There are devices you can buy to help control the work, but some simple things you can make are feather boards.

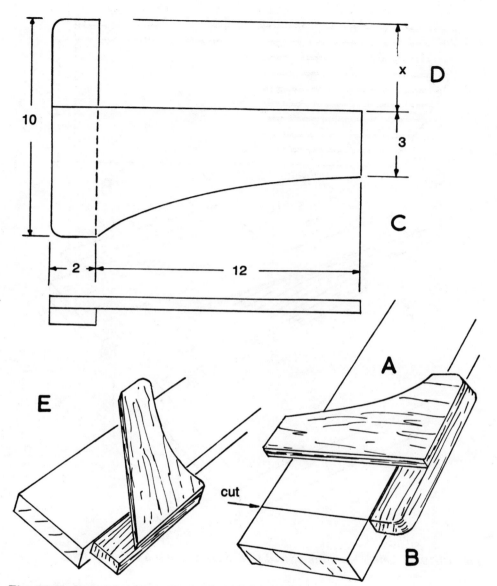

Fig. 10-9. *A special square will guide a portable circular saw.*

A *feather board* is a piece of wood with cuts in its end that gives some flexibility in the resulting arms or feathers that extend between the cuts. They are clamped to the bench or table so that they spring against the work and press it into place (Fig. 10-10A).

Feather boards can be made in many sizes and in various woods. They should be regarded as disposable, in any case, as you must expect them to wear and break. The specimen design could be made of softwood about ¾ inch thick (Fig. 10-10B). Avoid

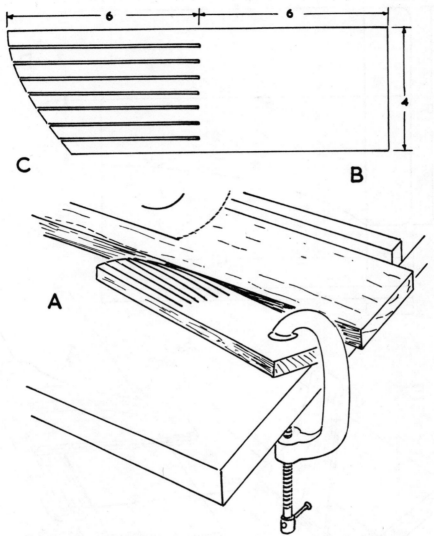

Fig. 10-10. *A feather board can be used to keep wood against a table saw fence.*

knots and choose a straight-grained part for the feathers. As shown, the cuts are about ½ inch apart, but spacing depends on the wood and the degree of flexibility you want. You will find it worthwhile making several feather boards from different woods, varying the thicknesses and spacing of the feathers.

Curve the board across the feathers (Fig. 10-10C). The amount of curve is not crucial. The ends of the feathers will wear after a little use.

To use the feather board, put the work to be held against the fence, then lightly clamp the feather board. Bend it until the feathers bend, then tighten the clamp. Adjust the amount of pressure to get the right degree of hold combined with ease of feeding the wood onto the saw.

11

Band Saw Accessories

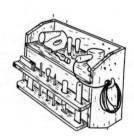

A band saw is regarded mainly as a means of cutting curves, but it can be used for many other types of cuts. When you have one, it tends to become your general-purpose saw, and you turn to it for cuts that might otherwise be done by handsawing or by using a portable circular saw on the bench. What it cannot do is make an internal cut, for which there is no access from outside the shape. A portable jigsaw might be the tool for that, but for any curved sawing for which it can be used, a band saw produces a better and more accurate edge than most jigsaws.

A selection of saw blades makes possible different types of cuts in various materials. Narrow blades are needed to follow tighter curves. Wider blades are suitable for straight cuts. Fine-pitch teeth leave smoother edges, but coarse teeth are needed for thick stock and some rough woods. For satisfactory cutting, there should usually be at least three teeth within the thickness of the wood. The ability to alter the machine speed is worth having if you want to cut metal and plastics as well as wood, but for most woodworking cuts, the standard speed set by the makers is suitable.

With these considerations in mind and a band saw that is basically equipped, you can increase its usefulness and efficiency by adding some of the suggested accessories in this chapter. Remember, though, that there is a limit to what work you can get out of a particular machine. Be careful not to overload it or expect it to perform functions its basic design does not suit.

A moving band saw blade might not be quite as dangerous as a rotating circular saw blade, but it cannot have guards that come into position when you are not cutting, so keep your fingers away. Some of the push sticks described for other saws can be used on a band saw. Avoid the temptation to flick bits of scrap wood out of the way with your fingers. It is better to keep a stick made like a push stick, but with its end taken almost to a point. If that touches the saw while pushing scraps out of the way, its end can be cut again—you cannot repair your finger.

RIPPING FENCES

In the average small shop, the band saw is capable of making deeper cuts than the table saw. Where you might be able to rip 2-inch stock on the table saw, the band saw can cope with twice that depth. It might not be very fast, but if that is the only way of dividing a 4-inch board in two, you have to accept that.

You need a broad blade for ripping. If you try to use a narrow blade, particularly on thick wood, it will wander. You will not only get a cut that does not follow the line, but one that might not be upright through the length of the cut.

Ripping freehand with reasonable accuracy might be possible with a short piece of wood, but for accurate results there must be a fence. Because not all band saws come with a fence, you might have to provide one.

Make your fence from carefully squared strip wood. For a small band saw, the wood could be 1-inch-×-2-inch section, preferably hardwood. Cut it slightly longer than the distance across the saw table. You could put C clamps at each end (Fig. 11-1A). There would be less risk of accidental tilting if you cut down the ends (Fig. 11-1B). Another

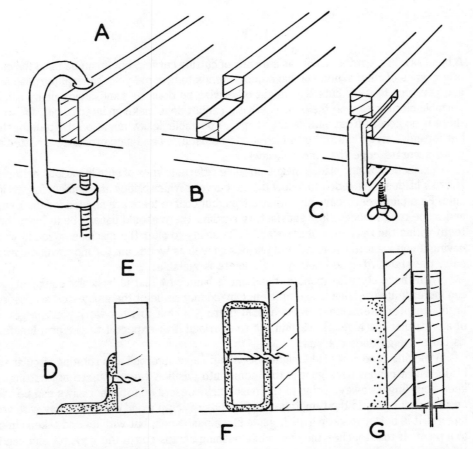

Fig. 11-1. *A wood fence can be clamped on the table of a band saw or added to a metal fence.*

method that keeps clamps out of the way is to use simple ones made from strip metal and cut notches for them (Fig. 11-1C).

A piece of angle iron will serve as a fence (Fig. 11-1D) to keep the clamps away from the working face. Front it with wood screwed on (Fig. 11-1E).

If a fence is supplied with the band saw, it might have to be adapted for some work. The fence supplied with at least one machine is tubular and its edges are rounded, which avoids marking work. If you want to rip very thin wood such as veneer, however, it will get under the curve. Screw on a wood face to prevent this (Fig. 11-1F).

The standard fence, or the one you make for normal use, might not be as high as a thick piece of wood you want to rip. If it is a board on edge, it needs support for its full height to keep it true throughout the cut (Fig. 11-1G). Tilting or wobbling a board on edge would cause the cut to wander. If possible, screw an auxiliary fence through the existing fence to keep screwheads from the working surface, but if you have to screw from the front, countersink or counterbore the screwheads deeply.

On most table saws there is a splitter or riving knife behind the blade to keep the cut open and prevent binding. When ripping on a band saw, the cut might tend to close behind the blade. Have some wedges ready, then if this happens, you can press one or more in to ease the friction on the blade. If you are cutting difficult wood, such as a very resinous type, oiling the blade is messy. You could lubricate it by rubbing a candle on it or letting it cut lightly into a candle. Adequate tension and correct positioning of the blade guides are important for accurate ripping with the minimum trouble.

TABLE EXTENSIONS

The band saw in most small shops is not large enough to stand on the floor, but it has to stand on a low bench to get it to working height. Its saw table might be less than 18 inches square, yet the work you do on it can be considerably bigger. At the maximum, you may want to manipulate an entire 48-inch- × -96-inch sheet of plywood to cut a curved end. To do that you need at least one helper or some good supports.

The outfeed roller for the table saw can be used, if it is the right height or can be adapted. You could clamp temporary supports to your trestles, but for satisfactory holding of large pieces where curves have to be cut, it is better to have flat surfaces than just local support.

Plywood Support

You can make a light folding support to take large work overhanging the band saw table from ½-inch plywood and a piece of 2-inch- × -4-inch wood (Fig. 11-2A). As drawn in Fig. 11-2B, this provides an area about 5 inches × 24 inches at the same level as the saw table, which should be enough to steady large overhanging work while being cut. When out of use, the support folds flat. A piece of rope controls the spread of the legs. You can alter the height by varying the length of knotted rope, making the support adaptable to supporting work on other machines.

The vertical size will have to be made to suit the height of table on your band saw, but other sizes can be left as shown. The three feet are 6 inches wide. This arrangement will stand firm better than four feet if there is slight unevenness in the floor.

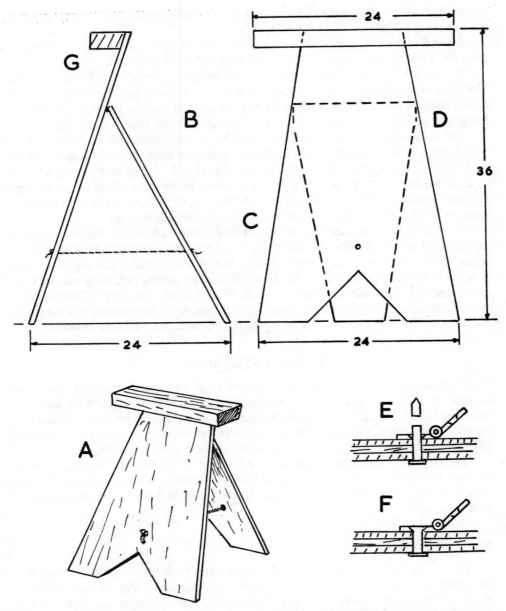

Fig. 11-2. *This folding stand made from plywood will support large pieces being cut on a band saw.*

Taper the main leg from 24 inches to 12 inches, with a notch to form the feet (Fig. 11-2C). Mark across 9 inches down where the top of the short leg will come. Make the top of the short leg to this width, tapering to a 6-inch foot (Fig. 11-2D). Adjust the length of this leg so that the top of the other leg will be centered when the legs are spread 24 inches.

Hinge the legs together. Two 3-inch hinges should be satisfactory, but ½-inch plywood does not provide sufficient thickness for screws to grip securely. Instead, you can rivet the hinges, using nails. Soft metal nails are easiest to use—copper is ideal. Drive the nails through undersized holes in the wood. Cut off with enough projecting to make a head in the countersink of the hinge (Fig. 11-2E). Support the nailheads on an iron block and spread the nail end into the countersink of the hinge (Fig. 11-2F).

Put the rope through matching centered holes and adjust its length between knots so that the top edge of the stand is level with your band saw table. Check the angle needed to give a horizontal top to the bearing surface and plane the top piece (Fig. 11-2G) to match. Nail or screw it on to complete the support.

Folding Extension Table

If your band saw is mounted on a low bench, you should be able to make an extension tabletop to support shaped work while you are manipulating it to make a curved cut. It can clamp onto the bench top. You will have to adapt the arrangements suggested to suit your bench and saw, but the drawing is for an extension table that has a bench edge approximately under the saw table with enough area for two C clamps (Fig. 11-3A). The top then comes level with the saw table. When out of use, it hinges against the upright, and there is a folding leg that reduces in length to fold against the other parts. If the bench is suitable, you might be able to arrange the extension to fit to the back or side of the machine, according to needs.

The key part is the upright (Fig. 11-3B and C). Its height should lift the extension tabletop level with the saw table, and its width can be the same as the saw table. Use ½-inch plywood, with a 1-inch-×-2-inch strip across the top. At the bottom, arrange two pieces of 2-inch-×-3-inch wood to extend enough to take clamps but with a gap at the center to clear the leg when folded (Fig. 11-3D).

The top is shown 24 inches long, but if your bench and table heights are very different, check that the top you make can fold over the upright (Fig. 11-3E). Where the top pivots on the upright, rivet through the hinges, as described for the plywood support. Put a strip of 1-inch-×-2-inch wood across the further end of the table for stiffness and to take the folding leg.

The leg could be a single piece, but that would extend a lot when the table is folded. As shown, the leg is in two parts (Fig. 11-3F). Hinge the top part to the center of the strip across the end of the table. Join the two parts with a ¼-inch bolt with a wing nut and two washers. This should provide enough friction to keep the leg upright, but you could make holes for two bolts and take one out when you fold the leg. The extension table is intended to serve as a steady and is not meant to take heavy loads, so the folding leg should be strong enough.

Try the assembly in position and see that the parts will fold onto each other. If the action is satisfactory, round all exposed edges and corners, then paint or varnish, if you wish.

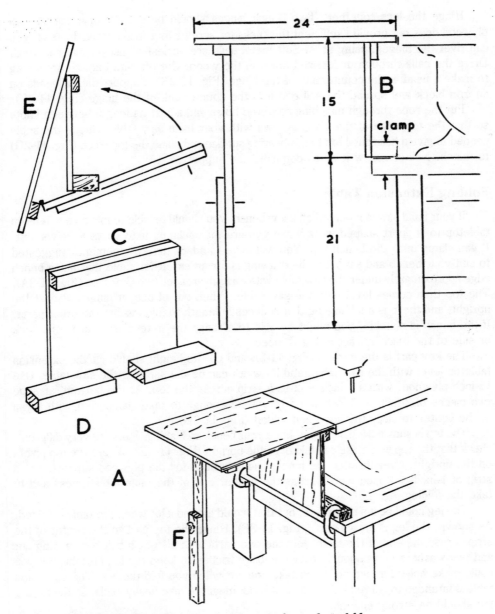

Fig. 11-3. *An extension table for a band saw can be made to fold.*

DEPTH STOPS

If you are engaged in repetition work that involves making cuts set distances into the wood, as you might when cutting various joints, it helps to have some means of stopping the cut from going too far. It is very easy when using a band saw to let a cut run away and not always easy to see a line marking the limit.

For one-off situations, you can clamp a board behind the saw blade at the distance you need to stop the cut, but an adjustable stop is more convenient, particularly if there will be several changes in the same job. A depth stop need only be directly behind the saw, as that is where the cut comes, and a few inches of width might help to keep work square, if that is what is wanted. If the cut is towards an irregular edge, however, a narrower stop will be better.

Two depth stops are suggested, both working in the same way, but one is made in metal and the other in wood. They clamp to the back of the table, and a stop blade can be adjusted behind the saw. Both blades can be reversed to give the option of a wide or narrow end. The sizes are shown as a guide, but you will have to alter them to suit the table of your band saw.

Wood Depth Stop

This depth stop should be made of compact hardwood. The blade must be long enough to reach from the back of the saw table to the saw, with a few inches extra, but for most machines the other parts can be to the sizes shown (Fig. 11-4A). The stock clamps to the rear of the table. The blade can be used with its broad T end towards the saw, or it can be reversed when a narrow stop is needed. Lock the parts with a screw, shown with a knurled head (Fig. 11-4B), or use a wing or a hexagonal head to take a wrench.

Make the blade first. It must be straight and parallel for easy action. The T end is a block notched to take the end of the blade (Fig. 11-4C). If it projects ¼ inch from the thickness of the blade, it will bear on the saw table. When the blade is reversed, the end will be ¼ inch above the table, which will not matter unless you are cutting wood under ¼ inch thick.

Notch the underside of the stock so that the blade will slide squarely across (Fig. 11-4D). The notch also has to take a sheet metal pressure plate (Fig. 11-4E). This could be brass or aluminum and need only be quite thin (22 gauge would do). Make it fit in the groove and turn it up enough to prevent slipping. When the blade and pressure plate are in the groove, the underside of the blade should be just below the surface of the stock.

For the locking screw, let a nut into the wood. Drill a clearance hole for a ¼-inch bolt through the center of the notch. Cut away for the nut, which can be square or hexagonal. You could make a hollow the shape of the nut, but it might be easier to make a fitted groove to the edge (Fig. 11-4F). The end of the groove will be hidden by the turned-up end of the pressure plate.

Make the bottom of the stock (Fig. 11-4G and H). Glue and screw it under the top part of the stock. Check the action of the blade. The stock could be left as it is, but it is better cut down at the ends for the clamps. Appearance is improved if all upper edges are well rounded and the whole depth stop is varnished.

Materials List for Wood Depth Stop

1 blade	¼	×	1	×	18
1 blade end	½	×	1	×	6
1 stock	1	× 1¼	×	7
1 stock	¼	× 1¼	×	7

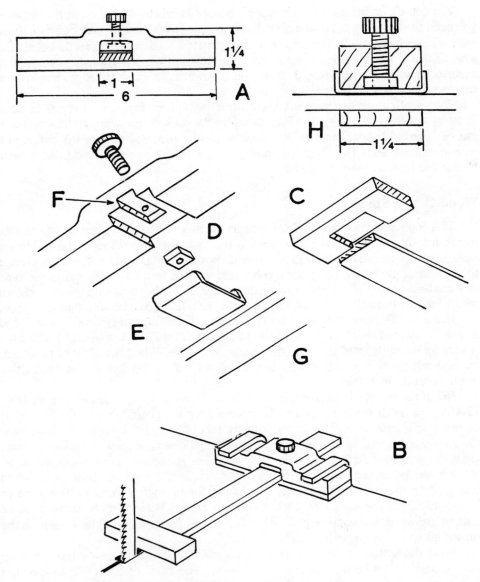

Fig. 11-4. *This wood depth stop limits the cut made by a band saw.*

Metal Depth Stop

A depth stop that works in the same way can be made from metal (Fig. 11-5A). The stock has a clamp built in. The blade is shown with a widened end, and it can be reversed in the same manner as the wood depth stop. The suggested sizes should suit most saws of moderate size. The blade length will have to be made to suit the particular saw table.

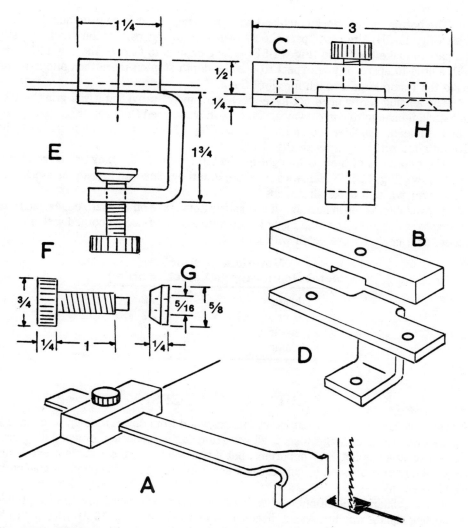

Fig. 11-5. This metal depth stop on a band saw works in the same way as the wood one in Fig. 11-4.

The blade is ⅛ inch × 1 inch through the notch. You could cut this from wider material to allow for bending the T end, or you could weld or braze a piece across the end of a parallel strip. The blade strip will be ¼ inch above the saw table, but the T end should be made to fit close to the table surface.

Cut a notch through the upper part of the stock (Fig. 11-5B), so the blade will slide through squarely with its surface just inside the edges of the notch.

The screw to hold the blade could be one you have in stock, or you could turn one with a ⅝-inch diameter knurled head and a ⁵⁄₁₆-inch screwed diameter (Fig. 11-5C). Thread it and drill and tap the stock to center it over the notch.

The bottom of the stock combined with the clamp is cut from plate about ³⁄₁₆ inch thick (Fig. 11-5D). Its cross part should match the upper part of the stock. Be sure the part to make the clamp (Fig. 11-5E) is long enough to fit over the saw table edge with a little to spare. If you expect to use the depth stop on more than one machine, make the clamp large enough for all of them.

The holding screw need not have much movement, providing it will grip the table and slacken enough to come away again. It is shown turned from rod (Fig. 11-5F) with a knurled head. Shoulder the end to fit a pad (Fig. 11-5G), into which it can be lightly riveted after screwing through the clamp.

The two parts of the stock might be riveted together, but they are shown joined with screws (Fig. 11-5H). Screws are secure, but they allow you to take the stock apart if you ever want to make alterations.

Try the depth stop in position. If it is satisfactory, take off all sharp edges and round the exposed corners. The stop might be left with just a surface smoothed with abrasive paper, or it could be protected with lacquer.

Materials List for
Metal Depth Stop (all steel or brass)

1 blade	⅛	×	1	×	12	
or	⅛	×	3	×	12	
1 stock	½	×	1¼	×	3	
1 clamp	³⁄₁₆	×	3	×	5	

CUTTING CYLINDERS

A band saw can be used for cutting cylindrical wood from dowel rods up to quite large logs, either across or lengthwise. If all you are doing is producing firewood from scrap pieces, accuracy is not very important, but if you want to make a straight cut along a large round piece of wood or cut across it squarely, you cannot depend on guiding the wood freehand.

For a cylindrical piece of wood within its capacity, you could use the jig intended for holding square wood being cut diagonally on a table saw (Fig. 10-3). Clamp it to the table so the blade is within the cut end and the feed direction is square to the saw.

With the ability to cut thicker wood, it is better to make a pair of guide strips to clamp on the saw table and keep the cylinder from rolling (Fig. 11-6A). The angles should be about 45 degrees, but this is not crucial providing they are both the same.

The separate guide strips work well for larger cylinders, but when you get down to dowel rods less than 1 inch in diameter, a more precise support is advisable. The table saw guide could be used, but support over a greater length is worth having. Also, you might have to deal with the problem of a cut closing behind the saw, so it pinches or the cut surfaces become uneven.

A suitable jig can be made to go right across the saw table (Fig. 11-6B). Keep the angles the same, but one side can be wider than the other for clamping at the ends. If you use 1-inch wood, it should suit all small round pieces up to 1¼-inch diameter. Make a cut along the bottom of the V equal to the distance of the saw from the front

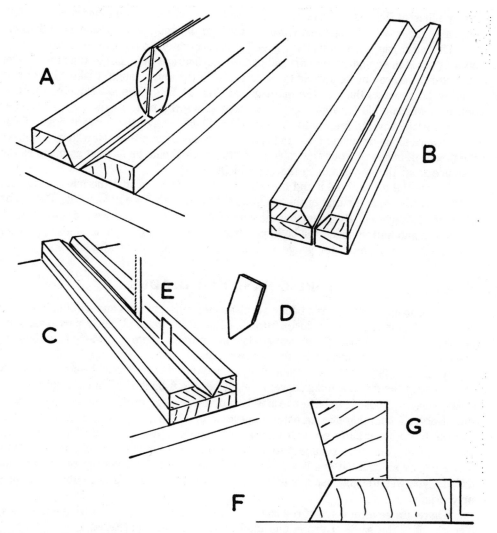

Fig. 11-6. *A trough guides cylindrical work being divided on a band saw (A-E). A special jig is used for cutting across (F, G).*

of its table. You will probably get a straighter cut if you do this on a table saw. In use, the jig is slid across the table from the back and clamped so that the cut end comes near the front edge (Fig. 11-6C).

You could use the jig as it is, but if you add a splitter, you remove the risk of the cut closing behind the blade and the rod twisting. The splitter is a piece of steel about the same thickness as the saw blade and standing as high as the deepest cut you expect to make. A piece of hacksaw blade with the teeth ground off is suitable. Start its hollow with a chisel, then if it has a pointed end (Fig. 11-6D), it can be driven in and held with epoxy adhesive (Fig. 11-6E) a few inches behind the saw. If you feed round rod in carefully until it engages with the splitter, it will be kept upright and the split open from then on.

The miter gauge set squarely will feed stock accurately to the saw for cross cutting, but it is not high enough to support and push any cylindrical wood larger than the smaller diameters. You can make a wood guide to use with the miter gauge. Make a lower part from wood about as thick as the miter gauge (Fig. 11-6F). Give it a slope of about 30 degrees. Make a block to go above it as high above the table as the largest cylinder you expect to have to feed onto the saw (Fig. 11-6G). Give the forward edge of this a downward slope or curve. Glue and screw these pieces together. How long you make the pieces depends on your saw table, but the length should be at least as much as the distance from the saw blade to the edge of the table.

To use the guide, hold it and the wood to be cut tight against the miter gauge set to 90 degrees, with the end of the gauge fairly close to the line of saw cut. The shape of the guide might not always match the curved rod exactly, but those it does not touch on the top and bottom faces will be kept down on the table. Push rods of less diameter than the height of the miter gauge with it without using the wood guide.

STORING BAND SAW BLADES

You will probably need several band saw blades for different cuts and widths. They can be stored as full circles or reduced into coiled smaller circles. Usually new blades are supplied in these compact three-part circles, and it might seem a mystery how they are made up in this way without kinking or twisting.

A band saw blade follows an even curve around the wheels. It must be stored carefully so a sharper bend is not induced, as it might be if you hung the full circle of steel on a single nail or hook. It is better to use two or three pegs made from dowels to hang the blade at something like its natural curve (Fig. 11-7A), especially if you expect to use the blade again fairly soon. If you do not expect to use the blade for some time, it is more convenient to reduce it to a three-part circular form and hang it safely on a single peg or store it flat in a box or drawer. When you have mastered the way to coil a blade, you will probably use this method, even when the blade is to be off the machine only briefly.

There are several ways of reducing the single circle of blade to a triple-circle ring. The result is the same. Here is one method that is easily mastered:

Wear gloves. Hold the blade in front of you with the teeth pointing away from you and your thumbs inside (Fig.11-7B). Bend the upper part outwards and downwards over the lower part (Fig. 11-7C). Keep the blade in this shape and pass one of the loops you are holding through the other (Fig. 11-7D). If you have done it correctly, you will see the crossed loops spring to overlap as three circles, which can be closed up (Fig. 11-7E). The teeth will all be the same way and there will be no twists. If kinks form, you have done something wrong. Open the blade out and start again. The three-part ring will keep its shape, but it is usual to put string or tape around at one place to prevent it from opening and uncoiling (Fig. 11-7F).

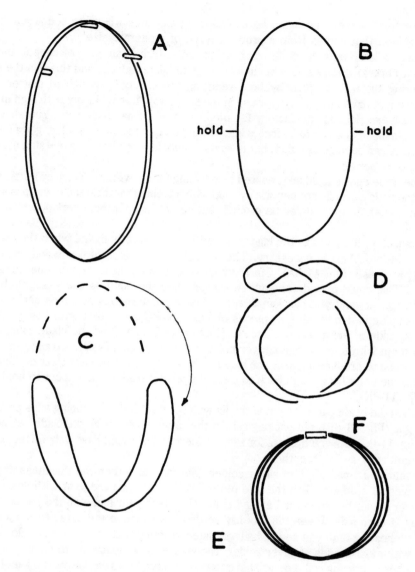

Fig. 11-7. *A band saw blade can be hung or coiled to a smaller size.*

BAND SAW REJOINING JIG

It is frustrating when a band saw blade breaks long before it has worn out by becoming blunt. It might have teeth that would cut for a long time yet, but unless you can join the broken ends, you will have to throw the saw blade away. It is possible to braze or silver solder the ends together to make a joint that should give a lot more use. As bought, the blade was probably made into a continuous curve by welding, but welding blades satisfactorily in a small shop is difficult. Brazing and silver soldering are basically the same process (sometimes called *hard soldering*) and they will make sound joints with only the heat that comes from a propane torch of moderate size.

Brazing is done with spelter or brazing rod, which is an alloy of copper and zinc (similar to brass). *Silver solder* is similar, but with silver added, and this has the effect of lowering the melting point without reducing the strength enough to matter. Your supplier might have other alloys for use in the same way, but avoid any with high melting points. Silver solder is satisfactory for the blades of a small band saw. You should be able to join blade ends up to ½ inch wide. When you buy the silver solder, get a suitable flux. Borax can be used as a flux, but it tends to bubble away from the metal; a prepared liquid flux is better.

The blade ends should be prepared by beveling for an overlap ¼ inch or a little more. Grind the ends carefully so they will overlap with matching teeth. If the overlap is slightly too thick when finished, it can be ground, but do not make a thin overlap, which would be weak.

Obviously, the parts of the blade have to be kept exactly in line when the ends are silver soldered. A jig is necessary. The base is a stout piece of hardwood, which can be held in a vise (Fig. 11-8A). Cut a 2-inch square from the center of one edge (Fig. 11-8B). This could provide enough clearance when the flame is used—slight charring will not matter, and you can join dozens of blades before this becomes serious.

Clamping is done with four pieces of ¹⁄₁₆-inch-×-1-inch steel strip that project ½ inch each side of the gap (Fig. 11-8C). They are held down and the blade clamped between them with four ¼-inch hanger bolts with nuts (Fig. 11-8D). Arrange the strips on the wood to produce a gap at one side for the saw teeth to be kept clear of the metal. Position the bolts far enough back to clear the widest blades you expect to hold in the jig (Fig. 11-8E).

When the blade parts are put in the jig with their ground overlapping ends positioned in the gap (Fig. 11-8F), put packings about the same thickness as the blade behind each bolt (Fig. 11-8G). As you prepare for silver soldering, you might have to bend the meeting ends until they spring together.

Hammer a small piece of silver solder thin—no more than the thickness of paper. Cut a piece a little less than the size of the join. Coat it and the joint with flux and put the silver solder between the beveled ends. Now play your flame on the joint. Start by heating at each side. When the flux has settled down, move the flame to the joint and continue heating until you see the silvery line indicating that the solder has flowed. By then, with most grades of silver solder, the steel will be beginning to glow red. If you use spelter or brazing rod, you will have to heat to a brighter red. Leave the joint to cool.

If the silver solder does not appear to have flowed through the joint, coat a piece of silver solder with flux to touch on the joint. Be careful this does not melt with a rush or you will finish with a thick blob over the joint that will have to be filed and ground off later. There is a risk that the parts might open, and you will get a thick joint or no joint. To prevent this, you have to clamp the joint before the silver solder hardens. It is no use squeezing with cold pliers. That is too drastic; the joint will chill and the parts will not unite. Keep an old pair of pliers for this job. While you are heating the joint, hold the end of the pliers in the flame. They need not glow red, but they should be fairly hot. If the saw blade ends stay together, all is well, but if they show signs of parting after the solder has melted, squeeze and hold with the hot pliers.

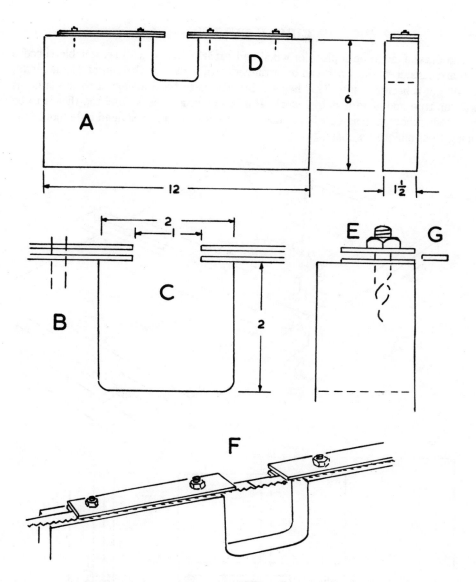

Fig. 11-8. *This jig will hold the parts of a band saw blade while being brazed.*

When the joint is cold, remove the blade from the jig and wash off any remaining flux. Check the thickness of the joint and grind if necessary, but be careful of overdoing it. File the back edge true. Touch up the teeth with a triangular file.

The blade circumference is now a little shorter than it was, but the machine adjustment will allow for that. Adjust tension as for a normal blade, but remember that it might have been previous overtensioning that broke it.

CIRCLE CUTTER

You can draw a circle on a piece of wood and cut it freehand with reasonable success if you are careful. If the wood can be arranged with a pivot at the center of the circle, you will get a better result. This helps if the disc is to be transferred to the lathe as it will run true and need less tool work. If it is something like a stool top that is to be completed without turning on a lathe, the accurately sawn disc will need little more than sanding to complete its shaping.

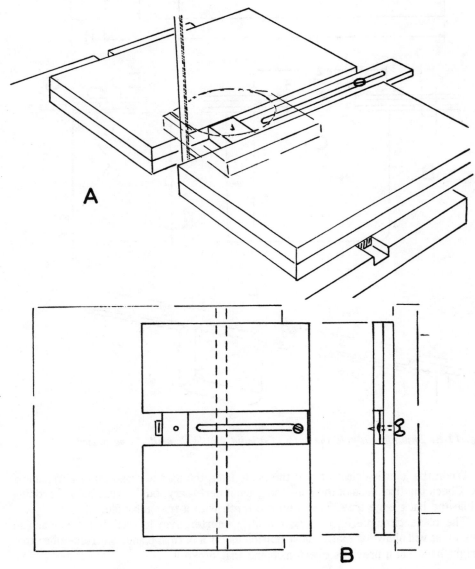

Fig. 11-9. *A jig will hold work that has to be cut into a circle on a band saw.*

A circle cutter is an auxiliary table, which fits on the band saw table, with a pivot pin that can be adjusted in relation to the saw blade. This circle cutter (Fig. 11-9A) is made mostly from ½-inch plywood and is intended to cut circles from about a 1-inch to 6-inch radius, though it could be made bigger. The size you make the circle cutter depends on the size of the band saw table; this one is assumed to be about 14 inches square.

The auxiliary table should be slightly less front to back than the saw table and wide enough to go round the saw blade about 1 inch and overhang the side enough to give clearance for the pivot slide clamping screw (Fig. 11-9B). It could be made wider to allow for cutting larger circles. It is built up from two thicknesses of ½-inch plywood.

Make the bottom part with a single piece of plywood and notch it 2 inches × 1 inch at the center of an edge (Fig. 11-10A). Make two pieces to fit on top and leave a 2-inch wide groove for the slide (Fig. 11-10B). Glue these parts together with a few screws or pins to locate them. Make a hardwood strip to fit the groove in the saw table. Fix it under the auxiliary table parallel with the edge and at a distance that brings the edge of the notch close to the saw blade (Fig. 11-10C). There must be a small clearance at the side of the saw blade, but if you start too close and the saw cuts away the notch, that does not matter.

Make the slide (Fig. 11-10D) from two thicknesses of ¼-inch wood, which could be plywood or solid wood, but the total thickness at the end when in the groove should

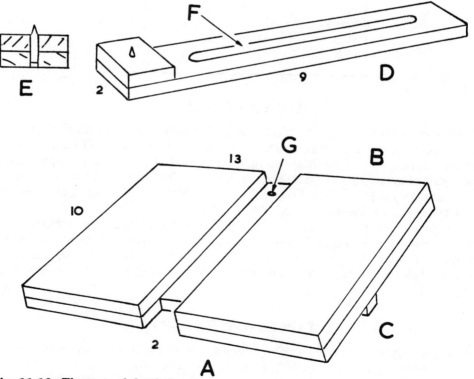

Fig. 11-10. *The parts of the circle cutter.*

come level with the auxiliary table surface. Allow for sliding in the width without excessive play. The length can be from the edge of the saw to the other edge, or a little longer. Make the pivot pin from a nail or a piece of ⅛-inch steel rod sharpened to a point (Fig. 11-10E). A projection of about 3/16 inch should suit most work. You can use a punch to alter the projection or drive the pin out for replacing.

Use a ¼-inch carriage bolt with a large washer and wing nut underneath to lock the slide. Make a groove to admit its square neck in the slide (Fig. 11-10F) and drill a hole to allow it through the end of the groove (Fig. 11-10G). That must be in the overhang of the auxiliary table, so you can turn the wing nut underneath.

To use the circle cutter, put it in position, then slide it along the saw table groove until the pivot pin is square to and in line with the teeth of the saw. Use one or two C clamps to hold the auxiliary table there. Set and lock the pivot pin at the radius you want from the saw. If the wood you are to cut the disc from is too oversized, cut off some of the waste.

Experimenting with scrap wood will show you how to rotate and cut the wood for the best results. Moving the base backwards or forwards a little in the saw table groove might be necessary to get a good cut without the saw binding or trying to wander. This depends on the particular saw blade.

Materials List for Circle Cutter

1 base	10	×	13	×	½	plywood
2 bases	5½	×	10	×	½	plywood
1 strip	¾	×	½	×	13	
1 slide	¼	×	2	×	15	

COPYING CURVES

If you want to cut several pieces of wood with the same curve, a straight piece of wood with one end rounded can make an adaptable auxiliary fence (Fig. 11-11A). If you want to cut several pieces with a simple curve, mark out and cut one curve freehand. Clamp your strip of wood to the saw table like a rip fence, but far enough from the saw to admit the thickness you have to cut. Feed the wood in with the curved edge against this and you will reproduce the same shape (Fig. 11-11B).

If the curve is partly concave and partly convex, you cannot use a straight fence. This is where the curved end of the piece is used. Cut one shaped edge on the wood freehand. Position the curved end opposite the saw at the distance you want and clamp it there. You can now follow the curve with the wood bearing against the rounded stop (Fig. 11-11C).

TAPERS AND WEDGES

If there is a rip fence supplied with your band saw or you have made one, it is possible to cut tapers or make wedges with the same jigs suggested for use with a table saw (Figs. 10-4, 10-5, and 10-6). The fence can be at the opposite side of the blade, which

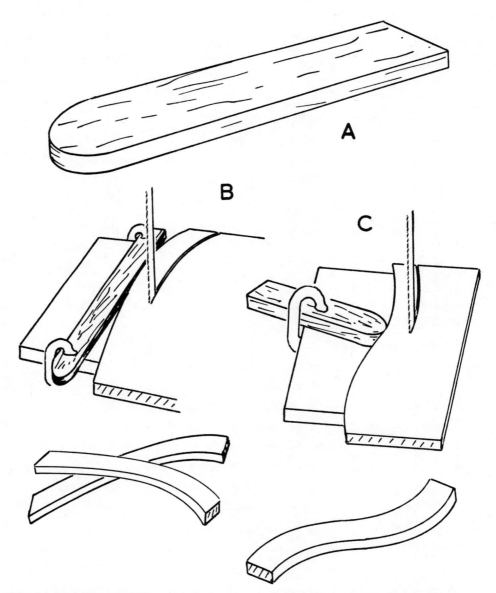

Fig. 11-11. *A board with a rounded end will guide curved parts being duplicated.*

means turning the jigs over, so if they are made one-sided, you will have to make more. It might be worthwhile making more, in any case, to suit the different size of the table and fence. Although the band saw will do the work, it might not be as easy to achieve accuracy on table legs and other long tapers as it is on a table saw. The band saw has the advantage, however, of being suitable for thicker wood, even if final surfacing has to be by planing.

12

Planing Aids

Traditionally boards were made smooth by fairly laborious hand planing. There are still a large variety of hand planes available, and a woodworking craftsperson will need some of them to tackle ambitious projects. Some of the finest finishes are the result of the use of sharp hand planes. However, much of the hard work has been taken out of routine planing by machines that produce true surfaces and correct thicknesses with a finish that is good enough for many purposes. Even if hand planing follows, the foundations of accuracy are there to work on.

There are portable power planes that are used like ordinary hand planes, but their scope is limited, and most planing is done by static machines over which the wood is moved. If the machine produces a flat planed surface, it is a *jointer*. If this is followed by planing the other surface to get the wood to a uniform thickness, it is done on a machine called a *planer*. Many of these power tools have a jointer on top, then the wood is fed underneath through a planer. There are few opportunities for making accessories for the planer, but some can be produced for use with a jointer.

FLAT PUSH STICKS

If you are planing fairly thick wood on a jointer, your hands on the wood are far enough away from the cutters. The bulk of the wood is also heavy enough to keep it flat while it is planed. With thinner wood, it is difficult to maintain this flatness on the feed table, and your fingers could come closer than is advisable to the cutters. You can use push sticks of various widths to spread pressure on the work and keep your hands in safe positions. Basically, a planer push stick is a notched piece of wood. It could just have a strip across the top as a handle (Fig. 12-1A). A push stick for the widest wood your jointer will plane can be made that way.

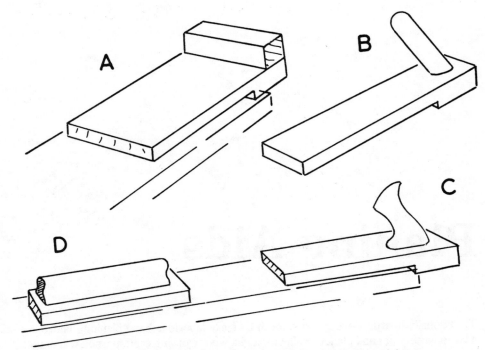

Fig. 12-1. Push sticks keep your hands at a safe distance when using a jointer.

You will probably want at least two narrower push sticks, which are better made with upright handles. You could use 1-inch dowel rod sloping forward (Fig. 12-1B) or use an old plane handle or a shape something like it (Fig. 12-1C). A notch ¼ inch deep should be enough. Anything less might ride over the work, and slipping hands are risky.

With each width of push stick, it is useful to have a matching pressure pad to use in the other hand to hold the wood down as it comes off the cutters. You might just press this with your fingers, or you could add a lengthwise handle (Fig. 12-1D).

THIN WOOD PUSH STICKS

Your table saw might cut wood down to ⅛ inch thick. For woven paneling for your yard, the sawn finish is adequate, but for furniture or where a good finish is required, you have to plane both sides. The best way to plane one side is to do it before sawing from a thicker board, then when that has been cut, plane a new surface for the next one. You still have to plane the second side.

You need a pressure pad as wide as the thin wood, and preferably as long, and stiff enough to remain flat. Prepare its surface on the jointer. Its other faces could be trued, but they are less important. You could glue a piece across the end of the pad for pushing (Fig. 12-2A). Do not be tempted to drive in nails or screws. Metal hitting planer cutters can ruin them.

It will probably be better to make a push stick to go over the pad (Fig. 12-2B) with a grip on top. The bottom might reach the jointer table, then it will be planed level with

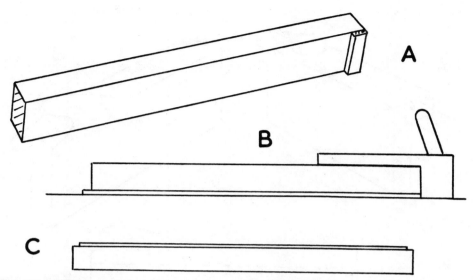

Fig. 12-2. Thin wood can be planed on a jointer with a thick pad and special push stick.

the thin wood. Press down with one hand on the pad while moving the job forward with your other hand on the push stick.

If you need to reduce the thickness as well as smooth the second side, add a backing to the thin wood (Fig. 12-2C); this can be the pad suggested for using on the jointer. Keep the first planer cuts very light, or you could finish with wood much thinner than you expected, or no wood at all!

FENCE PUSH STICK

After planing one surface of a length of wood, you usually have to plane an edge square to it using the fence as a guide. If the board is fairly wide and stands above the fence, you will have no difficulty in holding it against the fence with your fingers far enough away from the cutters. With narrower or smaller pieces you want to make square, the wood might not stand far above the feed table.

A push stick that travels on the fence can be used (Fig. 12-3A). Either notch solid wood over the fence or glue a top to the upright part. As shown (Fig. 12-3B), there is a shaped notch for pushing. You could fit a turned knob (Fig. 12-3C). Make this push stick the full depth at first. Plane its bottom edge at the first pass. Angle the edge that does the pushing so it is upright or has a slight downward slope to keep the wood tightly on the table (Fig. 12-3D).

SIDE PUSH STICK

The second step in planing wood on a jointer is usually planing one surface square to another by holding the first surface tight against the fence, which is set square to the table. Besides pushing forward, you have to hold the first surface flat on the fence. This

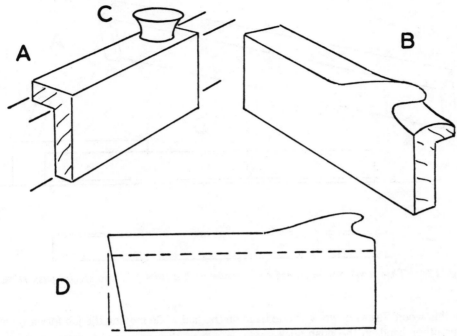

Fig. 12-3. *Fence push sticks guide wood being planed on edge.*

is easy to do with your hand in large sections but can be a problem with square stock of the sizes used in furniture, which are usually less than 2 inches square.

It helps to have a long push stick or pad with a notched edge, which you can press sideways with your left hand while you use another push stick with your right hand for forward motion. Use fairly thick wood at least 9 inches long and shape the outer edge to form a grip (Fig. 12-4A). You might make one for wood upwards of 1½ inches thick and a slimmer one for small sections (Fig. 12-4B).

JOINTER BLADE HONING

The rapidly rotating blades in a jointer or planer have comparatively thin edges, like chisels, but they strike wood hard at an enormous number of times per minute. Even if there are no extra hard flaws or particles of grit in the wood, the blades will soon be dulled from this heavy and frequent impact and must be sharpened more often than is usually the case. The ease, or otherwise, of removing the blades for sharpening depends on the machine, but it is a chore that is often delayed longer than sharpening should be. If you continue to force wood over blunt blades, the surface produced will be much poorer than it ought to be.

You can avoid removing the blades for sharpening for some time if you hone, or whet, them in position. There will come a stage when the blades have to be removed and reground, but before then you can restore the cutting edge with an oilstone. A waterstone might be used, but an abrasive stone with thin oil is more appropriate.

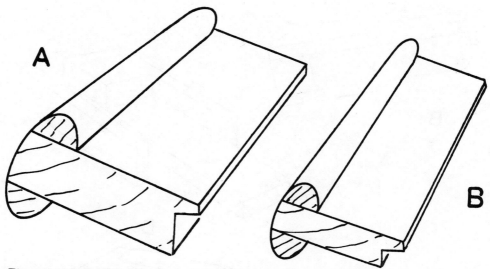

Fig. 12-4. *Side push sticks are helpful in keeping wood against the fence of a jointer.*

You can use any flat oilstone, but if there are nicks in a blade or if it is very dull, you need a coarse stone. The best edge will be obtained by following it with a fine stone. A double-sided stone is worth having because you can turn it over from coarse to fine. Size is not very important. The 8-inch-×-2-inch-×-1-inch size used for hand tools is suitable and shown in the drawing in Fig. 12-5, but you could use a smaller one. A good width of stone on the blade helps in keeping the edge straight. The stone will still be available for other purposes.

The honing case, or handle, is an open-ended box into which the oilstone fits (Fig. 12-5A). Parts of the box are narrowed to let you see the whole width of the stone in contact with the blade being sharpened. Make the hollow for the stone the same as its depth, then the edges are level (Fig. 12-5B).

To hone the blades, prepare the jointer by lowering both tables to allow each blade in turn to project as far as possible. Arrange a piece of thin sheet steel on the infeed table to make a stop for the blade being sharpened (Fig. 12-5C). Clamp it to the table. It will help if you can stop the blade block rotating, possibly by wedging or tying around the belt.

Wrap paper or thin plastic sheet around the enclosed part of the stone (Fig. 12-5D) to stop the stone from marking the table surface. Now use the stone flat on the table with a filing action and plenty of oil. Move with a circular action over the whole length of the blade edge to get an even wear even if you are tempted to work more where there is a nick in the edge. Keep the edge straight. After the first few rubs, check the angle of sharpening. You can adjust the angle a little by moving the sheet metal plate you are using as a stop.

Continue sharpening until you have removed nicks and can feel a burr, or wire edge, on the underside of the blade. Remove this by drawing a piece of hardwood on its side along the full length of the cutting edge. If you are now changing to a finer stone, wipe

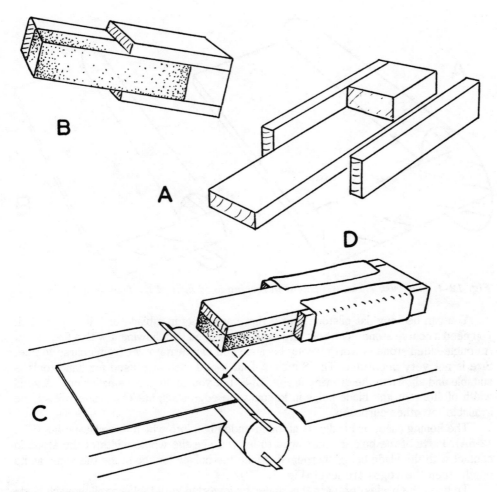

Fig. **12-5.** *Jointer blades can be honed with an oilstone in a holder.*

off the oil because it might contain particles of the coarser grit, then start again with a clean stone and more oil.

Sharpen all blades in this way and remove as much oil as possible. Reset the table heights for a first fine cut. Use the full width. Fine cutting will clear the blades before you resume normal planing.

PLANER BLADE GRINDING JIG

The cutting edge of a planer blade must be straight, otherwise the surface produced on wood will not be flat. You cannot grind on the stone commonly used for small tools because the risk of departing from a straight edge is too great. The blade has to be secured in some way so that it can be moved across the grinding surface in a straight line and at a constant angle.

The best grinder for sharpening planer blades is a cup stone on a vertical spindle, so the blade can be moved under it in a jig. Ideally, the cup stone is driven at a higher speed than the usual drill press can produce, which means using a vertical mill or something similar. If all you have is a drill press or a portable electric drill mounted in a vertical stand, then you might be able to grind a set of planer blades, providing you accept that the cup stone might wear excessively at the lower speeds.

On a milling machine, there will be the means of traversing the blade across the table below the grinding stone. On the usual drill press, however, you will have to arrange to traverse as well as secure the blade. Dense hardwood can be used for all parts of a jig for occasional use. Metal would have to be used if considerable sharpening is expected.

Sizes depend on the blades. The blade holder should be a little longer than a blade, and the trough for traversing should be twice as long as that. Sizes suggested are for a 6-inch blade.

Check the end shape and size of a blade. The slot in the holder must be at an angle that will bring the bevel horizontal (Fig. 12-6A) and will project the blade only enough for grinding when the blade rests on the bottom of the slot (Fig. 12-6B). The wood must be wide enough to remain stiff when the blade is screwed in place. Blades have different methods of fitting into machine blocks, but there should be some holes you can use. Counterbore and drill for at least two screws (Fig. 12-6C), which could be wood screws in a block intended for only occasional use.

Finish the 7-inch block 1¼ inches deep and 2½ inches wide. Make the 14-inch guide strips 1-inch square. How wide you make the base depends on how you will mount the

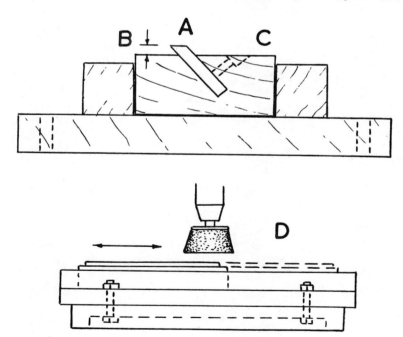

Fig. 12-6. This jig holds jointer blades for grinding.

jig. It has to be attached to the table of the drill press or milling machine with its center under the spindle center (Fig. 12-6D), then you can move the block and blade fully both ways under the cup grinding wheel. If there are slots in the table in suitable places, you can use bolts through them on extensions of the base, or you might have to use clamps.

When you have decided the size and shape of the base, screw and glue the guide strips to the base. The blade block should slide smoothly but without any more play than needed for necessary movement.

Setting up might take longer than actual grinding. Make sure the jig is secure and square to the spindle. Once it is positioned, it should be satisfactory for a set of blades. Lock the grinder setting at each depth and make a complete pass across the back before altering it to ensure a straight edge.

Rub the flat side of a blade on an oilstone a few times, then slice across the edge of a piece of scrap wood to remove any remaining burr. Whether the bevel needs honing or not depends on how fine the grit of the grinding wheel is, but you could remove grinding marks by honing in position, as previously described.

HAND PLANING HELPS

Shooting boards for use with hand planes are described in chapter 6 (Figs. 6-1 to 6-3). Some other equipment described in earlier chapters also can be used when hand planing.

13

Shaper and Router Accessories

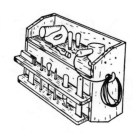

The shaper and router perform very similar functions, but the shaper is a static machine over which the wood is moved, while the router is a portable power tool that is moved over the wood. Both can take a variety of cutters to groove, mold, and make many shapes on edges, while the router is also suitable for shaping away from the edges. Both depend on the types of cutters that can be fitted rather than the way they are manipulated in relation to the wood. Because of this, the methods of feeding and controlling wood are usually settled by the design of the appliance, and there is not much scope for making additions to perform special functions as there are with some of the other shop power tools.

Accessories for the shaper are mainly concerned with convenience and safety. The guides and controls supplied with the machine will deal with normal functions and should not be interfered with.

Many routers have guides and fences that give control over a limited range. You can make guides to control other movements, so the tool can make cuts in many ways and do repetition work. Some guides can be improvisations to suit a particular job, but others can adjust to suit a variety of purposes. In a small shop, a router is a more valuable tool than a shaper, which is more suited to long runs in production. The router also occupies much less space.

SQUARE PUSH STICK

Some of the push sticks suggested for use on the table saw, band saw, and planer can be used on a shaper, but there are a few others worth making. Molding across end grain needs a firm feed because end grain is more inclined to jump and vibrate than side grain. You must also keep your hands away. If there is a miter guide, it can be set squarely and the wood fed by it, but it is better to use a wide square push stick.

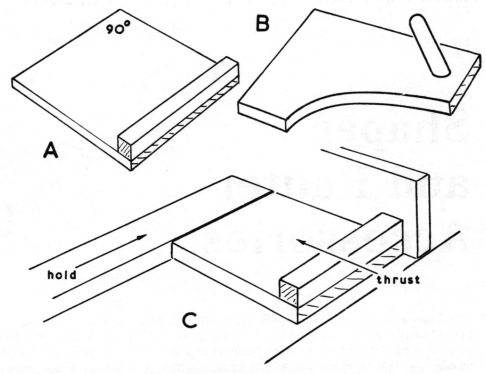

Fig. 13-1. *A square push stick holds wood being cut across the end on a shaper.*

A square push stick could be just a piece of wood with a square corner and a strip across to make a handle (Fig. 13-1A). You could shape it and put a handle nearer the edge where most thrust is needed (Fig. 13-1B). Hold the work and the push stick tight to the fence with one hand and feed forward with the other (Fig. 13-1C).

UPRIGHT PUSH STICK

If you want to use the shaper across the edge of a panel held upright, whether end or side grain, the length of an edge will be enough to keep it steady throughout the pass. If you want to work across the end of a long narrower piece, however, there will be difficulty in keeping it upright and square if you do not have a suitable push stick.

You can use a push stick similar to the one square one, but it helps to keep it upright if you broaden the bottom edge (Fig. 13-2A). You could make it to travel over the top edge of the fence (Fig. 13-2B). It would be useful to have another upright push stick about the height of the fence for smaller jobs (Fig. 13-2C).

ANGULAR PUSH STICK

When you need to feed a small piece of wood past the cutting head, you cannot hold it with your hand or use two push sticks. A notched angular push stick might be used

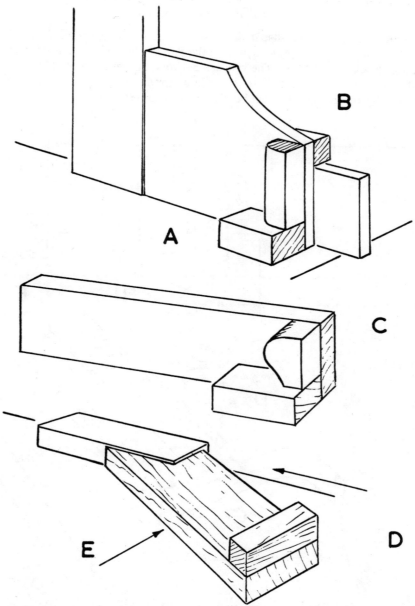

Fig. 13-2. *Special push sticks hold wood being fed through a shaper.*

instead (Fig. 13-2D). With two hands on it, you can press in as well as feed the work (Fig. 13-2E). One notch might not suit all work. If you make the stick long, you will be able to alter the notch or cut if off and start again without scrapping the stick.

CUTTER DEPTH GAUGE

When setting cutters in the shaper, it is useful to be able to measure the height above the table or the amount of projection from the fence. This can be done with a rule held in a gauge block (Fig. 13-3A). The rule can be wood or metal, but it should be marked in sixteenths of an inch or smaller. It could be graduated in millimeters. The rule is unaffected by the cutters and can be removed for other uses.

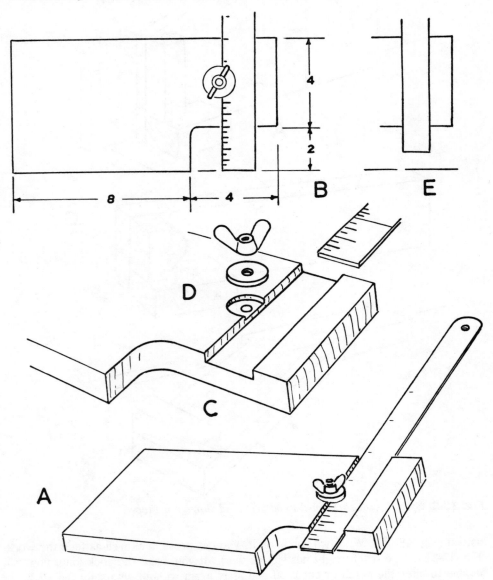

Fig. 13-3. *A simple gauge to hold a rule is useful when setting shaper cutters.*

Use hardwood. Plane one edge straight and square, then cut away (Fig. 13-3B) an exact depth (2 inches is suggested) to clear the greatest cutter setting you expect to check. Make a groove square to the edge in which the rule can slide (Fig. 13-3C).

To hold the rule, use a ¼-inch bolt with a large washer and a wing or knurled nut. Let the washer in deep enough to press on the rule and drill for the bolt close to the rule edge (Fig. 13-3D). Tightening the nut should prevent the rule from sliding.

In use, when setting the height or projection of a cutter, set the end of the rule to it. Read the measurement less than 2 inches at the notch edge (Fig. 13-3E).

SHAPER EXTENSION TABLE

The standard shaper table is large enough for most work, but for very long or wide work you will need a helper or additional support in the same way as when using a table or band saw. The roller stand suggested for the table saw or the folding table suggested for the band saw might work, but an independent table that can be used elsewhere in the shop, yard, or home might be better.

The table in Fig. 13-4 has a plywood top made like a shallow box onto which the crossed legs can fold. The important consideration is getting the height to match the height of the shaper table. Leg lengths, and therefore the size of the top onto which they fold, have to be adjusted to suit. Make the top about as long as the shaper table

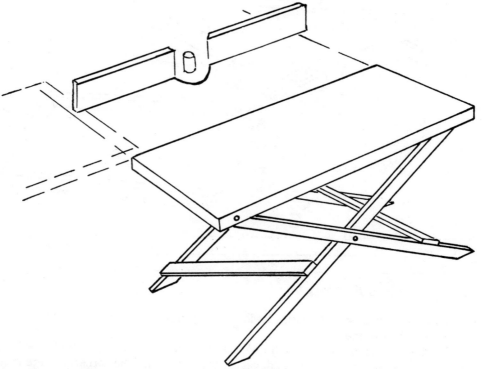

Fig. 13-4. A folding table can form an extension to a shaper.

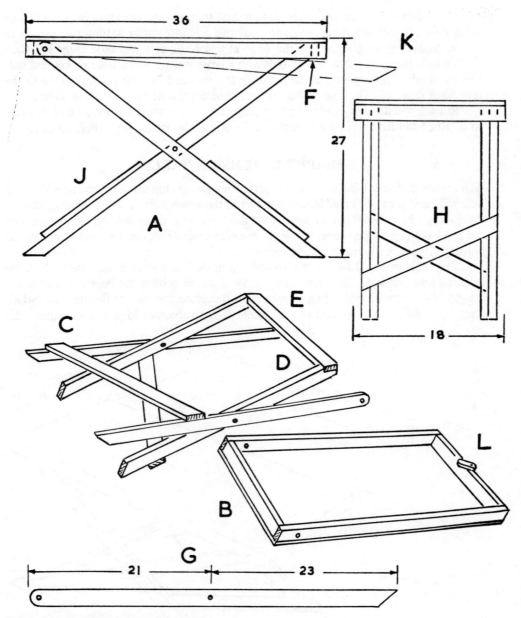

Fig. 13-5. *Details of the folding table.*

top and rather wider than its outfeed width. You can position it at the side or end of the machine to suit the work.

For the suggested sizes (Fig. 13-5A), the top is a shallow box with a plywood top (Fig. 13-5B). Anything from nails to dovetails can be used for the corners. There is an outer leg frame (Fig. 13-5C) that pivots on two bolts inside the top. The inner leg frame fits inside the other (Fig. 13-5D). It has a crossbar at the top to fit inside the box end (Fig. 13-5E and F).

Pivot two legs with bolts where they cross (Fig. 13-5G) and brace each pair of legs with diagonal struts arranged opposite ways (Fig. 13-5H) on what will be the outside surfaces when the legs are folded (Fig. 13-5J). Cut the angles of the feet to rest flat on the floor. The leg frames should fold into each other, then fold against the underside of the top (Fig. 13-5K). To help hold the legs in place when the table is erected, you can fit a wood turnbutton on the top (Fig. 13-5L).

Materials List for Shaper Extension Table

1 top	18 ×	36 ×	½ plywood
2 top frames	1 ×	2 ×	38
2 top frames	1 ×	2 ×	20
4 legs	1 ×	2 ×	48
2 diagonals	½ ×	2 ×	24

ROUTER SQUARE

One of the commonest uses of a portable router is cutting dadoes across the grain of a board, usually square to the edge, as in fitting shelves in a bookcase. The router has to be guided. This can be done by clamping a strip of wood, but it has to be positioned with a square. It saves time to make a square that is also a guide for the router.

This router square (Fig. 13-6A) is made like a T square but is widened to give ample area for gripping with a clamp. Size depends on your usual work, but this one (Fig. 13-6B) should suit most projects. The part of the stock projecting towards the router must not be long enough to interfere with the action of the router, or you will find your cutter going through it. Measure the distance from the center of your router to the edge that will rub along the guide and deduct about 1 inch, which should clear the largest dado cutter you will use.

Make the parts of hardwood and pay particular attention to the edge of the stock that will be against the wood edge and the edge of the blade where the router runs. Other parts can be shaped or rounded as you wish. Join with glue and screws. A hole at the end of the blade allows it to hang on a hook. Brass screws and a varnished hardwood will make an attractive square. The working edge could be thickened, if you wish (Fig. 13-6C).

Of course, the guide does not have to be square. Having a blade at a 45-degree angle for a miter cut (Fig. 13-6D) is an obvious additional form. You could make a pair for use at opposite ends of a board. Extending the blade to the other side of the stock allows work from either edge (Fig. 13-6E).

If you are making a staircase, you must cut dadoes at special angles. You can make a square to suit after you have laid out the staircase. This speeds your work and ensures all tread angles being the same. It is possible to make an adjustable square with a blade on a bolt, but it is liable to move unless clamped very securely.

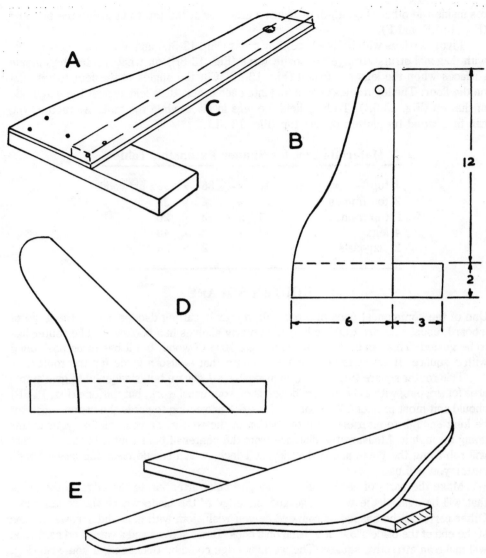

Fig. 13-6. *Squares can guide a portable router when cutting dadoes or other work.*

DOUBLE GUIDE

With a square as a guide, you have to hold the router tight against it to keep the cut straight. If you want to make sure the cut is kept straight without you needing this extra concentration, you can make a double guide in the form of a square with two blades. You can make it with a fixed end piece that gives clearance to the widest board you expect to work on (Fig. 13-7A), or you can make it adjustable (Fig. 13-7B) to bring the further piece close to the work. All parts could be 1-inch - × -2-inch softwood, or ¾-inch by 1½-inch hardwood, with ¼-inch carriage bolts with washers and wing nuts.

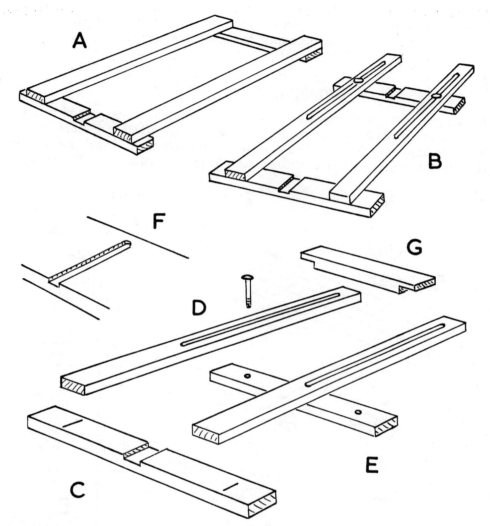

Fig. 13-7. *A double guide controls by touching both sides of a router base.*

Mark the stock (Fig. 13-7C). Cut across the center to clear the router cutter. Make the two blades with slots coming in to what you expect to be the narrowest width you will work on (Fig. 13-7D). Keep the ends of the slots closed. If you cut them right through, there is a risk of them opening, and this could bring the controlling edges out of parallel.

Fix the blades square to the stock with just enough space between for the router to travel across without sideways play. Make the further piece with holes to suit (Fig. 13-7E). In use, it might be possible to bring that piece tight against the wood so that the guide grips the work and you do not need a clamp, but normally it is wiser to use at least one clamp.

If you do not want a dado to show on the front edge, make it blind or stopped (Fig. 13-7F). The router will have to be halted at the same position in a series of dadoes.

A stop can be a simple notched piece of wood to clamp across the two blades (Fig. 13-7G). Let it go deep enough to stop the router, but it does not have to touch the surface of the work.

GRIPPING STRAIGHTEDGE

Many router cuts, whether dadoes, moldings or other decorations, have to be made straight. The router has to be controlled by a straightedge, whether the cut is across, along, or diagonal to the grain. You can take any available piece of straight wood and clamp it to the work, and in most circumstances that is quite satisfactory. To make sure

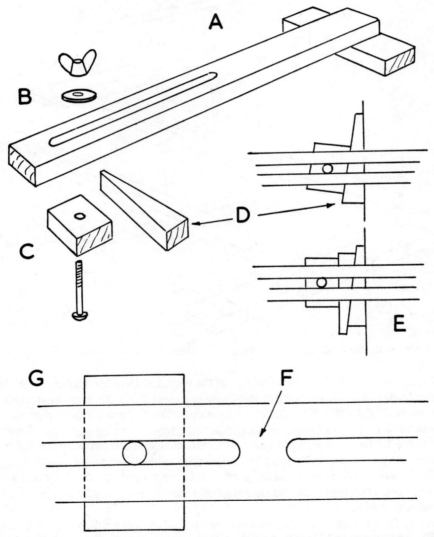

Fig. 13-8. *This straightedge can grip the wood when being used as a guide for a router.*

you always have a true straightedge available, it is worthwhile making one or more straightedges that can be arranged to grip the wood without adding clamps.

It is possible to use clamp-type screws built into the straightedges, but you can get similar results in a cheaper and simpler way by using wedges.

Use a piece of 1-inch-×-2-inch wood, planed straight and as long as you need. You might wish to make one, or a pair, of short ones and more at a greater length. At one end there is a piece fixed squarely across (Fig. 13-8A). The blade has a slot for a ¼-inch bolt (Fig. 13-8B). Under that goes a block to pivot on the bolt (Fig. 13-8C), against which goes a wedge to bear on the edge of the work (Fig. 13-8D). You might wish to use a pair of matching wedges opposite ways (Fig. 13-8E). The advantage of using these "folding" wedges is that there is less risk of moving the straightedge sideways when you tighten them.

If you make a long straightedge and want to slot it to give a considerable range of movement, it is inadvisable to make a very long single slot because that might allow the wood to bow outwards and no longer be straight. It would be better to divide the slot into sections no longer than 9 inches and leave short pieces of solid wood between (Fig. 13-8F). If the pivot block is longer one way than the other (Fig. 13-8G), it can be turned on its bolt to arrange a face to allow for bridging the width of the solid wood when wedging.

HINGE TEMPLATES

Letting a hinge into the edge of a door and its stile the correct amount can be difficult when you know the leaves of the hinge have to be let in just the right amount to give the necessary clearance when the door is closed. Using hand methods means careful work with chisels, but you might not get the bottom of the recess level and will have to resort to packings. This is a particular problem when the hinge is narrower than the door edge.

You can use the router to cut an accurate recess with the aid of a template. This has to be cut to suit the particular hinge, but you will find that you only use a few standard sizes and do not have to make a great many templates.

So the template gives a good bearing to the base of the router, let the template extend all ways (Fig. 13-9A). Put a strip underneath to bear against the face of the door or stile (Fig. 13-9B). Hollow its top enough to clear the router cutter, or let the cutter make the hollow during the first use of the template (Fig. 13-9C).

The recess will finish with a smooth level bottom and straight edges, but rounded corners (Fig. 13-9D). For the usual square hinges, trim the corners with a chisel. You can buy hinges with rounded corners. If you get them, choose a router cutter with the same radius as the hinge corners, then you will not have to do any hand toolwork at the corners.

ROUTER COMPASS

One way to form a round piece with a molded edge is to turn it on a lathe, then use a molding cutter in the router to apply the molding. How big this can be depends on the lathe. For something like a tabletop, you are unlikely to be able to turn the edge

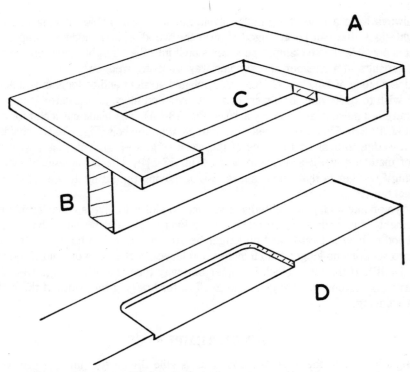

Fig. 13-9. *This jig guides a router when cutting a rabbet for a hinge.*

and will have to get it circular, as well as mold it, by other means. This can be done with your router.

A router compass (Fig. 13-10A) holds the router while it is drawn around an awl or nail that acts as a center. The size of circle possible depends only on the length of the arm. This could be several feet, if all you want is an arc of a circle at the edge of a piece of furniture, or it could be as small as a few inches for a pot stand.

Use ½-inch plywood to make a piece with a hole to fit around the base of your router (Fig. 13-10B). Allow about 1 inch around it and extend to one side to meet the arm. For cutting circles on the surface of wood, that might be all the holding arrangements needed, but at the edge of a piece of wood, there would be a tendency for the router to tilt. To prevent tilting, make a subbase to go below the router, with a hole to allow the cutter to pass through (Fig. 13-10C). That could be thin plywood, but sheet plastic about ¹⁄₁₆ inch thick would be better. Cut it to the same outline as the upper part and glue these pieces together.

Make the arm (Fig. 13-10D) to whatever length you need. Screw it to the router holder, then if you want to change it, you can. You could put a series of holes along the centerline of the arm, but it will be better to drill them as you need a particular radius. Prespaced holes will probably never be quite right.

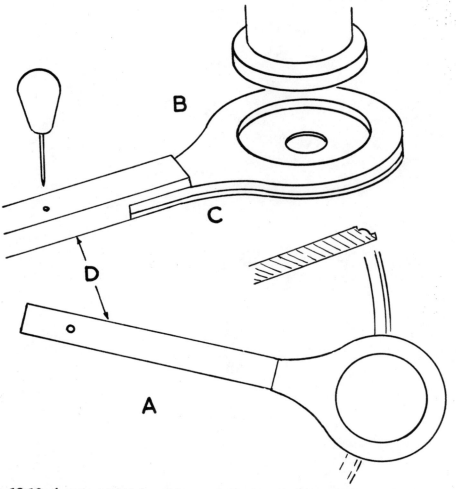

Fig. 13-10. *A router mounted on this arm works like a compass for circular cuts.*

A fine awl as the pivot point will hold firm but not leave a very obvious hole. If you must have a finished surface without even a fine center hole, temporarily attach a piece of veneer or thin wood at the center using rubber adhesive or other easily peeled glue. Push the awl point into that and peel it off when the work is finished.

Glossary

As anyone with even a little shop experience knows, there is almost another language to cover the techniques of working in wood and metal. There are whole books explaining the meaning of technical terms. The words that follow are a selection of those that might concern the reader of this book when tackling the projects described. I hope that the explanations will clarify the meanings of any terms that are unfamiliar.

alloy—A substance having metallic qualities; composed of one or more chemical elements, at least one of which is a metal.

anneal—To heat-treat a metal or alloy to soften it.

apron—The vertical part of the front of a bench or the carriage of a metalworking lathe.

back steady—Support for slender work that is being turned in a lathe.

bed—The support on which other parts of a machine are mounted, as on a lathe.

blind hole—A hole that does not go right through.

borax—A flux for hard soldering and brazing.

brass—A yellow alloy of copper and zinc.

brazing—Joining by melting hard solder or spelter.

butcher block—A form of furniture or bench construction that uses many strips glued together instead of solid wood. Named after the method of making a butcher's chopping block.

butterfly nut—A nut with projecting wings to grip for hand tightening or loosening. Also called a *wing nut*.

carriage bolt—Bolt with a shallow domed head and a square neck to prevent it turning in wood, used with a nut.

chipboard—Alternate name for particleboard.

cleat—Strip or block of wood used as a support or brace.

clench (clinch)—To turn over the projecting end of a nail.

counterbore—To drill a hole so the head of a screw is below the surface; used with short screws in thick wood or to permit covering the screwhead with a plug.

countersink—To bevel the opening of a hole to sink a flathead screw flush with the surface. The tool for doing this.

ellipsograph—Device for drawing an ellipse with a beam compass or trammel heads. The whole arrangement can be called *trammels*.

feather board—Strip of wood with its end cut like a comb that can be clamped to a saw table to keep the wood being cut close to a fence.

flux—Liquid or powder used to help a metal or alloy flow in welding, brazing, or soldering.

folding wedges—Two identical wedges driven in opposite directions to give a parallel thrust when tightening.

focus—(Plural is *foci*.) Point about which a curved shape is generated. The center of a circle is its focus. An ellipse has two foci.

galvanized iron—Iron or steel coated with zinc to protect it from rust.

gauge—Size. In metalwork particularly, the thickness of sheets or diameter of wire according to a recognized scale. The tool for measuring size. In woodworking, a tool for marking lines parallel to an edge.

graver—Cutting tool with triangular-sectioned cutting point.

haft—Long handle of a hammer or similar tool.

handed—Made as a pair.

hard solder—Copper and zinc alloy with other metals added to lower its melting point. It is melted to join metals. Silver solder is a hard solder.

holdfast—Tool that usually fits through a hole in the top of a bench to hold down wood being worked on.

honing—Final stage in sharpening. Rubbing the edge with a fine abrasive stone or abrasive powder on a leather strop. Also called *whetting*.

jig—Device for guiding a cut or other tool work on wood or metal.

joggle—Offset double bend in a strip of metal.

jointer—In woodworking, a machine for planing a surface level.

kerf—Slot made by a saw.

kicker—In a fitted drawer, a strip above a drawer edge that prevents the drawer from tilting downwards when it is partly pulled out.

lag screw—Large wood screw with its head shaped so it can be turned by a wrench.

laying out—Setting out details of design and construction, particularly large work. Marking out smaller parts is usually called *setting out*.

mandrel (mandril)—In turning, a round piece on which a part to be turned with a central hole can be mounted. Iron block on which metal parts can be shaped. Conical block used to true metal rings.

mild steel—Low carbon steel that cannot be hardened and tempered. Often loosely and incorrectly called iron.

miter—The angle between two parts, as in a picture frame where each end is at a 45-degree angle. It is a miter whatever the meeting angle.

nonferrous—Any alloy or metal that does not contain iron.

outfeed—The side of a machine where the work is led off.

particleboard—Board made by bonding wood chips with a synthetic resin. Also called *chipboard*.

pilot hole—A small diameter hole drilled first to guide the point of a large drill.

push stick—Any piece of wood used to push wood through a machine to avoid bringing hands too close to cutters.

rabbet (rebate)—Angular notch in the edge of a piece of wood, as at the back of a picture frame.

rake—Cutting angle of a drill or other tool.

ridge—Top or apex of a roof where the sloping sides meet.

rule—Measuring instrument. Not a "ruler."

screw—A *wood screw* has a tapered thread. A *self-tapping screw* has a similar action for cutting its way into sheet metal or wood. A fastening to take a nut that has threads almost to its head is also a screw, but if the threads are for a shorter distance from the end, it is a *bolt*.

setting out—Marking out parts, usually on the bench. Doing the same over a bigger area, as when marking the shape of foundations of a building, is called *laying out*.

shank—The neck or part of a tool between the handle and the blade.

shooting board (shuting board)—Device for holding wood so a plane will produce a square edge.

silicon gel—Chemical, obtainable as crystals or impregnated paper, that has the capacity for attracting moisture. When included with tools or steel stock, it reduces the tendency to rust.

soft solder—Alloy of lead and tin that has a low melting point; it can be melted to give a lower strength than hard solder when joining alloys or metals.

Spanish windlass—Method of twisting turns of rope with a lever to produce tension so it can be used for clamping.

spelter—Copper and zinc alloy used to join metals by brazing. When other metals are added to lower the melting point, it is called *hard solder*.

spline—Strip of wood of thin section used for checking or comparing sizes.

square—Besides an equal-sided rectangle, this also means corners at 90-degree angles.

swarf—The waste removed from metal by filing, turning, or other machining.

table vise—A vise with a flat base to bolt to the table of a drill press or other machine.

tang—Part of a tool that is driven into a handle.

tap—In metalworking, the tool used for cutting a thread inside a hole.

template (templet)—Pattern used to mark around to transfer an outline or to locate hole positions.

tilt bin—A box arranged to swing out on its base to give access to the contents.

V block—Block with V notch cut across to support a cylindrical piece, as when drilling across on a press.

vise—Two-jawed device with a tightening screw. Usually attached to a bench. A portable device with a similar action is a clamp.

Index

Index

Other Bestsellers of Related Interest

**DESIGNING AND BUILDING COLONIAL
AND EARLY AMERICAN FURNITURE,
With 47 Projects**—2nd Edition
—Percy W. Blandford

An internationally recognized expert in the field provides first-rate illustrations and simple instructions on the art of reproducing fine furniture. Every project in the volume is an exquisite reproduction of centuries-old originals: drop-leaf tables, peasant chairs, swivel-top tables, ladder-back chairs, tilt-top box tables, hexagonal candle stands, dry sinks, love seats, Welsh dressers, and more! 192 pages, 188 illustrations. Book No. 3014, $12.95 paperback only.

THE WOODTURNER'S BIBLE—3rd Edition
—Percy W. Blandford

Long considered the most comprehensive guide available on woodturning techniques, this book is an authoritative reference to every aspect of the craft, from choosing a lathe to performing advanced turning techniques. Blandford covers every kind of lathe and turning tool available, than gives step-by-step instructions on tool handling techniques and lathe applications. This expanded edition offers added coverage of turning wood patterns for metal-castings and tips on using high-speed steel tools. 272 pages, 210 illustrations. Book No. 3404, $16.95 paperback, $26.95 hardcover.

24 WOODTURNING PROJECTS
—Percy W. Blandford

Here are 24 ways to put your lathe and your wood-turning skills to work creating beautiful and useful objects from wood. You'll find projects ranging from the simple to the more advanced, including such items as candlesticks, bowls, floor lamps, canes, a round table, boxes and lids, vases, jewelry, and more. Each project provides a materials list and advice on wood choice, step-by-step instructions, detailed drawings, and a picture of the finished piece. 144 pages, 95 illustrations. Book No. 3334, $9.95 paperback, $18.95 hardcover.

**WOODWORKING JOINTS:
An Illustrated Handbook**—2nd Edition
—Percy W. Blandford

The most comprehensive book on woodworking joints is back in a widely expanded second edition. Learn how to create strong and durable joints in everything from furniture to boats, and more. Material was added on popular Japanese joints, plate and biscuit joints for simple power tools, and fence and log cabin joints, as well as methods for using green wood and materials such as particleboard. 380 pages, 384 illustrations. Book No. 3324, $17.95 paperback, $26.95 hardcover.

WOODWORKER'S 30 BEST PROJECTS
—Editors of *Woodworker* Magazine

A collection of some of the finest furniture ever made can be found within the pages of this project book. Designed for the woodworker who has already mastered the basics, the projects presented in this book are for the intermediate- to advanced-level craftsman. Each furniture project comes complete with detailed instructions, a materials list, exploded views of working diagrams, a series of step-by-step, black-and-white photos, and a photograph of the finished piece. 224 pages, 300 illustrations. Book No. 3021, $14.95 paperback only.

**DO-IT-YOURSELF'S GUIDE TO FURNITURE
REPAIR AND REFINISHING**—2nd Edition
—Percy W. Blandford
". . . more than helpful; it's challenging and inspiring."
—*Jersey Journal*

Precise directions and almost 200 illustrations show you how to reupholster, replace veneers, carve parts, simulate aged wood, imitate grains, reinforce joints, use woodburning, remove scratches, "antique" surfaces, rebuild panels, reglue parts, apply decals, and more! 192 pages, 198 illustrations. Book No. 2994, $12.95 paperback only.